Tools, Exercises, and Strategies for Coping With Complexity

Rune Storesund
Storesund Consulting, Kensington, USA

Ian I. Mitroff
Mitroff Crisis Management, Berkeley, USA

A volume in the Advances in Educational Marketing, Administration, and Leadership (AEMAL) Book Series

IGI Global
PUBLISHER of TIMELY KNOWLEDGE

Published in the United States of America by
IGI Global
Information Science Reference (an imprint of IGI Global)
701 E. Chocolate Avenue
Hershey PA, USA 17033
Tel: 717-533-8845
Fax: 717-533-8661
E-mail: cust@igi-global.com
Web site: http://www.igi-global.com

Library of Congress Cataloging-in-Publication Data

Names: Storesund, Rune, author. | Mitroff, Ian I., author.
Title: Tools, exercises, and strategies for coping with complexity / Rune Storesund, Ian Mitroff.
Description: Hershey, PA : Information Science Reference, [2024] | Includes bibliographical references and index. | Summary: "We live in a world in which every aspect of our existence is influenced by inordinate amounts of complexity. Technical Complexity, for example, is not necessarily the same as Economic Complexity although the two are related. Similarly, Public Health and Social Complexity are different as well. Nonetheless, one thing above all is a prominent feature of today's world; all the various types and forms of complexity are not only related, but deeply intertwined. Today, an idea can travel the globe in mere seconds thanks to the internet and social media! These factors make our world today so complex and extremely different from previous ages in history"-- Provided by publisher.
Identifiers: LCCN 2023000681 (print) | LCCN 2023000682 (ebook) | ISBN 9781668465639 (hardcover) | ISBN 9781668465646 (ebook)
Subjects: LCSH: Complexity (Philosophy)
Classification: LCC B105.C473 S86 2023 (print) | LCC B105.C473 (ebook) | DDC 117--dc23/eng/20230320
LC record available at https://lccn.loc.gov/2023000681
LC ebook record available at https://lccn.loc.gov/2023000682

This book is published in the IGI Global book series Advances in Educational Marketing, Administration, and Leadership (AEMAL) (ISSN: 2326-9022; eISSN: 2326-9030)

British Cataloguing in Publication Data
A Cataloguing in Publication record for this book is available from the British Library.

Advances in Educational Marketing, Administration, and Leadership (AEMAL) Book Series

Siran Mukerji
IGNOU, India
Purnendu Tripathi
IGNOU, India

ISSN:2326-9022
EISSN:2326-9030

MISSION

With more educational institutions entering into public, higher, and professional education, the educational environment has grown increasingly competitive. With this increase in competitiveness has come the need for a greater focus on leadership within the institutions, on administrative handling of educational matters, and on the marketing of the services offered.

The **Advances in Educational Marketing, Administration, & Leadership (AEMAL) Book Series** strives to provide publications that address all these areas and present trending, current research to assist professionals, administrators, and others involved in the education sector in making their decisions.

COVERAGE

- Educational Management
- Educational Marketing Campaigns
- Educational Leadership
- Marketing Theories within Education
- Educational Finance
- Academic Administration
- Advertising and Promotion of Academic Programs and Institutions
- Technologies and Educational Marketing
- Students as Consumers
- Academic Pricing

IGI Global is currently accepting manuscripts for publication within this series. To submit a proposal for a volume in this series, please contact our Acquisition Editors at Acquisitions@igi-global.com or visit: http://www.igi-global.com/publish/.

The Advances in Educational Marketing, Administration, and Leadership (AEMAL) Book Series (ISSN 2326-9022) is published by IGI Global, 701 E. Chocolate Avenue, Hershey, PA 17033-1240, USA, www.igi-global.com. This series is composed of titles available for purchase individually; each title is edited to be contextually exclusive from any other title within the series. For pricing and ordering information please visit http://www.igi-global.com/book-series/advances-educational-marketing-administration-leadership/73677. Postmaster: Send all address changes to above address.

Titles in this Series

For a list of additional titles in this series, please visit: http://www.igi-global.com/book-series/

Interrogating Race and Racism in Postsecondary Language Classrooms
Xiangying Huo (University of Toronto, Canada) and Clayton Smith (University of Windsor, Cnada)
Information Science Reference • © 2024 • 300pp • H/C (ISBN: 9781668490297) • US $215.00

Strategic Opportunities for Bridging the University-Employer Divide
William E. Donald (University of Southampton, UK & Ronin Institute USA)
Information Science Reference • © 2023 • 300pp • H/C (ISBN: 9781668498279) • US $225.00

Academic Framework for 21st-Century Schooling Promoting Global Peace and Harmony
Marmar Mukhopadhyay (Educational Technology and Management Academy Council, India) and Arnab Kundu (Chhinpur Jr. High School, India)
Information Science Reference • © 2023 • 349pp • H/C (ISBN: 9781668470053) • US $230.00

Promoting Crisis Management and Creative Problem-Solving Skills in Educational Leadership
Afzal Sayed Munna (University of Sunderland in London, UK) Uzoechi Nwagbara (University of Sunderland in London, UK) and Yahaya Alhassan (University of Sunderland in London, UK)
Information Science Reference • © 2024 • 300pp • H/C (ISBN: 9781668483329) • US $215.00

Becoming and Supporting Online Adjunct Faculty in a Gig Economy
Jennifer L. Robinson (University of Arizona Global Campus, USA)
Information Science Reference • © 2023 • 277pp • H/C (ISBN: 9781668477762) • US $215.00

Closing the Educational Achievement Gap for Students With Learning Disabilities
Florence Nyemba (University of Cincinnati, USA) and Rufaro Audrey Chitiyo (Tennessee Technological University, USA)
Information Science Reference • © 2023 • 454pp • H/C (ISBN: 9781668487372) • US $215.00

IGI Global
PUBLISHER of TIMELY KNOWLEDGE

701 East Chocolate Avenue, Hershey, PA 17033, USA
Tel: 717-533-8845 x100 • Fax: 717-533-8661
E-Mail: cust@igi-global.com • www.igi-global.com

Table of Contents

Detailed Table of Contents

The authors present an overview of the four phases of problem solving: (1) problem identification; (2) solution design; (3) implementation; and (4) evaluation. The four types do not of course exhaust all the various kinds of problems and types of complexity. They are merely a start. And it's definitively not the case that one cannot prefer one or more of the types at the same time. Nonetheless, typically, one prefers one more than the others. Likewise, while all four phases are of equal importance, the authors are primarily concerned with the problem identification phase. For if we end up "solving the wrong problem(s) precisely," then we only end up adding to complexity.

A System is an intentionally designed, systematically organized, whole entity (e.g., an automobile, computer, smart building, etc.) that has one or more essential functions so that an individual and/or groups of people are thereby able to accomplish a set of important purposes. Furthermore, the functions, not the parts, are critical in defining a System. By means of their functions, the parts exist to allow people to accomplish significant purposes, not the other way around. A critical distinction is that a System's parts have functions while only humans as purposive individuals have purposes.

The Jungian personality framework (JPF) was developed by Katherine Briggs and Isabelle Myer Brigg and is based on the pioneering work of the eminent Swiss psychiatrist/psychoanalyst Carl Jung. Jung observed that no matter what the field of human endeavor with which he was familiar—art, history, literature, psychology, etc.--the same basic differences in outlook emerged repeatedly. They represented the fundamental differences between how different people viewed any situation, field of human knowledge, and/or practice.

This tool is concerned with the different kinds of knowledge that are best suited for different kinds of problems. (1) Expert agreement—something is objective if and only if it's based on "hard Data, facts, or observations" and the "tight agreement" between different observers as to the data, etc. (2) True formula—something is objective if, and only if, it's based on logical reasoning from self-evident first principles or premises. (3) Multiple perspectives—something is objective if and only if it's the product and the result of multiple points of view. (4) Expert disagreement—something is objective if and only if it's the product and the result of (that is, it survives) the most intense debate between the most disparate points of view. And finally, (5) Systems thinking—something is objective if and only if it's the product and the result of the most intense effort of sweeping in knowledge from the arts, humanities, professions, philosophy, sciences, etc.

The authors present a general method known as assumptional analysis for uncovering and analyzing key assumptions. Assumptions are plotted on a two-dimensional chart. The horizontal dimension ranged from those assumptions on the left that were relatively unimportant to those on the right that were extremely important to a strategy's success. The vertical dimension ranged from those assumptions on the top that were felt to be certain to those on the bottom that were felt to be uncertain. They were as likely to be false as they were to be true.

Chapter 6

There are basically five different ways or modes of handling conflict. Two underlying dimensions are at the basis of the model: assertiveness and cooperativeness. The first dimension, assertiveness, is the extent to which a person tries to satisfy his or her needs or concerns irrespective of those of others. The second dimension, cooperativeness, is the extent to which a person tries to satisfy another person's needs or concerns irrespective of his or hers. Combining the two dimensions in all ways results in five basic modes: Competing (high in assertiveness and low in cooperativeness), accommodating (low in assertiveness and high in cooperativeness), compromising (moderate in both assertiveness and cooperativeness), avoiding (low on both dimensions), and collaborating (high on both dimensions).

Chapter 7

The authors present Stephen Toulmin's incredibly powerful framework for analyzing the structure of arguments: the Toulmin argumentation framework, or TAF for short. Every argument terminates in a claim, the end conclusion of an argument. Every argument also makes use of evidence of some kind. In short, the evidence is the evidentiary support upon which an argument is built. The warrant, which is the because part of an argument, is the bridge between the evidence and the claim. The backing is the deeper set of background reasons why the warrant should be accepted. Finally, every argument has a rebuttal. The rebuttal is the full set of counter-arguments against every part of the main argument, for example, why the claim is dubious and makes no sense at all, why the evidence is flawed and therefore doesn't support the claim, why the warrant is deficient, and why the backing doesn't support the warrant.

Foreword

The world is a complex place and is getting more so with each emerging technical and social innovation. As our technologies and markets become more sophisticated and our communication and transport systems become more interconnected, innovations—and failures—can spread with dizzying speed. Advances in artificial intelligence are leading to the rapid development and deployment of autonomous and self-directed systems that look set to add further layers of complexity to our health, transport, financial and other systems in ways that may bring enormous benefits, and enormous harm. A dramatically changing climate is (or should be) introducing new complexities to almost every decision in almost every sector. And our health and care systems are confronting the complexity of new diseases while needing to find ways to implement innovative—and complex—new ways of treating old ones. Complexity has become one of the defining characteristics of modern societies, and of the challenges that modern society confronts.

This process of complexification demands that we complexify our own thinking and practical approaches to strategy, leadership, management and control. In the spirit of Ashby's (1958) law of requisite variety: a complex system can only be understood and controlled by a system of equivalent complexity. This book represents an attempt to assist in that process, providing as it does a wealth of practical tools and frames for thinking, seeing and acting in a complex world. What we are often confronted with when we engage with complexity is something that can, at first blush, look like a mess. One of the most fundamental challenges that must be confronted in coping with complexity is to recognise, frame and bring structure to the ill-structured problems that characterise many of the most important problems in modern society (Simon, 1973). Structuring ill-structured problems requires a unique set of skills which must be applied from the earliest and most tentative phases of problem solving, and which demand systemic, holistic, creative and collaborative modes of inquiry and synthesis.

Engaging with complexity inevitably depends more on a process of iterative and cautious sensemaking rather than of definitive and confident decision-making (Weick, 1995). In this book, Rune Storesund and Ian Mitroff do particularly well to bring together a diverse and practical set of models, tools and concepts that can be used for collective sensemaking and collaborative action. The tools and ideas presented in this book reach back to the definitive systems theory of organizational theorist Russ Ackoff (1971), and even further to some of the founding explorations of personality psychology which have more recently found popularity in some commercial applications. They also draw on more recent innovations in important areas such as the analysis and resolution of conflict, the foundational systems and principles of inquiry, the structure and analysis of arguments, and the strategic analysis of assumptions. It is the latter that can remain the most readily hidden and, if not surfaced and understood, the most damaging. Decades of work—and countless organizational disasters—have dramatically illustrated the insidious threat posed by hidden assumptions (Turner, 1976). These threats are only amplified—and rendered harder to identify—by increasing sociotechnical complexity.

In bringing together a set of practical tools for thinking and acting on, in and through complexity, Storesund and Mitroff develop a genuinely pragmatic approach to one of the defining challenges of our age. Pragmatism represents a practical, collaborative, incremental and learning-oriented approach to engaging with the world; one that is focused on problem solving, reflexive engagement with knowledge and assumptions, and deliberative and open modes of inquiry (Ansell, 2011). This book is awash with practical ideas, useful lenses, tangible methods and engaging examples that span from the management of wildfires to the development of health policy. It represents a rich portfolio of tools, and an illustrative compendium of the requisite variety that will be needed to underpin our collective efforts directed at coping with complexity.

Carl Macrae
University of Nottingham, UK

REFERENCES

Ackoff, R. L. (1971). Towards a system of systems concepts. *Management Science*, *17*(11), 661–671. doi:10.1287/mnsc.17.11.661

Ansell, C. (2011). *Pragmatist Democracy: Evolutionary Learning as Public Philosophy*. Oxford University Press. doi:10.1093/acprof:oso/9780199772438.001.0001

Ashby, W. R. (1958). Requisite variety and its implications for the control of complex systems. *Cybernetica*, *1*, 83–99.

Simon, H. A. (1973). The structure of ill-structured problems. *Artificial Intelligence*, *4*(3-4), 181–201. doi:10.1016/0004-3702(73)90011-8

Turner, B. (1976). The organizational and interorganizational development of disasters. *Administrative Science Quarterly*, *21*(3), 378–397. doi:10.2307/2391850

Weick, K. E. (1995). *Sensemaking in Organizations*. Sage.

Preface

We live in a world in which every aspect of our existence is influenced by inordinate amounts of complexity. Technical Complexity, for example, is not necessarily the same as Economic Complexity although the two are related. Similarly, Public Health and Social Complexity are different as well. Nonetheless, one thing above all is a prominent feature of today's world; all the various types and forms of complexity are not only related, but deeply intertwined. Today, an idea can travel the globe in mere seconds thanks to the internet and social media! These factors make our world today so complex and extremely different from previous ages in history.

And yet, for the most part, our educational system has lagged seriously behind in helping to arm us with strategies, and methods to grapple, and thereby cope with complexity. This book exists to meet this pressing need. We present tools, methods, and strategies (Tools), which, if they are used correctly, can aid us in Coping with Complexity. The key to Coping with Complexity is to arm oneself with methods and strategies to be able to structure problems that are not oversimplified, but well-defined enough and representative of the complex situation, so that informed decisions are made, and purposeful actions taken that yield the intended outcomes.

We start (Chapter 1) by presenting an initial take on problems with which we are presented in everyday life. These problems can be crisp, clear, and straightforward (what we will refer to as "exercises"), but they can also be convoluted, unclear, and seemingly impossible to grapple (what we refer to as "messes"). We offer guidance on how to frame complex problems, an overview of problem treatments, as well as introduction to the four phases of problem solving.

Next, Chapter 2 introduces the concept of Systems, which recognizes and acknowledges the multi-faceted composition of the larger world in which we live in. The notion of Systems is more than a concept; it is an intellectual way of life, a worldview, a concept of the nature of reality and how to investigate it without oversimplifying and committing "E3 Errors," or solving the wrong problem precisely. Having an understanding of the larger picture is critical to confronting Complexity because it is the only framework that allows for the full consideration of the unbounded nature of complex messes.

Our perceptions, beliefs, and attitudes towards different kinds of problems are a major part of the book and a recurring theme. For this reason, we explore in detail how different attitudes and mental states directly affect our ability to confront different kinds of problems (Chapter 3). The Jungian Personality Framework (JPF) is fundamental in understanding why different Personality Types relate differently to problems.

Knowledge is a key component in Coping with Complexity, so Chapter 4 outlines the use of Inquiry Systems (ISs) to collect relevant knowledge to the complex challenge at hand. Namely, what kinds of Knowledge Producing Systems are most appropriate and thereby are needed for which kinds of problems?

We cannot emphasize enough the importance of fundamental assumptions when it comes to basis for making decisions. For this reason, Chapter 5 describes a general method known as Strategic Assumption Surfacing And Testing or (SAST) for uncovering and analyzing key assumptions. Assumptions are pivotal in structuring productive discussions when faced with differing opinions and thoughts on decisions needing to be made.

When it comes to navigating problems and the associated suite of decisions needing to be made, one can never escape conflict. Intense conflict can result in "Fight, Flight, or Freeze." We present an overview of various conflict modes and provide available modes of addressing and confronting conflict (Chapter 6), which can overcome the immobilizing sense of 'Freezing," the fear-induced "Flight" response, or conflict escalating "Fight" response.

Chapter 7 presents the Toulmin Argumentation Framework (TAF), which is crucial in examining the different types of arguments that people give in responding to different types of problems and issues in general. The TAF provides a powerful framework for analyzing the structure of arguments and can be used to outsmart Complexity by appropriately structuring arguments that integrate the multiple Tools presented in this book and honing in on solutions to problems that are not oversimplified and speak to the many different associated perspectives and beliefs.

Chapter 8 provides a synthetic case study that applies the concepts presented in the book to one hypothetical complex messy problem: future increase in hurricane frequency and intensity because of climate change. The highly interrelated nature of the topic is outlined and acknowledge that it's an ill-defined, unstructured, and unbounded problem. Problem treatment approaches and mitigation solution timeframes. This evaluation helps break down the larger problem into smaller components as well as assisting us in providing some definition, structure, and boundary. The initial complex problem is considered from multiple perspectives (ISTJ, ENFP, and INTJ)\, where each offers valuable insights, emphasizing the importance of integrating diverse perspectives in understanding and approaching complex problems.

In the end, we are dealing with Complex, Messy Systems. To cope with them as effectively as we can demands that we not only be aware of, but master four essential activities. First, we not only need to acknowledge, but to accept that much in our lives is Complex and Messy. We should acknowledge and accept our role in contributing to both the Complexity and Messiness of the world. In other words, we need to accept social responsibility for our actions as well as our inactions. Second, we need to leverage and advance Tools for Coping with Complex, Messy Systems. Third, we need to apply the Tools as best we can. We also need to accept that we cannot go it alone. Coping requires the intense cooperation of others. It requires us to give up the idea that we and we alone "own" certain parts of problems. Fourth, we need to assess how the Tools are working in aiding our Coping, and to go back and Reapply the Tools if need be. In short, Coping with Complexity is an on-going, if not never-ending process.

One thing is above all is abundantly clear. We either learn to face up to complexity and deal with it, or it will not only overwhelm, but ultimately defeat us. Let us not be immobilized by complexity but leverage the presented Tools to navigate and overcome the challenges of complexity.

Rune Storesund
Storesund Consulting, Kensington, USA

Ian I. Mitroff
Mitroff Crisis Management, Berkeley, USA

Introduction

This book is aimed to assist decision makers avoid E3 errors (solving the wrong problem precisely), which typically occurs when 'complex' problems are oversimplified in order to become more manageable. We all have experience in making decisions based on simple and straight-forward problems (which we refer to as Exercises), but when it comes to multifaceted and inter-related problems (which we call Messes), we can quickly and easily be overwhelmed by the complexity as well as the lack of similar experiences. These constraints manifest themselves into decisions and actions based on beliefs formed from previous experiences and not based on the needs of the actual complex problem at hand.

We aim to arm decision makers with additional cognitive and decision-making tools to confront complexity and apply structured decomposition to articulate a well-specified problem to which a series of exercises can be applied that will responsibly inform the decision maker to make decisions and take actions that are compatible with the characteristics and attributes of the 'mess.'

Chapter 1
Introduction to Framing and "Solving" Problems

ABSTRACT

The authors present an overview of the four phases of problem solving: (1) problem identification; (2) solution design; (3) implementation; and (4) evaluation. The four types do not of course exhaust all the various kinds of problems and types of complexity. They are merely a start. And it's definitively not the case that one cannot prefer one or more of the types at the same time. Nonetheless, typically, one prefers one more than the others. Likewise, while all four phases are of equal importance, the authors are primarily concerned with the problem identification phase. For if we end up "solving the wrong problem(s) precisely," then we only end up adding to complexity.

"The greatest challenge to any thinker is stating the problem in a way that will allow a solution." — Bertrand Russell

Learning Objectives

- Define what constitutes a 'mess', 'problem', and 'exercise'
- Differentiate a 'mess' from an 'exercise'
- Identify steps to frame a 'problem'
- List four different problem treatments
- Describe the three elements of Ends Planning
- Explain the Diamond Model's four phases of problem solving

DOI: 10.4018/978-1-6684-6563-9.ch001

INTRODUCTION

In a small coastal town named Seaville, residents began noticing peculiar changes. The local beach, where families spent their summers building sandcastles and picnicking, started shrinking. Each year, there was less and less space to lay out a beach towel, and some of the oldest beachfront cafes had to be abandoned due to increasing water levels. The town's fishermen, who had fished the nearby waters for generations, began complaining about decreasing fish catches and the unpredictability of the weather.

Meanwhile, inland, farmers faced their own set of challenges. Unpredictable rain patterns meant that some months saw intense flooding, while others brought drought-like conditions. Crops that once thrived in Seaville started failing, and the apple orchard that held the town's annual apple-picking festival produced fewer apples each year. Residents also started experiencing hotter summers and colder winters, with many elderly citizens finding it particularly challenging to cope with the extreme temperatures.

All these changes in Seaville weren't isolated incidents but were interconnected symptoms of a larger issue: climate change. The rising sea levels affected the beach and fishing patterns, while the changing weather patterns impacted agriculture and daily life. Seaville's challenges were not singular problems that could be tackled individually but a complex web of interrelated issues—a true "mess". Addressing one concern without considering the others would only provide temporary relief and potentially exacerbate other problems.

Let's delve deeper into the complex web of interrelated issues Seaville faces due to climate change:

Rising Sea Levels

Seaville: As the global temperatures rise, polar ice caps melt and cause sea levels to increase. In Seaville, this results in the gradual loss of beachfront. The increased salinity from seawater intrusion can contaminate freshwater sources and affect local aquifers, making freshwater less available for the community.

Farmer's Fields: Farmlands near the coast experience saltwater intrusion, which damages the soil quality, making it less fertile and harder for crops to thrive.

Changed Rainfall Patterns

Seaville: Inconsistent rain affects the town's infrastructure. Sudden heavy rainfall can cause local flooding, affecting homes and businesses, while prolonged dry periods can deplete local reservoirs, leading to water shortages.

Farmer's Fields: Erratic rainfall makes it challenging for farmers to predict the best times for planting and harvesting. Floods can drown crops, while drought conditions can wither them away.

Shifts in Biodiversity

Seaville: As sea temperatures change, certain marine species that the local fishermen rely upon move to colder waters or die out, affecting the fishing industry. New, sometimes invasive species might move in, affecting the balance of the local ecosystem.

Farmer's Fields: Changes in local biodiversity can introduce new pests or diseases that attack crops. The decrease in beneficial insects, like bees, affects pollination and reduces yields.

Temperature Extremes

Seaville: Hotter summers mean residents consume more energy for cooling, straining the local power grid. The elderly or those without proper housing face health risks during heatwaves. Colder winters increase heating costs and can disrupt the regular activities of the town.

Farmer's Fields: Extreme temperatures can kill crops or reduce their growth period. Certain crops might no longer be viable if temperatures continue to rise.

Economic Strains

Seaville: As the beach shrinks and fishing yields decrease, tourism and fishing, two primary sources of income for the town, decline. This can lead to job losses and reduced income for many families.

Farmer's Fields: Reduced yields and the unpredictability of crops mean farmers face financial instability. Some might need to change their farming methods or the crops they cultivate, requiring investment and new skills.

Each of these challenges does not stand alone but is connected in myriad ways. For example, economic strains in Seaville due to reduced tourism can mean fewer people buying local produce, further impacting the already struggling farmers. This intricate interplay of issues exemplifies a "mess", where problems are interconnected, and addressing one in isolation is extremely unlikely to lead to a comprehensive solution.

If we think of a spectrum of discreteness both in the structure and boundaries of a perceived problem or challenge, then at one end of the spectrum, we have exercises. These are well-bounded, well-structured; you basically know what the answer will be, but not necessarily the magnitude. At the other end of the spectrum, we have 'messes.' These are unbounded, unstructured, and highly interconnected... there is no clear end or beginning. Bridging between 'exercises' and 'messes' are 'problems.' Problems are instances where one can extract a representation of an aspect of a mess that can then be broken down into a series of exercises (which can be solved) and thus become the basis for decisions to be made. It is important to note that messes can be extremely challenging to confront due to the ambiguity in who the actual stakeholders are. Table 1 presents a summary of the attributes of exercises, problems, and messes.

Table 1. Differences between exercises, problems, and messes

EXERCISES	PROBLEMS	MESSES
*Bounded *Structured *Well-Defined *Existing Algorithms *Established "Rules" *All stakeholders in strong agreement	*Establish base assumptions *Questions to be answered *Abstracted from messes *Well-Specified *Identify plausible "Rules" *Requires Effective Communication	*Unbounded *Unstructured *Ill-Defined *Heuristics (judgment) *No established "Rules" *Strong Stakeholder Disagreement *Ineffective Communication
*Apply to all stakeholders (stakeholder independent)	*Discover stakeholders	*Involves hidden/improbable/ignored stakeholders

This chapter arms the reader with knowledge so that they are not either (a) immobilized by indecision when faced with a mess or (b) oversimplify the problem so as to 'solve the wrong problem precisely', but rather arm them with the tools to confront and responsibly navigate the complexities of messes and extract representative problems upon which exercises can be applied and decisions made and/or solutions implemented.

RECOGNIZING MESSES

Messes are unbounded (having no apparent beginning or end), unstructured (lacking an obvious and/or explicit organization), and ill-defined (having a high degree of vagueness, ambiguity, and lack of clarity), which as a result, routinely have hidden, improbable, and ignored stakeholders. As a result of the hidden, improbable, and ignored stakeholders, the stakeholder group is largely undefined and the ability to promote "solutions" to problems is greatly constrained because you don't really know who you're talking to or what decision criteria they are using to arrive at any particular decision. On the other hand, Exercises are bounded, structured, and well-defined, which means the stakeholder groups are more explicitly defined and their decision-making criteria are more straight-forward, resulting in 'easier' decisions.

The concept of a 'Mess' stems back to Russell L. Ackoff, who originally appropriated the word 'Mess' (Ackoff, 1971, 1977, 1999) to stand for a whole system of problems that were so interconnected such that one couldn't take any of the so-called individual problems out of the Mess and attempt to analyze it on its own without doing irreparable damage both to the so-called individual problem and entire Mess of which it was an integral part. In short, the problems that constitute a Mess are so interconnected such that they are constantly changing in response to one another. Given their complexity and constantly changing nature, one never "solves Messes," certainly not in the ways that one does Bounded, Well-Structured Exercises. The best one does is to cope with Messes as best one can.

PROBLEM TREATMENTS

As discussed above, from Ackoff's perspective, a "mess" is a complex web of interrelated issues that cannot be solved individually; they must be managed as a whole. The first step in dealing with a mess is to understand its scope and its interconnected components. Ackoff would advocate for a systems-thinking approach, where one maps out the elements of the mess and the relationships between them. This mapping not only provides a comprehensive view but also highlights areas where specific problems could be extracted for more targeted interventions.

Once the mess is understood systemically, the next step is to identify specific "problems" within the mess that are sufficiently independent to be treated individually. These problems should be 'bite-sized,' meaning their solutions should be actionable and measurable, but they should also be 'juicy,' meaning solving them would create noticeable positive change within the larger system. For example, in the case of climate change affecting the coastal town Seaside, one identified problem could be the erosion of the beachfront, which is easier to tackle compared to the entire mess of climate-related issues affecting the town.

After extracting a problem, Ackoff would suggest applying problem treatments, or solutions, specifically designed for it. Using established methodologies and tools, one can devise strategic plans, set measurable objectives, and allocate resources to tackle the problem effectively. However, Ackoff would remind us that solving one problem should be seen as a part of the overall strategy for managing the mess, not as an end in itself. Therefore, any solution applied should be continually assessed for its impact on the other components of the mess, ensuring that solving one problem does not inadvertently make another problem worse. Understanding that one can't necessarily solve a mess, but one may be able to treat problems

There are four ways of treating problems: absolving, resolving, solving, and dissolving (Ackoff, 1999).

- Absolving a problem is ignoring a problem and hoping it will just go away or self-resolve itself. No active problem solving occurs.
- Resolving of a problem is an action(s) that yields an outcome that is satisfactory. An attempt is made to find the cause of the problem and the remove or suppress it.
- Solving a problem is an action(s) that optimizes an outcome that is desirable.
- Dissolution of a problem eliminates it by redesigning the system that contains it so that the context for the problem is removed.

Problem treatments vary based on the complexity of the problem (Table 2). Exercises, for example, lend themselves for resolving and solving. These types of problems, because they are well-structured, bounded, well-defined, and with clear stakeholders can typically be solved directly or resolved to great satisfaction of all involved parties. Messes on the other hand, tend to employ absolving and dissolving due to the nature of the mess where the actual problem (or problems) are ill-defined, unbounded, and unstructured. Well formulated problems tend to lend themselves to resolving, solving, and dissolving.

Table 2. Summary of problem treatments

PROBLEM TREATMENT	EXERCISES	PROBLEMS	MESSES
Absolving	Less Relevant	Less Relevant	Very Relevant
Resolving	Relevant	Relevant	Very Relevant
Solving	Very Relevant	Very Relevant	Less Relevant
Dissolving	Less Relevant	Relevant	Very Relevant

Additionally, there are some problems that require more time to address than others. In these instances, one can leverage the concepts of Ends Planning (Ackoff, 1999), which consists of designing a desired future and extracting from it those ends that can be achieved in incremental temporal steps:

Goals – Ends that are expected to be obtained within the near-term (timeframe of months to years);

Objectives – Ends that are expected to be immediately achieved, but rather through a series of goal sessions (timeframe of years to decades); and

Ideals – Ends that are believed to be 'unattainable' in that one makes continuous progress to achieve or maintain, without a formal 'end' (ie being safe, being a good parent, being financially responsible).

Ends Planning enables one to take more complicated and/or complex problems that span years if not decades and divide them up into a series of sequential mini problems that can be managed in a reasonable period of time. This approach enables one to take otherwise daunting or intimidating problems and break them down into smaller more doable problems.

Consider the issue of water pollution affecting both Seaville's residents and the nearby farmer's fields. This is a complex problem with multiple, interconnected causes such as agricultural runoff, industrial waste, and poor sewage management. Here are examples of actions that can be taken in the short term, medium term, and long term:

Goals: Short Term (i.e., Within One Year)

- Public Awareness Campaign: Start an immediate awareness campaign on water conservation and the dangers of water pollution. Share steps for safe water use and ways to minimize pollution.
- Water Quality Testing: Implement rigorous water testing in Seaville and the farmer's fields to identify pollution levels and sources.
- Emergency Filtration Systems: Install temporary water filtration units at critical points where water pollution is highest.
- Regulatory Enforcement: Strengthen and enforce existing regulations on industrial waste discharge and agricultural runoff.

Objectives: Medium Term (i.e., Three to Five Years)

- Upgrade Sewage System: Begin upgrading the sewage treatment plants to better handle contaminants.
- Natural Filtration Systems: Collaborate with farmers to establish buffer zones with plants that naturally filter water before it enters local rivers or groundwater.
- Local Legislation: Pass laws that require agricultural and industrial operations to adopt cleaner practices, with incentives for early compliance.

- Community Monitoring: Establish a community-led water monitoring system that allows residents to report issues or test water quality.

Ideals: Long Term (i.e., More Than Ten Years)

- Large-Scale Infrastructure: Build a state-of-the-art water treatment facility capable of handling the water needs for both Seaville and the surrounding agricultural areas.
- Sustainable Farming: Promote and subsidize sustainable farming practices that not only increase yield but also minimize water pollution.
- Education: Integrate water conservation and pollution control into educational curriculums from elementary school through high school.
- Green Urban Planning: Redesign urban spaces in Seaville to include more green areas that naturally filter water and decrease the likelihood of floods, which can exacerbate water pollution.

By taking targeted actions in the short, medium, and long term, it's possible to make substantial progress in addressing the complex issue of water pollution in Seaville and the farmer's fields.

SENSEMAKING

Sensemaking was a concept introduced by Karl Weick in the 1970s who argued that organizations are central arenas for making sense of things due to their inherent complexities. It can be understood as a methodology to structure the unstructured and give meaning to experiences that are initially perceived as random or chaotic. It's a process through which individuals or groups come to understand and give meaning to complex or unfamiliar situations. When faced with such situations, individuals engage in data collection, interpretation, and interaction, reflecting on their findings, and then decide on a course of action. Feedback loops are integral, allowing for adjustments based on new data or outcomes.

Key Concepts

1. **Retrospection**: Sensemaking often occurs post-event, reflecting on experiences to understand them.
2. **Identity**: Who we are shapes how we interpret events.
3. **Enactment**: Through actions, individuals can shape their environments.

4. **Ongoing**: Sensemaking is continuous; as we get more information, interpretations may change.
5. **Social**: Interactions with others play a significant role in how we make sense of events.
6. **Cues**: Small details or cues can significantly shape understanding.
7. **Plausibility over Accuracy**: People tend to prioritize narratives that make sense over those that are necessarily accurate.

Sensemaking is a vital cognitive and social process where individuals and groups interpret ambiguous situations. Over the past five decades, it has been a key area of academic exploration, revealing the complex interplay of individual cognition, social interactions, and organizational contexts in shaping how we understand the world around us.

Imagine a coastal community that, over the years, has experienced hurricanes but generally of manageable magnitudes. However, in recent years, they've observed an uptick in the frequency and intensity of these hurricanes, leading to more frequent evacuations, greater damage, and more prolonged recovery periods. This change disrupts the community's previous understanding and expectations.

1. **Disruption**: The community recognizes a pattern of more frequent and more intense hurricanes.
2. **Data Gathering**: Community leaders gather historical weather data, consult climate scientists, and review records of local hurricane impacts over the past decades.
3. **Interpretation**: Initial data suggests a link between global climate change and the rising intensity of hurricanes. Warmer ocean temperatures might be fueling more powerful storms.
4. **Interaction**: Community forums are held where residents share their personal experiences. Scientists present their findings, and local emergency services share their challenges. There's a consensus that this is not a temporary anomaly but possibly the new norm.
5. **Reflection**: The community realizes that while immediate disaster response is crucial, there's a need for long-term strategies to adapt to this new reality, such as improved infrastructure, updated evacuation plans, and better public education on hurricane preparedness.
6. **Action**: They decide to allocate funds to bolster sea defenses, revise building codes for new constructions to be more hurricane-resistant, launch a public awareness campaign about hurricane preparedness, and collaborate with neighboring communities for coordinated evacuation plans.

7. **Feedback Loop**: After implementing the changes, the community closely monitors the effects of subsequent hurricanes, assesses the efficacy of their preparations, and remains open to revising their strategies based on real-world outcomes and evolving scientific understanding.

As these strategies are implemented, the community would then monitor their effectiveness during subsequent hurricanes, adjusting as needed based on outcomes and updated scientific insights. Through sensemaking, this community could better understand, adapt to, and prepare for their changing reality. In this scenario, the coastal community uses sensemaking to understand and adapt to the changing patterns of hurricanes, leading to both immediate and long-term strategies to enhance resilience and safety.

CONCEPTUAL MODELS

A conceptual model serves as a representation of a system (or sub-system), capturing its significant elements and the relationships among them. Think of it as a mental map or a simplified sketch that outlines a system's structure and behavior. Unlike detailed models, which may be laden with specifications and intricate calculations, a conceptual model focuses on the broader picture, highlighting key components and their interactions.

The idea of conceptual modeling is not new. Its roots can be traced back to ancient civilizations where rudimentary diagrams or physical models were used to depict various systems, from the arrangement of celestial bodies to architectural plans of significant structures. However, the term gained more formal recognition in the mid-20th century, notably within the realms of systems theory and computer science. Here, conceptual models emerged as vital tools, aiding in the design of complex systems, software, and even aiding scientific understanding by providing abstract representations of phenomena.

Conceptual models play an indispensable role in multiple disciplines, from natural sciences to social sciences and engineering. They help stakeholders visualize and understand a system, making complex ideas more digestible. By highlighting primary elements and their interconnections, such models enable improved communication, fostered collaboration, and streamlined decision-making. Moreover, they often serve as foundational blueprints upon which more detailed, quantitative models can be built.

Before diving into the creation of a conceptual model, it's paramount to define its purpose. Is it being developed to understand a natural ecosystem, design a software interface, or perhaps guide policy decisions? Once the purpose is clearer, the scope can be delineated, determining which components of the system should be included and which can be overlooked for the sake of simplicity.

With a clear understanding of the purpose and scope, the next step is to identify the major components or entities of the system. This is often an iterative process, involving brainstorming sessions, literature reviews, and consultations with experts. Once these elements are pinned down, their relationships or interactions need to be charted out, considering how one component affects or is affected by another.

Creating a conceptual model is rarely a linear, one-off endeavor. Instead, it's an iterative process, where the model is continually refined as more information becomes available or as feedback is received from stakeholders. A well-constructed conceptual model, rooted in clarity and simplicity, can be an invaluable tool, bridging the gap between complex realities and comprehensible representations, aiding understanding, and paving the way for more detailed analyses.

Conceptual models are visual representations, and a variety of techniques are utilized to effectively convey the structure and dynamics of a system or concept. Here are some common techniques used to illustrate conceptual models:

1. **Flowcharts**: These diagrams represent processes or systems using boxes of various shapes to depict specific stages, activities, or entities. Arrows guide the viewer, showing the flow or sequence of steps.
2. **Mind Maps**: Originating from brainstorming sessions, mind maps radiate from a central concept or idea. Branching out, they illustrate sub-concepts or related ideas, providing a hierarchical view of the system.
3. **Venn Diagrams**: Used primarily to showcase relationships between different sets, Venn diagrams utilize overlapping circles or other shapes to indicate shared characteristics or intersections between entities.
4. **System Dynamics Diagrams**: These models, often used in systems thinking, represent feedback loops, stocks, and flows. They are particularly useful for depicting how components of a system interact and influence one another over time.
5. **Spider Diagrams**: Similar to mind maps but more structured, spider diagrams branch out from a central theme, capturing main ideas and then further sub-ideas or details.
6. **Concept Maps**: These are structured graphs that illustrate the relationships between concepts, usually shaped as circles or boxes. They differ from mind maps by their structure and the nature of the relationships they depict. They may include labeled arrows or linking phrases like "gives rise to" or "results in" to describe the nature of the relationship between concepts.

7. **Matrix Diagrams**: Using rows and columns, matrix diagrams showcase the relationships or connections between two or more lists. This is particularly useful when you want to depict how different elements correlate or interact.
8. **SWOT Analysis**: Often utilized in business and strategy development, SWOT diagrams segment information into Strengths, Weaknesses, Opportunities, and Threats, providing a clear overview of the internal and external factors affecting an entity.
9. **Storyboarding**: Originating from film and animation, storyboards sequence images or panels in a linear fashion to depict the flow of events, user interactions, or system processes.
10. **UML (Unified Modeling Language) Diagrams**: Widely adopted in software engineering, UML diagrams come in various forms (like use case diagrams, sequence diagrams, and class diagrams) to represent different aspects of software systems.

Selecting the right technique depends on the specific needs of the project, the nature of the system being modeled, and the audience's familiarity with the method of representation.

VENN DIAGRAMMING MESSES TO PROBLEMS

It can be helpful to provide some boundary and structure to enable logical and structured framing of problems. One can take a very broad subject and break it down into smaller, more manageable components that are still consistent with the nature and characteristics of the mess but allow for the application of more explicit definition as well as the ability to separate out subtopics.

Venn diagrams offer a visual way to segment and organize the components of a "mess" by representing them as overlapping circles. Each circle can represent a different aspect or factor within the larger system. The points where these circles overlap indicate areas of intersection or interrelation among the issues at hand. For example, if you're dealing with a mess related to community health, one circle might represent healthcare access, another could represent local environmental factors, and yet another might symbolize economic conditions. The overlapping regions could reveal specific problems like inadequate healthcare for low-income families in polluted areas, which combines elements from all three circles.

By isolating these overlapping regions in a Venn diagram, one can identify specific problems that might be more manageable than trying to tackle the entire mess at once. These intersections often present themselves as "key leverage points" where intervention can produce the most significant impact on the system as a whole.

Once you've used a Venn diagram to break the mess down into these more specific, intersecting problems, you can apply targeted treatments to each. For instance, in our community health example, focused efforts could be made to improve healthcare access specifically in low-income, high-pollution areas. These more contained issues are easier to define, measure, and solve, making a Venn diagram a useful tool for translating a complex mess into actionable problems.

Consider the following. Martha is a single mother struggling to support herself and her two children. As a low-skilled worker, she earns only $3000 a month. Unfortunately, she needs a minimum of $3500 to adequately feed, clothe, and house herself and her two children. Martha's problem is not merely the difference between $3500 and $3000. The real problem is not one of arithmetic or Finance alone. Martha already knows too well the amount she's short every month. The real problem is multi-faceted and layered. Does Martha get support from the father of the children? Does she have access to child-care? Does it even exist? Why, why not? How can Martha's family help? Do they even want to? Can she enroll in an educational program or programs that will give her the true skills she needs to get a better paying and more rewarding job? Can Social Services help? Can a Social Worker steer her to the right programs?

If we examine Martha's story, she was in a situation where she had $3500 in expenses each month, but only $3000 in income. If we consider this equivalent to Martha's Financial State, we observe that there are many facets to her situation. Use of Venn diagrams can be a useful way to organize the various elements, acknowledge interrelationships, and then address individual components that would then impact the overall condition of Martha's financial state. A Venn diagram uses overlapping circles or other shapes to illustrate the logical relationships between two or more sets of items and graphically organize things, highlighting how the items are similar and different.

Figure 1 presents an example where differing elements that contribute to Martha's financial state can be inventoried and illustrate relationships. If we start with Martha's Employment and draw a circle is largely influenced by her current job (Job #1), but also by her educational background (Education). Her credit is impacted by her employment as well as her expenses. While these are simple illustrations, they do show the utility of using Venn diagrams to aid in 'making sense of the mess' and providing structure and boundaries to what would otherwise be a jumble of issues and topics.

Figure 1. Organization of differing elements that contribute to Martha's financial stat using a Venn diagram

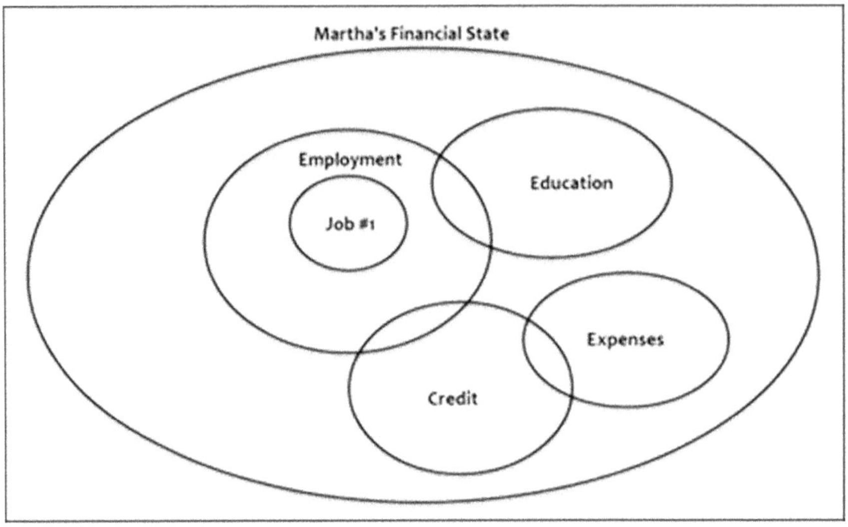

DIAMOND MODEL

The Diamond Model is most associated with Michael E. Porter, a renowned economist and professor at Harvard Business School. The model was originally developed to analyze competitive advantage among nations and industries, aiming to explain why some industries in certain nations are competitive internationally while others are not. The framework was introduced in Porter's seminal work, "The Competitive Advantage of Nations," published in 1990. Over time, the Diamond Model has been adapted for various other contexts beyond international competitiveness, including problem-solving and strategy development in a wide array of fields.

The Diamond Model has found a second life as a strategic framework for problem-solving across various domains. The model's emphasis on interconnected factors that contribute to a particular outcome has proven applicable to complex problem-solving situations. Its four-point structure, which encompasses problem identification, solution design, implementation, and evaluation, has been employed to systematically dissect and address intricate issues beyond trade and industry competitiveness. Whether it's tackling environmental challenges, healthcare inefficiencies, or organizational dilemmas, the Diamond Model provides a structured approach to identify key leverage points and to design, implement, and evaluate targeted interventions, thereby offering a comprehensive and flexible strategy for problem-solving.

Problem Identification is the first and foundational step in the Diamond Model process where the issue at hand is clearly defined and scoped out. Through data gathering, stakeholder interviews, and analytical tools, the problem is not just identified but also quantified to understand its extent and impact. Example outcomes of the problem identification step might include: (a) A comprehensive report outlining the high attrition rate in a company; (b) A health impact study identifying the specific areas most affected by air pollution; or (c) A needs assessment survey showing a community's lack of access to clean drinking water.

Once the problem identification step has concluded, the Solution Design stage begins. At this stage, various alternative solutions are brainstormed, assessed, and compared to identify the most effective and efficient way to address the problem. Criteria such as cost, feasibility, and long-term impact are considered. In the Solution Design phase of the Diamond Model, constructing an 'exact model' can be an invaluable approach for creating a detailed and accurate representation of the problem at hand and the potential solutions. This model, often crafted through mathematical formulas, simulations, or specialized software, serves as a blueprint that captures essential variables and their relationships. For instance, if the problem is traffic congestion, an exact model could use real-time data and algorithms to simulate how different solutions like widening roads or implementing a new public transit system would impact traffic flow. The model helps in anticipating potential bottlenecks, costs, and other issues before actual implementation, thereby aiding in the selection of the most effective solution. By creating an exact model, stakeholders can scrutinize each option under conditions that closely mirror reality, thus significantly reducing uncertainties and providing a robust basis for decision-making. Outcomes from the Solution Design process might include things such as: A shortlist of three potential engineering solutions to improve a city's public transportation system; A detailed proposal for implementing remote working policies to reduce attrition in a company; or An environmental impact assessment for different methods of reducing air pollution in a specific area.

Once a solution is chosen, a detailed plan is developed for its execution and the Implementation phase begins. This implementation plan includes resource allocation, timelines, and responsible parties. Then the plan is put into action. Implemented solutions might include actions such as: (a) Construction of a new light rail system in a city, based on the selected engineering solution; (b) The rollout of a new remote working policy, complete with training sessions and IT infrastructure upgrades; or (c) The installation of air purifiers and green spaces in areas identified as most polluted.

The final step of Evaluation involves assessing the outcomes against the objectives set during the problem identification and solution design stages. This helps in understanding the effectiveness of the solution and provides insights for future endeavors. Evaluation findings might include: A post-implementation study showing a 20% increase in public transportation usage; Employee surveys and attrition data showing a 30% reduction in turnover after the remote working policy was implemented; or Air quality measurements showing a 15% improvement in the targeted areas following the environmental interventions.

Each step of the Diamond Model is critical for ensuring that the problem is not just addressed but solved in a manner that is sustainable and beneficial in the long term.

Figure 2. Overview of the Diamond Model and the four problem solving phases

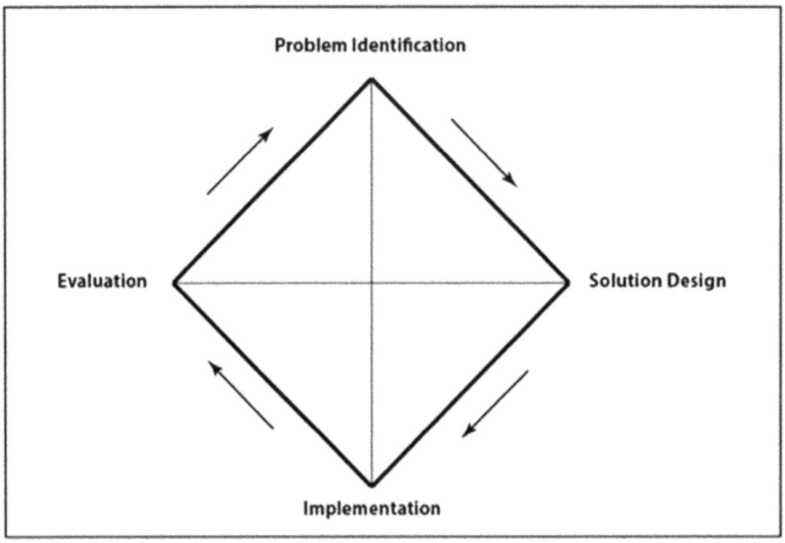

Let's examine two example case studies utilizing the Diamond Model as a framework.

Diamond Model Example One: Poor Elevator Service

The manager of a large office building was receiving mounting complaints about poor elevator service such that he felt he had no choice but to call in an outside consultant to help him with the problem. The consultant recommended putting in new elevators with different ones going to different floors. The trouble with this is that it proved so costly that it was cheaper to tear down the current building and build a new one from scratch. Fortunately, one of the clients in the building was a Clinical Psychologist. When she heard about the problem, she approached the manager with a very different solution. She recommended putting mirrors in the lobby so that people could basically occupy themselves while waiting for the elevators. Today, we would of course put in large TVs so people could watch CNN. The cost of putting in TVs is substantially less than putting in new elevators such that it doesn't even come close.

The important point of this example is that there is all difference in the world between saying the problem is fundamentally in the building versus in the people. The initial problem being sensed was that of submitted complaints for poor elevator service. One perception centered around structural deficiencies, while the other centered around the feelings of poor service, where a distraction would likely remedy the perception of poor service much more efficiently and cost-effectively than rebuilding the entire elevator bank with new elevators. Of course, at some point, new elevators may be needed, but it's more than worth it to try TVs first.

The Solutions phase forms an Exact Model of the problem that allows for quantitative analyses and bounded uncertainties. The initial system structure, boundaries, stakeholders, and assumptions are further developed and refined. A formal listing of stakeholder requirements is required. Operational assumptions are clearly identified and inventoried. There is frequently substantial data collection and development of numerical models to inform anticipated outcomes. This stage of the process is largely quantitative, and the goal is to minimize uncertainties as much as possible. Elements of the solution process are analyzed, such as operational timelines, costs, and required resources.

In developing the Exact Model, success criteria (how can one ascertain if the implemented solution remedies the sensed problem) need to be defined explicitly. Criteria for success will then be monitored during the later Implementation Phase to confirm that the implemented solution fully remedies the initial problem.

In the case of our elevator scenario, the Syntactic Phase would collect user data, develop quantitative models to analyze the optimal number of TVs required, where they are placed, what shows are made available to which groups of elevator riders. The success criterion would be a reduction of complaints by (for example) 80% per year.

The Solution Phase consists of extracting the optimal solution from "Exact Model." During this phase, one will aim to satisfy as many of the stakeholder criteria as possible. Key decision-makers review the options generated during the Syntactic Phase and choose the selected Solution configuration for implementation.

For the elevator scenario, this would encompass the building management team reviewing the evaluated scenarios and final recommendation for the number of TVs required, where they are placed, what shows are made available to which groups of elevator riders. The building management team would then either concur with the final recommendation or request a return to the Syntactic Phase if they felt some elements were either omitted or inadequately evaluated.

Diamond Model Example Two: Seaville Erratic Rainfall Patterns

Let's apply the Diamond Model to one specific issue from Seaville and the farmers' fields: erratic rainfall patterns leading to both flooding and drought first discussed in this chapter.

The first step is Problem Identification, which aims to clearly identify and understand the problem. In Seaville and the surrounding farmland, erratic rainfall is causing both flooding and drought, which in turn affects residential areas, agriculture, and local businesses. Data on rainfall patterns, flood occurrences, and drought periods would be gathered and analyzed to quantify the extent of the problem. Community input could also be collected to understand the human impact, such as property damage or reduced crop yields.

Having identified that the problem of interest is erratic rainfall, the Solution Design stage begins where various potential solutions are brainstormed and compared. For example, one solution could involve building a dam and reservoir system to store excess rainwater, which could then be released during dry periods. Another option might be to implement green infrastructure solutions like rain gardens and permeable pavements in Seaville to help manage stormwater and reduce flooding. For the farmland, drought-resistant crop varieties could be considered. Each option's cost, feasibility, and potential impact would be assessed.

Once a solution has been chosen—let's say the dam and reservoir system—it's time to move into action, which is the Implementation phase. This phase involves detailed planning, securing funding, and actual construction. Local authorities would work with engineers, environmental scientists, and the community to implement the system.

After the dam and reservoir are operational, the effectiveness of this solution would be assessed as part of the Evaluation phase. Key performance indicators might include reduced instances of flooding, more consistent water supply for agriculture, and overall community satisfaction. If the system does not meet these objectives, then the reasons for its shortcomings can be identified.

The Diamond Model allows for iterative problem-solving; the evaluation phase could reveal new insights that necessitate revisiting earlier stages. Perhaps the dam and reservoir successfully prevent flooding but don't sufficiently address drought conditions in the farmland. In that case, the model guides stakeholders back to the drawing board for refining or supplementing the initial solution, ensuring that the approach remains flexible and adaptable.

CLARITY TEST

Problem delineation and formulation can greatly benefit from the 'clarity test.' The 'clarity test' is a means by which to sharpen a problem statement so it is 'well-specified.' Well-specified refers to a situation where complete information is given so that there would be agreement that the event or topic had or had not occurred. The example given is (Henrion, 1990):

Imagine a clairvoyant who could know all the facts about the universe, past, present, and future. Given the description of the event or quantity, could she say unambiguously whether the event will occur (or has occurred), or could she give the exact numerical value of the quantity? If so, it is well-specified.

Thus, the "price of gasoline" would not pass the clarity test. The clairvoyant would want to know what kind of gasoline, sold where and when, before she could give its exact value. An adequate specification of the quantity might be "the average retail price of regular unleaded gasoline in dollars per gallon observed at service stations in the northeastern United States on January 1, 1990." Without such precision, vagueness about what the parameter represents is liable to get confounded with uncertainty about its true value.

The Clarity Test can be a very useful tool to aid in the configuration of success criteria for the implemented solution. This technique forces specificity of the outcome(s) and helps achieve alignment across multiple stakeholder groups.

ADAPTIVE MANAGEMENT AND LEARNING

Learning is near impossible unless one is aware of the possible and actual errors or the skew between the anticipated outcome vs the actual outcome. During the implementation phase, it is critical that the deployed solution be monitored to ascertain the skew between the anticipated outcome vs the actual outcome. When the assumed and actual conditions are in general agreement, no action is required. However, if there is a significant skew or deviation (on the order of 20% or more), something may have gone wrong or gone exceptionally right. In such situations, diagnostic evaluations can be very helpful to find what generated the skew and identify potential corrective actions. There are four primary mechanisms for generation of significant skew (Ackoff, 1999):

1) The information used in making the decision was in error;
2) The decision-making process may have been faulty;
3) The decision may not have been implemented as intended; and
4) The environment may have changed in a way that was not anticipated.

Reviewing these four questions in instances with significant skew between the actual outcome(s) and the intended outcome(s) will almost always provide valuable insights into explaining what went wrong and why and what corrections are needed. The Adaptive Management process (Figure 3) allows for updating and refinement of data, assumptions, and even formulation of the problem. This iterative process is followed until the skew between the actual outcome(s) and the intended outcome(s) is reduced to a tolerable level.

Figure 3: Inclusion of adaptive management and refinement based on feedback during the implementation phase...did the developed solution dissolve the sensed problem?

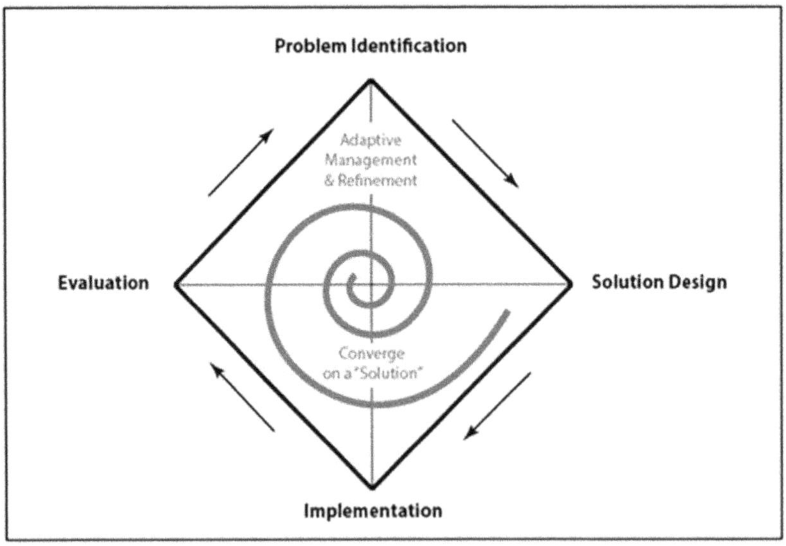

ADDITIONAL TOOLS, METHODS, AND STRATEGIES

Confronting messes, especially in the context of systems thinking and complexity, requires a variety of tools and methods. A summary of ten notable tools/methods, their primary developers, and their associated time periods is presented below:

Systems Thinking - A holistic approach that focuses on the interrelationships between components of a system rather than individual parts in isolation.

Developer: Ludwig von Bertalanffy

Time Period: 1950s-1960s

Example Applications:

- Environmental management: Understanding the interactions between species, climate, and human intervention in an ecosystem.
- Healthcare: Viewing hospitals as systems to better understand patient care paths, workflow, and resource allocation.
- Urban planning: Addressing the interconnected issues of transportation, housing, infrastructure, and the environment in growing cities.

Additional Readings (Ludwig von Bertalanffy):

- General System Theory: Foundations, Development, Applications
- Robots, Men, and Minds: Psychology in the Modern World
- Problems of Life: An Evaluation of Modern Biological Thought

Soft Systems Methodology (SSM) - A process used to understand and deal with complex problems by viewing them as systems to be explored and modeled.

Developer: Peter Checkland

Time Period: 1970s

Example Applications:

- Business process re-engineering: Identifying inefficiencies in company operations and designing better workflows.
- Community development: Engaging stakeholders in designing interventions for community challenges.
- Information systems design: Understanding user needs and requirements in software development.

Additional Readings (Peter Checkland):

- Systems Thinking, Systems Practice
- Soft Systems Methodology: A Thirty Year Retrospective
- Information, Systems and Information Systems: Making Sense of the Field (with Sue Holwell)

Scenario Planning - Strategic planning method used to make flexible long-term plans by considering various possible future scenarios.

Developer: Herman Kahn, with development in corporate contexts by Royal Dutch Shell

Time Period: 1960s-1970s

Example Applications:

- Energy sector: Predicting future energy needs and potential shifts to renewable sources.

- Financial forecasting: Planning for potential economic downturns or global market changes.
- Pandemic preparedness: Anticipating various disease outbreak scenarios and planning responses.

Additional Readings (Herman Kahn):

- On Thermonuclear War
- The Year 2000: A Framework for Speculation on the Next Thirty-Three Years (with Anthony J. Wiener)
- Thinking About the Unthinkable

Strategic Option Development and Analysis (SODA) - Uses cognitive mapping to capture individual or group perceptions and structure complex decision-making situations.

Developer: Colin Eden and Fran Ackermann

Time Period: 1980s

Example Applications:

- Corporate strategy development: Aligning team perceptions and mapping organizational goals.
- Conflict resolution: Structuring and understanding points of contention in negotiations.
- Project management: Understanding and planning complex projects with multiple stakeholders.

Additional Readings (Colin Eden):

- Making Strategy: The Journey of Strategic Management (with Fran Ackermann)
- Cognitive Mapping: A Step Towards Feasible Management of Complexity
- On the Nature of Cognitive Maps (with Fran Ackermann)

Horizon Scanning - A method to systematically identify opportunities and threats in the distant future.

Developer: Various contributors across multiple fields, particularly in governmental foresight

Time Period: Late 1990s onwards

Example Applications:

- National security: Identifying potential threats or geopolitical shifts.
- Technology forecasting: Anticipating technological advancements and their implications.
- Environmental conservation: Recognizing emerging threats to biodiversity or habitats.

Cross-Impact Analysis - A method to estimate how changes in one variable affect changes in other variables in a system.

Developer: Theodore Gordon and Olaf Helmer
Time Period: 1960s
Example Applications:

- Product development: Estimating how changes in product features might impact sales or market reception.
- Environmental policy: Gauging how interventions might affect various environmental metrics.
- Social policy evaluation: Understanding how policy changes might affect various societal indicators.

Additional Readings (Theodore Gordon):

- The Delphi Method: Techniques and Applications (with others)
- Future Studies: Qualitative and Quantitative Methods (with Jerome C. Glenn)
- Environments of the Future (with Olaf Helmer)

Causal Loop Diagrams (CLD) - Visual tools used to explore and display how different variables in a system are interrelated.
Developer: Jay W. Forrester and others in the field of system dynamics
Time Period: 1950s-1960s
Example Applications:

- Climate change research: Modeling the interactions between greenhouse gas emissions, temperature rises, and feedback loops.
- Economic modeling: Understanding the factors driving inflation, employment, and growth.
- Population studies: Analyzing birth rates, death rates, and migration patterns.

Additional Readings (Jay Forrester):

- Industrial Dynamics
- Principles of Systems
- Urban Dynamics

Morphological Analysis - A method to systematically structure and investigate complex problem spaces.
Developer: Fritz Zwicky
Time Period: 1960s
Example Applications:

- Product design: Exploring potential design configurations and innovations.
- Astrobiology: Analyzing potential life-form structures in extraterrestrial environments.
- Military strategy: Evaluating potential tactical scenarios and approaches.

Additional Readings (Fritz Zwicky):

- Discovery, Invention, Research: Through the Morphological Approach
- Morphological Astronomy
- Entdecken, Erfinden, Forschen im Morphologischen Weltbild

Multi-Criteria Decision Analysis (MCDA) - A tool that helps in making decisions involving multiple criteria, often used when dealing with complex scenarios.

Developer: Various developers in operational research

Time Period: 1970s onwards

Example Applications:

- Infrastructure development: Prioritizing projects based on cost, benefit, environmental impact, and other criteria.
- Pharmaceutical R&D: Deciding which drugs to develop based on potential impact, profitability, and ethical considerations.
- Natural resource management: Evaluating land use options considering ecological, economic, and social factors.

The Cynefin Framework - A decision-making framework that helps to understand the nature of complex problems and how to approach them.

Developer: Dave Snowden

Time Period: 1990s

Example Applications:

- Organizational change: Guiding companies in navigating change based on the complexity of their situations.
- Crisis management: Assisting leaders in responding to unforeseen events or emergencies.
- Innovation strategy: Helping organizations decide whether to pursue incremental improvements or radical innovations based on the nature of their challenges.

Additional Readings:

- Complex Acts of Knowing: Paradox and Descriptive Self-awareness (journal article)
- A Leader's Framework for Decision Making (with Mary E. Boone in Harvard Business Review)
- Storytelling: An Old Skill in a New Context (in Business Information Review)

While many of these methods have roots in earlier periods, they have been refined and evolved over time, often borrowing from each other and merging with contemporary thinking. Each of these tools and methods have the potential be applied in various sectors and contexts, depending on the nature and complexity of the challenges faced.

Figure 4. Summary of the problem-solving sequence to traverse from a potentially overwhelming mess to implemented solutions, as outlined in this chapter

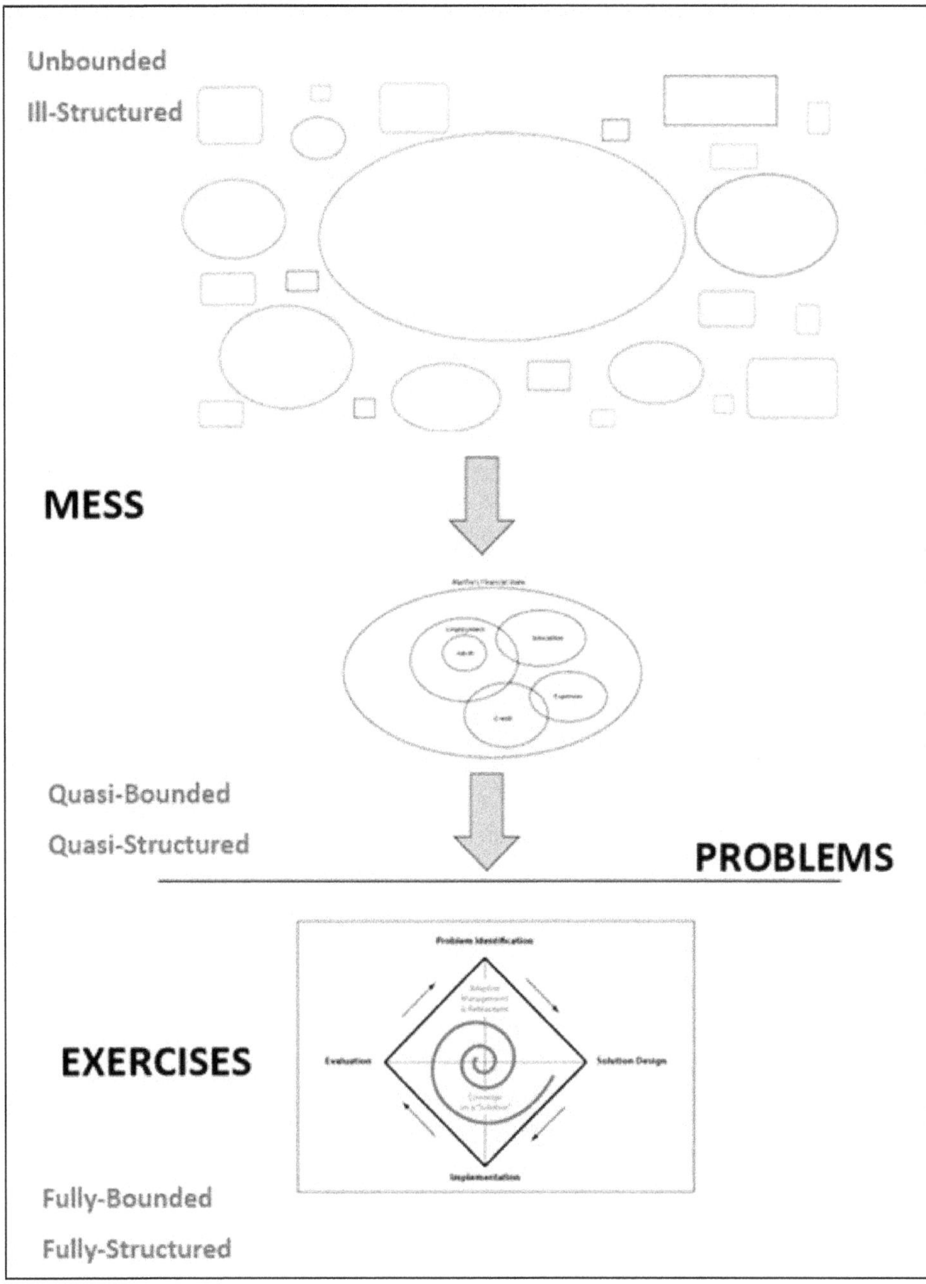

CONCLUSION

This chapter introduced the concept of exercises, problems, and messes. Exercises are well-bounded, well-structured; you know what the answer will be, but perhaps not the magnitude. Messes are unbounded, unstructured, and highly interconnected… there is no clear end or beginning. Bridging between 'exercises' and 'messes' are 'problems.'

For situations where we find ourselves in a 'mess' (unbounded, ill-structured), we can extract from the mess a subset of conditions using tools such as Venn diagrams, to frame quasi-bounded and quasi-structured "problems" to which the Diamond Model approach to problem solving can be applied. This problem-solving approach provides more explicit structure and boundaries so that a series of exercises can be applied to develop a conceptual model; then a more exacting model from which a preferred solution can be identified and implemented, with success criteria in place so that if significant skew between the intended and actual outcomes occur, we have the ability to refine and revise using adaptive management approaches. Figure 4 shows a summary of the problem-solving sequence to traverse from a potentially overwhelming mess to implemented solutions, as outlined in this Chapter.

COMPREHENSION EXERCISES

1) Which of the following best defines a 'problem'?
   a. A situation that is already perfectly understood and resolved.
   b. A situation with a specific challenge that seeks resolution.
   c. Multiple interrelated situations without clear solutions.
   d. An everyday routine that requires no critical thinking.
2) When employing Ackoff's method of "Resolving", what is the primary goal?
   a. To ignore the problem.
   b. To find the absolute best answer regardless of consequences.
   c. To implement good enough solutions, not necessarily the best or optimal ones.
   d. To redesign the system entirely to prevent the problem's occurrence.
3) Why is the Evaluation step important in the Diamond Model?
   a. To brainstorm alternative solutions
   b. To gather data about the problem
   c. To implement the chosen solution
   d. To assess the effectiveness of the implemented solution

4) Which scenario best exemplifies a 'problem'?
   a. Navigating the interwoven socio-economic challenges of an entire continent.
   b. Finding a way to prevent a particular chemical reaction in a science experiment.
   c. Addressing all the factors of urbanization in growing cities globally.
   d. Living daily life without any specific challenges.
5) According to Ackoff, which of the problem treatments seeks the best possible answer but might inadvertently lead to the emergence of new problems?
   a. Resolving
   b. Solving
   c. Dissolving
   d. Absolving
6) What activities are typically carried out during the Implementation phase of the Diamond Model?
   a. Identifying problems
   b. Brainstorming solutions
   c. Executing the chosen solution
   d. Evaluating the effectiveness of solutions
7) What is the primary focus of the Solution Design step in the Diamond Model?
   a. Implementing the chosen solution
   b. Evaluating the effectiveness of various solutions
   c. Brainstorming and comparing various alternative solutions
   d. Identifying the scope and impact of the problem
8) Why are structured methodologies often useful in addressing problems?
   a. Problems are typically broad and undefined.
   b. Problems require consideration of countless interconnected issues.
   c. Problems usually present specific challenges that can be tackled systematically.
   d. Problems don't require any systematic approach.
9) Which of the following is a characteristic of a problem?
   a. Lack of any clear objectives.
   b. Defined parameters and boundaries.
   c. No potential solutions exist.
   d. Always evolving without any potential for resolution.
10) If a company is trying to determine why a particular software keeps crashing, they are trying to solve a:
   a. Mess.
   b. Routine.
   c. Problem.
   d. General concept with no specifics.

11) Which of the following best defines a 'mess' in a systemic context?
    a. A single, well-defined problem with a straightforward solution.
    b. An easy-to-understand situation with clear boundaries.
    c. A complex situation comprised of multiple interrelated problems without a single well-defined solution.
    d. A routine task with predetermined steps.
12) Which scenario best exemplifies a 'mess'?
    a. Solving a linear equation in mathematics.
    b. Determining the best route for a road trip.
    c. Addressing climate change and its impacts on global ecosystems, economies, and societies.
    d. Baking a cake by following a specific recipe.
13) In the context of Ackoff's problem treatments, which approach involves hoping the problem will vanish on its own without any active intervention?
    a. Dissolving
    b. Resolving
    c. Absolving
    d. Solving
14) Why is addressing a mess often challenging?
    a. It requires only one specialist's expertise.
    b. It can be solved by a single formula or method.
    c. It is static and doesn't evolve over time.
    d. It involves interconnected issues and solving one may impact or complicate others.
15) Which of the following is NOT a characteristic of a mess?
    a. Dynamic and ever-changing nature.
    b. Interrelated sets of problems.
    c. Clear boundaries and singular solutions.
    d. Difficulty in defining completely.
16) If a city is dealing with economic decline, rising crime, failing education systems, and social unrest all at once, it is likely facing what?
    a. A straightforward problem.
    b. An exercise.
    c. A mess.
    d. A defined task with a clear solution.
17) In which step of the Diamond Model is data gathered to define the scope and impact of the issue?
    a. Evaluation
    b. Solution Design
    c. Implementation
    d. Problem Identification

18) What are the four key steps of the Diamond Model for problem-solving?
    a. Research, Planning, Execution, Feedback
    b. Problem Identification, Solution Design, Implementation, Evaluation
    c. Input, Process, Output, Feedback
    d. Assessment, Planning, Execution, Review
19) Which of the following IS NOT, according to Ackoff, an element that may cause significant skew between the actual outcome and the intended outcome?
    a. The information used in making the decision was perfect
    b. The decision-making process was perfect and flawless
    c. The decision may not have been implemented as intended
    d. The environment may have changed in a way that was not anticipated
20) In Ackoff's problem treatments, which method involves redesigning the system to eradicate the conditions causing the problem?
    a. Absolving
    b. Resolving
    c. Solving
    d. Dissolving

REFERENCES

Ackoff, R. L. (1974). *Redesigning the Future: A Systems Approach to Societal Problems*. John Wiley & Sons.

Ackoff, R. L. (1978). *The Art of Problem Solving: Accompanied by Ackoff's Fables*. John Wiley & Sons.

Ackoff, R. L. (1981). *Creating the Corporate Future: Plan or Be Planned For*. John Wiley & Sons.

Ackoff, R. L. (1999). *Ackoff's Best: His Classic Writings on Management*. John Wiley & Sons.

Ackoff, R. L., & Emery, F. E. (1972). *On Purposeful Systems*. AldineTransaction.

Ackoff, R. L., & Gharajedaghi, J. (1971). Towards a System of Systems Concepts. *Management Science*, *17*(11), 661–671. doi:10.1287/mnsc.17.11.661

Ackoff, R. L., & Rovin, S. (2003). *Redesigning Society*. Stanford University Press.

Axelrod, R., & Cohen, M. D. (2000). *Harnessing Complexity: Organizational Implications of a Scientific Frontier*. Free Press.

Brillinger, D. (2002). John Tukey: His Life and Professional Contributions. *Annals of Statistics*, *30*(6), 1535–1575. doi:10.1214/aos/1043351246

Checkland, P. (1981). *Systems Thinking, Systems Practice*. John Wiley & Sons.

Churchman, C. W. (1968). *The Systems Approach*. Dell.

Churchman, C. W. (1979). *The Systems Approach and Its Enemies*. Basic Books.

Dewey, J. (1963). *Experience and education*. Collier Books.

Edwards, A. W. F. (2004). *Cogwheels of the mind: The story of Venn diagrams*. Johns Hopkins University Press. doi:10.56021/9780801874345

Euler, L. (1768). *Lettres à une Princesse d'Allemagne sur divers sujets de physique et de philosophie*.

Flood, R. L., & Carson, E. R. (1993). *Dealing with Complexity: An Introduction to the Theory and Application of Systems Science*. Plenum Press. doi:10.1007/978-1-4757-2235-2

Forrester, J. W. (1961). *Industrial Dynamics*. MIT Press.

Gharajedaghi, J. (2005). *Systems Thinking: Managing Chaos and Complexity: A Platform for Designing Business Architecture*. Butterworth-Heinemann.

Grimaldi, R. P. (2004). *Discrete and Combinatorial Mathematics: An Applied Introduction*. Addison-Wesley.

Henrion, M. G. (1990). *Uncertainty: A Guide to Dealing with Uncertainty in Quantitative Risk and Policy Analysis*. University of Cambridge.

Holland, J. H. (2014). *Complexity: A Very Short Introduction*. Oxford University Press. doi:10.1093/actrade/9780199662548.001.0001

Holt, J. (1902). A Set of Postulates for the Logic of Classes. *Transactions of the American Mathematical Society*, *3*(3), 343–370.

Kesten, H. (1968). *An Introduction to Probability Theory and Its Applications* (Vol. 1). John Wiley & Sons.

Meadows, D. H. (2008). *Thinking in Systems: A Primer*. Chelsea Green Publishing.

Minsky, M. L. (1967). *Computation: Finite and Infinite Machines*. Prentice-Hall.

Mitroff, I. I., & Linstone, H. A. (1993). *The Unbounded Mind: Breaking the Chains of Traditional Business Thinking*. Oxford University Press.

Morin, E. (2008). *On Complexity*. Hampton Press.

Raiffa, H. (1968). *Decision Analysis: Introductory Lectures on Choices Under Uncertainty*. Addison Wesley.

Richardson, G. P., & Pugh, A. L. III. (1981). *Introduction to System Dynamics Modeling with DYNAMO*. MIT Press.

Rittel, H. W. J., & Webber, M. M. (1973). Dilemmas in a general theory of planning. *Policy Sciences*, *4*(2), 155–169. doi:10.1007/BF01405730

Senge, P. M. (1990). *The Fifth Discipline: The Art & Practice of The Learning Organization*. Currency Doubleday.

Simon, H. A. (1969). *The Sciences of the Artificial*. MIT Press.

Stacey, R. D. (1996). *Complexity and Creativity in Organizations*. Berrett-Koehler.

Sterman, J. D. (2000). *Business dynamics: Systems thinking and modeling for a complex world*. Irwin/McGraw-Hill.

Tufte, E. R. (1983). *The Visual Display of Quantitative Information*. Graphics Press.

Ulrich, W. (1983). *Critical heuristics of social planning: A new approach to practical philosophy*. Haupt.

Venn, J. (1880). On the Diagrammatic and Mechanical Representation of Propositions and Reasonings. *The London, Edinburgh and Dublin Philosophical Magazine and Journal of Science*, *9*(59), 1–18. doi:10.1080/14786448008626877

Waldrop, M. M. (1992). *Complexity: The Emerging Science at the Edge of Order and Chaos*. Simon & Schuster.

APPENDIX- COMPREHENSION EXERCISES: SOLUTIONS

1) Which of the following best defines a 'problem'?
   a. A situation that is already perfectly understood and resolved.
   b. A situation with a specific challenge that seeks resolution.
   c. Multiple interrelated situations without clear solutions.
   d. An everyday routine that requires no critical thinking.

Recommended Answer: b. A situation with a specific challenge that seeks resolution.

2) When employing Ackoff's method of "Resolving", what is the primary goal?
   a. To ignore the problem.
   b. To find the absolute best answer regardless of consequences.
   c. To implement good enough solutions, not necessarily the best or optimal ones.
   d. To redesign the system entirely to prevent the problem's occurrence.

Recommended Answer: c. To implement good enough solutions, not necessarily the best or optimal ones.

3) Why is the Evaluation step important in the Diamond Model?
   a. To brainstorm alternative solutions
   b. To gather data about the problem
   c. To implement the chosen solution
   d. To assess the effectiveness of the implemented solution

Recommended Answer: D

4) Which scenario best exemplifies a 'problem'?
   a. Navigating the interwoven socio-economic challenges of an entire continent.
   b. Finding a way to prevent a particular chemical reaction in a science experiment.
   c. Addressing all the factors of urbanization in growing cities globally.
   d. Living daily life without any specific challenges.

Recommended Answer: b) Finding a way to prevent a particular chemical reaction in a science experiment.

5) According to Ackoff, which of the problem treatments seeks the best possible answer but might inadvertently lead to the emergence of new problems?
   a. Resolving
   b. Solving
   c. Dissolving
   d. Absolving

Recommended Answer: b) Solving

6) What activities are typically carried out during the Implementation phase of the Diamond Model?
   a. Identifying problems
   b. Brainstorming solutions
   c. Executing the chosen solution
   d. Evaluating the effectiveness of solutions

Recommended Answer: c. Executing the chosen solution

7) What is the primary focus of the Solution Design step in the Diamond Model?
   a. Implementing the chosen solution
   b. Evaluating the effectiveness of various solutions
   c. Brainstorming and comparing various alternative solutions
   d. Identifying the scope and impact of the problem

Recommended Answer: c. Brainstorming and comparing various alternative solutions

8) Why are structured methodologies often useful in addressing problems?
   a. Problems are typically broad and undefined.
   b. Problems require consideration of countless interconnected issues.
   c. Problems usually present specific challenges that can be tackled systematically.
   d. Problems don't require any systematic approach.

Recommended Answer: c) Problems usually present specific challenges that can be tackled systematically.

9) Which of the following is a characteristic of a problem?
   a. Lack of any clear objectives.
   b. Defined parameters and boundaries.
   c. No potential solutions exist.
   d. Always evolving without any potential for resolution.

Recommended Answer: b) Defined parameters and boundaries.

10) If a company is trying to determine why a particular software keeps crashing, they are trying to solve a:
    a. Mess.
    b. Routine.
    c. Problem.
    d. General concept with no specifics.

Recommended Answer: c) Problem.

11) Which of the following best defines a 'mess' in a systemic context?
    a. A single, well-defined problem with a straightforward solution.
    b. An easy-to-understand situation with clear boundaries.
    c. A complex situation comprised of multiple interrelated problems without a single well-defined solution.
    d. A routine task with predetermined steps.

Recommended Answer: c. A complex situation comprised of multiple interrelated problems without a singular solution.

12) Which scenario best exemplifies a 'mess'?
    a. Solving a linear equation in mathematics.
    b. Determining the best route for a road trip.
    c. Addressing climate change and its impacts on global ecosystems, economies, and societies.
    d. Baking a cake by following a specific recipe.

Recommended Answer: c. Addressing climate change and its impacts on global ecosystems, economies, and societies.

13) In the context of Ackoff's problem treatments, which approach involves hoping the problem will vanish on its own without any active intervention?
    a. Dissolving
    b. Resolving
    c. Absolving
    d. Solving

Recommended Answer: c. Absolving

14) Why is addressing a mess often challenging?
    a. It requires only one specialist's expertise.
    b. It can be solved by a single formula or method.
    c. It is static and doesn't evolve over time.
    d. It involves interconnected issues and solving one may impact or complicate others.

Recommended Answer: d. It involves interconnected issues, and solving one may impact or complicate others.

15) Which of the following is NOT a characteristic of a mess?
    a. Dynamic and ever-changing nature.
    b. Interrelated sets of problems.
    c. Clear boundaries and singular solutions.
    d. Difficulty in defining completely.

Recommended Answer: c. Clear boundaries and singular solutions.

16) If a city is dealing with economic decline, rising crime, failing education systems, and social unrest all at once, it is likely facing what?
    a. A straightforward problem.
    b. An exercise.
    c. A mess.
    d. A defined task with a clear solution.

Recommended Answer: c. A mess.

17) In which step of the Diamond Model is data gathered to define the scope and impact of the issue?
    a. Evaluation
    b. Solution Design
    c. Implementation
    d. Problem Identification

Recommended Answer: d. Problem Identification

18) What are the four key steps of the Diamond Model for problem-solving?
    a. Research, Planning, Execution, Feedback
    b. Problem Identification, Solution Design, Implementation, Evaluation
    c. Input, Process, Output, Feedback
    d. Assessment, Planning, Execution, Review

Recommended Answer: b. Problem Identification, Solution Design, Implementation, Evaluation

19) Which of the following IS NOT, according to Ackoff, an element that may cause significant skew between the actual outcome and the intended outcome?
    a. The information used in making the decision was perfect
    b. The decision-making process was perfect and flawless
    c. The decision may not have been implemented as intended
    d. The environment may have changed in a way that was not anticipated

Recommended Answer: a. The information used in making the decision was perfect

20) In Ackoff's problem treatments, which method involves redesigning the system to eradicate the conditions causing the problem?
    a. Absolving
    b. Resolving
    c. Solving
    d. Dissolving

Recommended Answer: d. Dissolving

Chapter 2
Understanding Systems

ABSTRACT

A System is an intentionally designed, systematically organized, whole entity (e.g., an automobile, computer, smart building, etc.) that has one or more essential functions so that an individual and/or groups of people are thereby able to accomplish a set of important purposes. Furthermore, the functions, not the parts, are critical in defining a System. By means of their functions, the parts exist to allow people to accomplish significant purposes, not the other way around. A critical distinction is that a System's parts have functions while only humans as purposive individuals have purposes.

"A system is never the sum of its parts; it's the product of their interaction." – Russell Ackoff

Learning Objectives

- Define 'system'
- List the attributes of a SocioTechnical System
- Explain 'systems thinking'
- Describe an E3 error

DOI: 10.4018/978-1-6684-6563-9.ch002

INTRODUCTION

We cannot overemphasize the importance of Systems and Systems Thinking. It's at the very core of this entire book. In a series of seminal books spanning a lifetime, no one has done a more commanding job than Russ Ackoff and his colleagues in identifying and laying out the precise definition and nature of Systems ((Ackoff, 1999) (Ackoff, 1999) (Ackoff & Rovin, 2003) (Ackoff & Greenberg, 2008) (Gharajedaghi, 2006) (Mitroff & Linstone, 1993)).

SYSTEMS

First, we start with an overview of Systems. Ackoff describes Systems as more than a concept. It is an intellectual way of life, a worldview, a concept of the nature of reality and how to investigate it. A system is defined as a set of two or more elements that satisfies the following three conditions (Ackoff, 1999):

- *The behavior of each element has an effect on the behavior of the whole;*
- *The behavior of the elements and their effects on the whole are interdependent;*
- *However subgroups of the elements are formed, each has an effect on the behavior of the whole and none has an independent effect on it.*

The first condition is that a System cannot accomplish its defining function(s) without its essential parts, and persons. A car engine is an essential part for locomotion but a cigarette lighter is not. Similarly, the brain, heart, and lungs are essential parts of humans, but as Ackoff notes, the appendix is not. This is in fact why it is termed an "appendix."

The second condition is that by itself an essential part cannot affect a System independently of at least one other essential part. The essential parts are not only interconnected, but they interact. Thus, the heart affects the lungs and vice versa. Indeed, they don't exist without the other. In other words, without interactions and interdependencies, there is no System.

The third condition is that no group of a System's essential parts—that is, no subsystem—has an independent effect on the whole System. Once again, the nervous and metabolic subsystems of humans do not have independent effects on the whole human body as a System.

By means of their functions, the parts exist to allow people to accomplish significant purposes, not the other way around. That is, people do not exist for the parts or the System(s) in which they are embedded, although the parts can certainly give rise to new functions and purposes than the System's designers anticipated or intended. This is increasingly true of Technology where the unintended consequences produce effects that negate its positive benefits.

A critical distinction is that a System's parts have functions while only humans as purposive individuals have purposes. Thus, a car has major functions (e.g., transportation, the ability to change direction and speed when directed by a purposeful individual, etc.) that allow humans to satisfy purposes in the form of desired outcomes.

Only humans purposefully create specific means to accomplish intended outcomes or ends. In brief, humans (and of course certain other animals) are purposeful beings and thus exhibit purposive behavior even if they are not completely self-contained, i.e., autonomous.

Individual humans are not autonomous because they only exist by virtue of being members of even larger Systems, e.g., families, organizations, and societies. For one, infants do not have the innate ability to survive on their own. In short, the lines between individuals and the society of which they are members is thin at best. In fact, neither exists without the other.

To take another example, the heart and lungs have essential functions, but they don't have independent purposes, let alone an existence of their own apart from the entire human body. Similarly, the engine in a car obviously has an important function, but it doesn't have a purpose of its own independently of the combined human-machine system, i.e., NT. But once again, it wouldn't function without the necessary support of NF and SF. By themselves, wheels do not exhibit purposeful motion. They only carry out their intended function by being part of the car as a whole System that not only includes, but is directed by a purposeful being.

Improvement in the parts taken separately does not improve a System overall as a whole. Indeed, it often leads to its failure and complete destruction. Merely improving an engine without the careful coordination of and simultaneous improvements in the suspension and transmission does not improve the overall performance of a car. If anything, it can cause a car to spin dangerously out of control.

Lastly, a System has defining properties that none of its parts have. Thus, purposeful motion is a property of the combined (i.e., interactive) human-machine System that is a car. It is not a function of the engine or wheels alone. Indeed, without a driver or human interaction of some kind, NF and SF, e.g., remote control, a car cannot exhibit purposeful motion. Similarly, no amount of analysis of the parts would reveal a car's property as a social status symbol.

A car's function is to allow people to accomplish specific purposes, e.g., move to a desired set of locations by a preferred set of routes in specific times. Cars also have additional functions such as to enable people to engage in a form of entertainment and relaxation. Driving a car also allows people to "blow off steam" under "semi controlled conditions" even though it can very easily lead to road rage, which can be deadly.

SOCIOTECHNICAL SYSTEMS

The concept of sociotechnical systems originated in the early 1950s, primarily through the work of researchers at the Tavistock Institute in London, particularly Eric Trist and Fred Emery. These researchers were focused on understanding the interplay between people and technology in work environments. Their groundbreaking studies, particularly in coal mining operations, illuminated that optimizing work performance required not just technological improvements but also considerations of social factors like work relations, communication, and organizational structure. This led to the understanding that technical and social systems are interdependent and must be designed and evaluated in concert to achieve optimum performance and well-being. Over the years, the concept has expanded across disciplines and sectors, evolving to address complex modern systems where people and technology coexist and interact.

Sociotechnical systems stress the intertwined nature of social and technical elements in organizations, emphasizing complexity, adaptability, ethics, inclusivity, resilience, human-centricity, emergent properties, feedback mechanisms, and interdisciplinary collaboration.

Sociotechnical Systems: Timeline of Key Milestones

1940s-1950s:

Origin of Concept: During post-World War II coal mine studies in the UK, researchers from the Tavistock Institute (notably Eric Trist and Fred Emery) observed the interdependence of social and technical systems in work settings.

1960s:

Diamond Model: Harold J. Leavitt introduces his diamond model, stressing the connections between tasks, structures, people, and technology in organizations. STSD (Sociotechnical Systems Design): Emery advances STSD as a methodological approach to design work systems that optimize both the social and technical components.

1970s:

Ethical Dimensions: Geoffrey Vickers and others start to discuss the ethical considerations and values inherent in sociotechnical designs. Broadened Applications: The principles of sociotechnical systems begin to be applied beyond industrial settings to areas like healthcare, education, and public administration.

1980s:

Knowledge Organizations: Karl-Erik Sveiby emphasizes the role of knowledge in organizations, treating it as an asset and linking the social and technical aspects of knowledge management. Computer-supported Collaborative Work (CSCW): With the rise of computing technology, research focuses on how computer systems can support cooperative work, marking a significant intersection of the sociotechnical domain with technology.

1990s:

Information Systems: The importance of the sociotechnical approach becomes increasingly evident in the design and implementation of information systems. Human-Centered Design: The shift towards designing technology around human needs becomes more pronounced, emphasizing the balance between technical efficiency and human well-being.

2000s:

Digital Sociotechnical Systems: Brian Whitworth and others describe the World Wide Web as a sociotechnical system, emphasizing the co-evolution of technology and societal norms in the digital age. Ethical Dimensions Expanded: Lucas Introna and others further explore the ethical implications of sociotechnical systems, particularly in the realm of digital technology and artificial intelligence.

2010s:

Complex Systems Theory: With increasing technological advancements and challenges, the sociotechnical approach is intertwined with complex systems theory, considering emergent properties and nonlinear interactions. Interdisciplinary Collaboration: Boundary spanning becomes crucial as sociotechnical challenges require expertise from various disciplines to address complex societal problems effectively.

Key Attributes of SocioTechnical Systems

- **Systems Perspective**: Recognizes organizations as integrated entities where technology and social elements are interdependent.
- **Complexity:** Emphasizes the multifaceted nature of organizations, challenging simplistic solutions to intricate problems.
- **Adaptability:** Highlights the need for systems to evolve with changing environmental conditions and stakeholder demands.
- **Ethical Considerations:** Stresses the importance of addressing moral implications of technology within social contexts.
- **Stakeholder Engagement:** Prioritizes inclusive decision-making, acknowledging diverse interests within the system.
- **Resilience:** Focuses on the system's capacity to absorb disturbances and reorganize, maintaining core functions.

- **Human-Centered Design:** Advocates for designing technologies with human needs and capabilities at the forefront.
- **Emergence:** Recognizes that system properties can arise unpredictably from interactions of simpler elements.
- **Feedback Loops:** Emphasizes the importance of understanding and monitoring the reciprocal influences within systems.
- **Boundary Spanning**: Encourages interdisciplinary collaboration to address multifaceted challenges effectively.

A number of researchers have made foundational contributions to the sociotechnical systems theory, from its inception at Tavistock to its evolution in the digital age, emphasizing the interplay between social and technical elements, organizational values, ethics, and knowledge management. These researchers include:

- **Eric Trist & Fred Emery**: Pioneers from the Tavistock Institute who introduced the sociotechnical systems concept, emphasizing the mutual adjustment of the social and technical systems for optimal performance and human fulfillment.
- **Karl-Erik Sveiby**: Recognized for his work on knowledge organizations and treating knowledge as an asset, intertwining social and technical aspects.
- **Geoffrey Vickers:** Contributed to the understanding of "appreciative systems," a way of understanding organizations through values, understandings, and intentions, with a sociotechnical lens.
- **Harold J. Leavitt**: Introduced the diamond model emphasizing the interaction between tasks, structure, people, and technology in organizations.
- **Brian Whitworth & Tong Liu**: Explored the concept of sociotechnical systems in the context of the digital age, particularly considering the web as a complex sociotechnical system.
- **Lucas Introna:** Delved into the ethical dimensions of sociotechnical systems, particularly in the context of information systems and technology.

The concept of sociotechnical systems has been applied in a wide range of settings. Here are five examples across diverse sectors that emphasize the significance of considering both social and technical components when implementing changes or innovations in diverse settings.

Coal Mining in the UK (1940s-1950s)

Background: This is where the sociotechnical approach originated. Researchers from the Tavistock Institute studied the effects of new machinery and work processes in coal mines.

Findings: Teams with autonomy and flexible work structures, combined with the new technology, resulted in increased productivity and worker satisfaction compared to traditional hierarchical setups.

Authors: Eric Trist and Ken Bamforth from the Tavistock Institute.

Publications: "Socio-Technical Systems" and "Organizational Choice" are key publications that discuss the principles emerging from these studies.

Volvo's Uddevalla Factory (1980s)

Background: Volvo implemented a sociotechnical approach in their Uddevalla car assembly plant in Sweden.

Findings: Instead of assembly lines, teams of workers constructed entire cars, which led to increased skill development, job satisfaction, and adaptability, even though it wasn't necessarily the most cost-effective method of production.

Author: Åke Sandberg (among others).

Publications: Sandberg has various publications discussing the sociotechnical approach at Volvo, including "Enriching Production: Perspectives on Volvo's Uddevalla plant as an alternative to lean production."

The Implementation of Electronic Health Records (EHRs) in Healthcare

Background: With the rise of digital technology, many healthcare institutions have transitioned from paper to electronic records.

Findings: Successful implementation of EHRs depends not just on the technology, but on training healthcare professionals, reconfiguring work practices, considering patient-doctor interactions, and addressing privacy concerns. The sociotechnical perspective helps in understanding and navigating these challenges.

Authors: Multiple researchers have investigated this, but Joan Ash, Dean F. Sittig, and Hardeep Singh are notable.

Publications: Articles such as "The Extent and Importance of Unintended Consequences Related to Computerized Provider Order Entry" provide insights into the sociotechnical dimensions of EHR implementation.

The London Ambulance Service Computer-Aided Dispatch System (1990s)

Background: An attempt to modernize the ambulance dispatch system in London resulted in a catastrophic failure, causing significant delays and, reportedly, several deaths.

Findings: A post-mortem analysis using a sociotechnical lens revealed that while there were technical glitches, the failure was largely due to organizational and human factors like inadequate training, poor system design with respect to actual user needs, and lack of involvement of end-users in system development.

Authors: Tom W. Simpson, David Wastell, and others.

Publications: Various analyses exist, but Simpson's "London Ambulance Service Computer-Aided Dispatch System" provides a comprehensive view.

The Introduction of Smart Grid Technology in Energy Systems

Background: With the push for sustainable energy, there's been interest in smart grids, which use ICT to enhance the reliability and efficiency of electrical grids.

Findings: The deployment and effectiveness of smart grids depend on a variety of factors beyond just the technology, including regulatory policies, consumer behaviors, and the integration with existing infrastructure. Sociotechnical studies have emphasized the importance of these factors and their interplay for successful smart grid implementation.

Authors: Multiple authors have studied this topic, but Stephen M. Rinaldi is one of the notable figures.

Publications: While Rinaldi has worked more broadly on critical infrastructure, publications like "Modeling and Simulating Critical Infrastructures and Their Interdependencies" touch on aspects relevant to sociotechnical systems in smart grids.

While these authors and publications provide a starting point, it's worth noting that many of the topics, especially popular ones like EHRs and smart grids, have been studied by a broad range of researchers, each providing their insights and perspectives.

TYPES OF SYSTEMS AND MODELS

There are three basic types of systems and models of them. Additionally, there is an overarching ecological 'meta-system' that contains all three parts as part of it. These basic systems include (Ackoff, 1999):

1. Deterministic Mechanical Systems: These systems are rule-bound and predictable, following fixed laws. For example, a clock operates based on mechanical principles, with every part having a predefined function. A Car Engine: Functions based on mechanical laws, converting fuel into kinetic energy. A Windmill: Harnesses wind energy to perform tasks like grinding or pumping water. A Lever: Operates on the principle of mechanical advantage to lift or move objects.
2. Animated Systems: These are biological entities with self-preservation instincts and goals, but lack shared purpose. An example is a dog seeking food, shelter, and social interaction, but not contributing to a collective aim. A Fish: Swims, feeds, and reproduces but doesn't contribute to a larger collective purpose. A Tree: Absorbs nutrients and sunlight to grow and reproduce. A Bird: Seeks food, builds nests, and migrates based on instinctual behavior.
3. Social Systems: Comprised of people working towards shared objectives, these systems feature intentionality and purpose. A corporation, with its hierarchy and coordinated activities aimed at profit, exemplifies a social system. A Family: Members contribute to the well-being and goals of the family unit. A School: Comprised of teachers, students, and staff working towards educational objectives. A Government: Functions to provide services and governance, guided by laws and public policy.
4. Ecological Systems: These are complex networks of animated and social systems coexisting in a shared environment. A coral reef, for instance, involves numerous species and their interactions, forming a larger ecological web. A Forest Ecosystem: Consists of trees, animals, and microorganisms interacting in a complex web. A River System: Includes water, fish, plants, and human activities like fishing or pollution. A Desert Ecosystem: Involves hardy plants, animals, and microorganisms adapted to harsh conditions.

These examples illuminate the range and complexity of systems, reinforcing the academic focus on a holistic and interdisciplinary understanding of systems and their types.

The utility of Ackoff's four system types lies in their ability to provide a structured framework for understanding the complexity and interrelationships inherent in different kinds of systems. Deterministic mechanical systems offer insights into rule-bound, predictable interactions, serving as the foundational building blocks for more complex systems. Animated systems introduce the concept of individual goals and self-preservation instincts, broadening our understanding of biological intricacies. Social systems elevate this further by adding collective intentionality and shared objectives, a crucial aspect for understanding organizational behavior, governance, and societal structures. Ecological systems encapsulate all these elements, showing how both animated and social systems co-exist and interact within a shared environment, providing a comprehensive lens for studying sustainability, co-dependence, and environmental impact.

Understanding these types as separate yet interconnected allows for a multidisciplinary approach to problem-solving and knowledge acquisition. For instance, studying a river system (ecological) may require insights into mechanical principles for understanding water flow, biological knowledge for understanding fish behavior (animated), and social considerations for managing human activities like fishing or pollution control (social). This interconnectedness suggests that solutions in one area may have cascading effects on others, emphasizing the need for a holistic approach. By categorizing systems into these four types, one can better grasp the scope and implications of interactions within and across system boundaries, which is invaluable in fields ranging from engineering and biology to social sciences and environmental studies.

SYSTEMS THINKING

The essence of systems thinking is synthesis, or putting things together, which is opposite to conventional analytic thinking, where the thing to be explained is treated as a whole to be taken apart (decomposition). In synthetic thinking, the thing to be explained is treated as part of a containing whole. Synthesis consists of these three steps and is a pre-requisite to any analysis within the framework of Systems Thinking (Ackoff, 1999):

- Identifying a containing whole (system) of which the thing to be explained is a part;
- Explaining the behavior or properties of the containing whole; and
- Then explaining the behavior or properties of the thing to be explained in terms of its role(s) or function(s) within its containing whole.
- Synthesis focuses on function and aims to reveal why things operate as they do, whereas conventional analysis focuses on structure and reveals how things work. Analysis yields knowledge, whereas synthesis yields understanding.

Russell Ackoff's notion of systems thinking provides a comprehensive framework for understanding complex problems by looking at how different components interact within a larger system. Instead of isolating issues, this holistic approach promotes the idea that the behavior and characteristics of any part of a system can only be fully understood in relation to the larger system. This perspective is immensely useful for problem-solving and decision-making across various disciplines, as it encourages us to examine the interconnectedness and interdependencies that often govern outcomes.

Systems thinking can illuminate the intricacies of everyday phenomena that may otherwise seem unrelated or random. Take, for example, your daily commute to work. Instead of merely attributing traffic congestion to a high number of cars, a systems perspective would consider urban planning, public transportation availability, school timings, and even weather conditions as contributing factors. Similarly, if you find that you're always tired during the day, instead of solely blaming a lack of sleep, systems thinking would have you examine other variables like diet, stress, exercise, and mental health. Even in household chores like doing laundry, a systems approach would go beyond the simple act of washing clothes to consider efficient ways of sorting, detergent use, machine maintenance, and energy conservation. By applying systems thinking to day-to-day occurrences, one can gain a richer understanding of the complexities involved and identify more effective solutions or improvements.

For practical, everyday application, consider these additional scenarios:

1. Health and Diet: Instead of focusing solely on calorie intake for weight loss, systems thinking would have you consider exercise, mental well-being, and lifestyle factors that also impact your health.
2. Household Budget: Rather than just cutting expenses in one area like entertainment, consider how saving in multiple areas can collectively impact your financial stability and long-term goals.
3. Car Maintenance: Instead of merely fixing a faulty engine, think about how regular oil changes, tire rotations, and brake checks can prolong your car's lifespan.
4. Gardening: A systems approach would not just look at watering plants but consider soil quality, sunlight, and pest control to maintain a healthy garden.
5. Parenting: Systems thinking in parenting means not just addressing a child's misbehavior but also considering its underlying causes, such as school environment, peer influence, and family dynamics, for a more effective and comprehensive solution.

These examples illustrate how systems thinking can offer a more nuanced and effective approach to solving problems and improving various aspects of everyday life. Additional discussion of Systems Thinking is presented in Chapter 4 – Inquiry Systems.

AVOIDING E3 ERRORS

The Error of the Third Kind or E3 is the error associated with "solving the wrong problem(s) precisely." Errors of the First Kind (rejecting a null hypothesis when it's true) and Second Kind (accepting a null hypothesis when it's false) are well known in statistics. Indeed, they are part of everyday, normal scholarly practice. But there is a more important error of which far too many academics miss altogether. This is The Error of the Third Kind or E3. The concept of The Error of the Third Kind or E3 was first proposed by the eminent statistician John Tukey and the renowned decision theorist Howard Raiffa. E3 is defined as the "probability of solving the 'wrong problem' precisely." In brief, E3 causes us to engage in "meaningless activity," often at great costs in time, money, and wasted energy.

The following is a partial list of the different types of E3. Because they are highly interdependent, the different types overlap:

- Picking the "wrong/flawed" initial definition of a problem and adhering to it despite growing evidence to the contrary.
- Enforcing "narrow/restricted" definitions/contexts/boundaries of problems.
- Ignoring and suppressing multiple, sharply differing definitions of a problem.
- Ignoring the linkages with other problems and definitions of a problem.
- Taking the definition of a problem as fixed, singular, and static instead of as multiple, dynamically changing, variable, and emergent as one works on it.
- Ignoring other variables, theoretical perspectives, and the linkages between them that bear on a problem.
- Enforcing one disciplinary and theoretical perspective while ignoring and suppressing others.
- Regarding a problem as well structured when it is in fact ill structured. And, perhaps most important of all,
- Failing to raise to the surface, and hence challenge, basic assumptions and key issues that influence the selection and formulation of all problems.

Examples of E3 errors based on Ian Mitroff's work in the realm of organizational and strategic management:

Overreliance on Reductionist Models: One classic E3 error is the tendency for organizations to overly rely on reductionist models when making strategic decisions. By simplifying complex situations into manageable parts, organizations can inadvertently miss the interconnectedness and interdependencies among various factors. This error arises when decision-makers focus solely on isolated components of a problem while neglecting the intricate relationships that exist within the larger system. This can lead to misguided decisions and an inadequate understanding of the potential consequences.

Failure to Anticipate Emergent Properties: Organizations may commit an E3 by failing to anticipate emergent properties that can arise from complex systems. Emergent properties are outcomes that are not directly evident from the individual components but emerge as a result of their interactions. Neglecting to consider emergent properties can result in unforeseen challenges and unintended consequences. For example, introducing a new technology without fully understanding how it interacts with existing processes might lead to disruptions that were not initially apparent.

Neglecting Socio-Cultural Context: Disregarding the socio-cultural context in which an organization operates is another E3 error identified by Mitroff. Organizational decisions and strategies should be attuned to the values, norms, and expectations of the surrounding environment. Ignoring these factors can lead to public relations crises, legal issues, and reputational damage. An organization that fails to consider the cultural nuances of a new market may inadvertently offend local stakeholders and customers, jeopardizing its success.

Ignoring Weak Signals: Mitroff highlights the E3 error of ignoring weak signals – early indicators of potential disruptions or crises. Organizations that dismiss these signals may find themselves unprepared when a significant issue eventually emerges. For instance, a company ignoring subtle shifts in customer preferences or competitive landscape trends could be blindsided by changes that lead to a decline in market share. By failing to heed these weak signals, organizations miss valuable opportunities to proactively address challenges and innovate.

These examples underscore the essence of E3 errors, illustrating the importance of taking a more holistic, systemic, and contextually sensitive approach to organizational decision-making and management.

E3 errors can trigger a cascade of undesirable consequences that hinder effective problem identification and resolution within organizations. These errors often manifest in the misallocation of resources through the reliance on overly simplistic models. Consider a retail chain basing restocking decisions solely on historical sales data, ignoring emerging shifts in consumer preferences, leading to product shortages and dissatisfied customers. Additionally, overlooking socio-cultural context can give rise to damaging misunderstandings. For instance, a software company launching a global marketing campaign without considering local cultural sensitivities could inadvertently alienate potential customers. Furthermore, E3 errors can obstruct the detection of early warning signals, impeding timely intervention. Imagine a logistics company ignoring initial signs of delivery delays, which then escalate into widespread supply chain disruptions. Lastly, these errors can lead to the pursuit of strategies misaligned with the organization's goals. An educational institution might implement a new curriculum without consulting faculty, resulting in reduced student engagement. By recognizing these pitfalls, management can adopt a holistic approach to problem-solving, mitigating E3 errors and facilitating more effective identification and resolution of challenges.

For effective leadership and sustainable success, it's essential to recognize the substantial utility and value that lies in avoiding E3 errors. By actively avoiding E3 errors, one can ensure that decisions are grounded in a holistic understanding of complex situations. Embracing a systemic perspective enables one to consider the interconnectedness of various factors and predict potential ripple effects that might otherwise be overlooked. This, in turn, empowers leaders/managers to allocate resources more efficiently, optimize processes, and make strategic choices that align with our overarching goals.

Steering clear of E3 errors enhances the organization's responsiveness to dynamic environments. Neglecting socio-cultural context can lead to costly misinterpretations and strained relationships. By acknowledging and accounting for the diverse backgrounds and perspectives that shape the operating landscape, an environment of inclusivity and cultural competence is fostered. This can translate into improved stakeholder relations, enhanced customer satisfaction, and a stronger organizational reputation.

Perhaps most crucially, sidestepping E3 errors enables the organization to detect and address emerging challenges before they escalate into full-blown crises. Early warning signals often offer subtle insights that can guide preemptive actions. Recognizing these signals ensures that the organization remains nimble in its decision-making, preventing major disruptions and preserving our ability to adapt to unforeseen circumstances.

CONCLUSION

Systems are complex networks of interrelated components that work together to achieve a common goal or function. Sociotechnical systems add another layer of complexity by integrating both social elements, like human behavior and organizational culture, and technical elements, such as machinery or software. These systems are prevalent in various sectors, from healthcare and transportation to information technology, and understanding them requires an interdisciplinary approach that considers both the human and technical factors at play.

Russell Ackoff's four system models—deterministic mechanical, animated, social, and ecological—offer a structured way to dissect the complexity inherent in different kinds of systems. His categorization helps in understanding how individual elements interact within a larger context, whether it's the predictable parts of a mechanical system, the goal-directed behaviors in animated systems, the collective objectives in social systems, or the intricate interdependencies in ecological systems. Ackoff's models enable problem-solvers and decision-makers to approach issues from a holistic standpoint, enhancing effectiveness and reducing unintended consequences.

One common pitfall in dealing with complex systems is making E3 errors: errors due to oversimplification, misplaced emphasis, and excessive reductionism. Ackoff cautioned against these by advocating for a systems thinking approach. Only by being cognizant of the larger system can one avoid E3 errors and develop solutions that are both effective and sustainable. Failing to do so often results in superficial solutions that may solve immediate problems but create more issues in the long run. Thus, the essence of systems thinking, encapsulated in Ackoff's models, lies in its capacity to provide a robust framework that minimizes the risk of oversimplification and E3 errors, ultimately enabling more comprehensive and effective problem-solving.

COMPREHENSION EXERCISES

1) Which of the following systems is rule-bound and operates based on fixed laws?
   a) A Family
   b) A Clock
   c) A Coral Reef
   d) A Dog
2) In which type of system do entities have self-preservation instincts but do not share a collective aim?
   a) Deterministic Mechanical Systems
   b) Animated Systems
   c) Social Systems
   d) Ecological Systems

3) Which type of system consists of complex networks of animated and social systems coexisting in a shared environment?
   a) Deterministic Mechanical Systems
   b) Animated Systems
   c) Social Systems
   d) Ecological Systems
4) What do social systems primarily emphasize?
   a) Predictability
   b) Self-Preservation
   c) Shared Objectives
   d) Ecological Balance
5) Which error is likely to occur if one fails to adopt a systems thinking approach according to Ackoff?
   a) A1 Error
   b) E3 Error
   c) X5 Error
   d) Z2 Error
6) What are the main components of a sociotechnical system?
   a) Mechanical and Biological
   b) Social and Mechanical
   c) Social and Technical
   d) Ecological and Animated
7) Which of the following is a real-world example of a sociotechnical system?
   a) A Rock
   b) A Waterfall
   c) A Hospital
   d) A Tree
8) Why are sociotechnical systems considered complex?
   a) They involve only social elements.
   b) They involve only technical elements.
   c) They integrate both social and technical elements.
   d) They are simple and straightforward to understand.
9) What is the primary focus when optimizing a sociotechnical system?
   a) Maximizing Technical Efficiency Only
   b) Maximizing Social Relationships Only
   c) Balancing Technical Efficiency and Human Factors
   d) Ignoring Human Factors

10) In a sociotechnical system, what can occur if human factors are ignored?
    a) Increased Efficiency
    b) Reduced Complexity
    c) Increased User Satisfaction
    d) Reduced System Effectiveness
11) What does the term 'E3 errors' refer to?
    a) Errors due to Emotional, Ethical, and Economic factors
    b) Errors due to Excessive reductionism, misplaced Emphasis, and oversimplification
    c) Errors due to External, Environmental, and Experiential factors
    d) Errors due to Execution, Evaluation, and Effectiveness
12) Which of the following scenarios is most likely to result in an E3 error?
    a) Considering multiple factors when solving a complex problem
    b) Focusing only on the technical aspects of a social-technical system
    c) Employing a multidisciplinary approach to address an issue
    d) Analyzing the overall ecosystem to solve an ecological problem
13) In the context of systems thinking, how can one avoid making E3 errors?
    a) By reducing the problem to its simplest components
    b) By ignoring the interconnectedness of different system parts
    c) By focusing only on immediate problems
    d) By taking a holistic view of the system and its interdependencies
14) Which of the following can be a consequence of E3 errors?
    a) Improved System Efficiency
    b) Reduced Unintended Consequences
    c) Increased Risk of Superficial Solutions
    d) Increased Interdisciplinary Collaboration
15) What does the 'E' in E3 errors stand for?
    a) Effective
    b) Errors
    c) Explanatory
    d) Engaging

REFERENCES

Ackoff, R., & Greenberg, D. (2008). *Turning learning right side up putting education back on track*. Wharton School Pub.

Ackoff, R. L. (1999). *Ackoff's Beset His Classic Writings on Management*. John Wiley & Sons.

Ackoff, R. L. (1999). *Re-creating the corporation: a design of organizations for the 21st century*. Oxford University Press.

Ackoff, R. L., & Rovin, S. (2003). *Redesigning Society. Stanford*. Business Books.

Bar-Yam, Y. (1997). *Dynamics of Complex Systems*. Addison-Wesley.

Beyer, H., & Holtzblatt, K. (1998). *Contextual Design: Defining Customer-Centered Systems*. Morgan Kaufmann Publishers.

Bostrom, R. P., & Stephen Heinen, J. (1977). MIS Problems and Failures: A Socio-Technical Perspective, Part I: The Causes. *Management Information Systems Quarterly*, *1*(3), 17–32. doi:10.2307/248710

Checkland, P. (1981). *Systems Thinking, Systems Practice*. John Wiley & Sons.

Cherns, A. (1976). The Principles of Socio-Technical Design. *Human Relations*, *29*(8), 783–792. doi:10.1177/001872677602900806

Clegg, C. W. (1988). Psychology of Employee Lateness, Absence, and Turnover: A Methodological Critique and an Empirical Study. *The Journal of Applied Psychology*, *73*(1), 88–101. doi:10.1037/0021-9010.68.1.88

Coakes, E. (2011). *Sociotechnical and Soft Approaches to Information Requirements Elicitation in the Post-Millennium Era*. Researching the Future in Information Systems.

Dumas, J. S., & Redish, J. C. (1993). *A Practical Guide to Usability Testing*. Intellect Books.

Emery, F. E., & Trist, E. L. (1965). The Causal Texture of Organizational Environments. *Human Relations*, *18*(1), 21–32. doi:10.1177/001872676501800103

Forrester, J. W. (1961). *Industrial Dynamics*. MIT Press.

Gharajedaghi, J. (2006). *Systems thinking: managing chaos and complexity: a platform for designing business architecture*. Elsevier.

Gould, J. D., & Lewis, C. (1995). Designing for usability: Key principles and what designers think. *Communications of the ACM*, *28*(3), 300–311. doi:10.1145/3166.3170

Holland, J. H. (1998). *Emergence: From Chaos to Order*. Oxford University Press.

Introna, L. D. (2005). Disclosive Ethics and Information Technology: Disclosing facial recognition systems. *Ethics and Information Technology*, *7*(2), 75–86. doi:10.100710676-005-4583-2

Introna, L. D. (2011). Phenomenological Approaches to Ethics and Information Technology. In E. N. Zalta (Ed.), *The Stanford Encyclopedia of Philosophy*. Stanford University.

Introna, L. D. (2014). Towards a post-human intra-actional account of sociomaterial agency (and ethics). In J. McIntyre-Mills (Ed.), *Systemic Ethics and Non-Anthropocentric Stewardship* (pp. 31–53). Springer.

Kauffman, S. A. (1995). *At Home in the Universe: The Search for the Laws of Self-Organization and Complexity*. Oxford University Press.

Keeney, R. L., & Raiffa, H. (1976). *Decisions with Multiple Objectives: Preferences and Value Tradeoffs*. Wiley.

Klein, J. K., & Delbridge, M. A. (1996). Sociotechnical Criteria for Designing Integrated IT Systems. *Management Information Systems Quarterly*, *20*(1), 31–44.

Leavitt, H. J. (1965). Applied Organizational Change in Industry: Structural, Technological and Humanistic Approaches. In J. G. March (Ed.), *Handbook of Organizations* (pp. 1144–1170). Rand McNally.

Leavitt, H. J., & Pondy, L. R. (1964). Leadership: A Special Type of Role. In H. J. Leavitt, (Eds.), *Readings in Managerial Psychology* (pp. 58–71). University of Chicago Press.

Meadows, D. H. (2008). *Thinking in Systems: A Primer* (D. Wright, Ed.). Chelsea Green Publishing.

Mitroff, I. I., & Linstone, H. A. (1993). *The Unbounded Mind, Breaking the Chains of Traditional Business Thinking*. Oxford University Press.

Mumford, E. (1983). Designing Human Systems. In *The ETHICS method*. Manchester Business School.

Nielsen, J. (1993). *Usability Engineering*. Morgan Kaufmann Publishers. doi:10.1016/B978-0-08-052029-2.50007-3

Norman, D. A. (1990). *The Design of Everyday Things*. Basic Books.

Pasmore, W. A. (1988). *Designing Effective Organizations: The Sociotechnical Systems Perspective*. John Wiley & Sons.

Preece, J., Rogers, Y., & Sharp, H. (1994). *Human-Computer Interaction*. Addison-Wesley.

Prigogine, I., & Stengers, I. (1984). *Order out of Chaos: Man's New Dialogue with Nature*. Bantam Books.

Raiffa, H. (1968). *Decision Analysis: Introductory Lectures on Choices Under Uncertainty*. Addison-Wesley.

Raiffa, H., Richardson, J., & Metcalfe, D. (2002). *Negotiation Analysis: The Science and Art of Collaborative Decision Making*. Harvard University Press.

Senge, P. M. (1990). The Fifth Discipline: The Art & Practice of The Learning Organization. Doubleday/Currency.

Shneiderman, B. (1998) Designing the User Interface: Strategies for Effective Human-Computer Interaction. (3rd ed.). Addison Wesley Longman.

Sveiby, K.-E. (1987). *Managing Knowhow: Increase Profits by Harnessing the Creativity in Your Company*. Bloomsbury.

Trist, E. L. (1981). *A Socio-Technical Critique of Scientific Management*. Knowledge and Action.

Trist, E. L., & Murray, H. (1990). *The Social Engagement of Social Science: A Tavistock Anthology*. University of Pennsylvania Press.

Tukey, J. W. (1962). The future of data analysis. *Annals of Mathematical Statistics, 33*(1), 1–67. doi:10.1214/aoms/1177704711

Tukey, J. W. (1977). *Exploratory Data Analysis*. Addison-Wesley.

Vickers, G. (1965). *The Art of Judgment: A Study of Policy Making*. Chapman & Hall.

Vickers, G. (1968). *Value Systems and Social Process*. Basic Books.

Vickers, G. (1970). *Making Institutions Work*. John Wiley & Sons.

Vickers, G. (1972). *Freedom in a Rocking Boat: Changing values in an unstable society*. Penguin.

Vickers, G. (1980). *Responsibility – Its Sources and Limits*. Intersystems Publications.

Vickers, G. (1983). *Human Systems are Different*. Harper & Row.

Waldrop, M. M. (1992). *Complexity: The Emerging Science at the Edge of Order and Chaos*. Simon & Schuster.

Whitworth, B., & Whitworth, A. P. (2010). The social environment model: Small heroes and the evolution of human society. *First Monday, 15*(11), NP–NP. doi:10.5210/fm.v15i11.3173

Winograd, T. (Ed.). (1996). *Bringing Design to Software*. Addison-Wesley. doi:10.1145/229868

APPENDIX - COMPREHENSION EXERCISES: SOLUTIONS

1) Which of the following systems is rule-bound and operates based on fixed laws?
    a) A Family
    b) A Clock
    c) A Coral Reef
    d) A Dog

Recommended Answer: B) A Clock

2) In which type of system do entities have self-preservation instincts but do not share a collective aim?
    a) Deterministic Mechanical Systems
    b) Animated Systems
    c) Social Systems
    d) Ecological Systems

Recommended Answer: B) Animated Systems

3) Which type of system consists of complex networks of animated and social systems coexisting in a shared environment?
    a) Deterministic Mechanical Systems
    b) Animated Systems
    c) Social Systems
    d) Ecological Systems

Recommended Answer: D) Ecological Systems

4) What do social systems primarily emphasize?
    a) Predictability
    b) Self-Preservation
    c) Shared Objectives
    d) Ecological Balance

Recommended Answer: C) Shared Objectives

5) Which error is likely to occur if one fails to adopt a systems thinking approach according to Ackoff?
    a) A1 Error
    b) E3 Error
    c) X5 Error
    d) Z2 Error

Recommended Answer: B) E3 Error

6) What are the main components of a sociotechnical system?
   a) Mechanical and Biological
   b) Social and Mechanical
   c) Social and Technical
   d) Ecological and Animated

Recommended Answer: C) Social and Technical

7) Which of the following is a real-world example of a sociotechnical system?
   a) A Rock
   b) A Waterfall
   c) A Hospital
   d) A Tree

Recommended Answer: C) A Hospital

8) Why are sociotechnical systems considered complex?
   a) They involve only social elements.
   b) They involve only technical elements.
   c) They integrate both social and technical elements.
   d) They are simple and straightforward to understand.

Recommended Answer: C) They integrate both social and technical elements.

9) What is the primary focus when optimizing a sociotechnical system?
   a) Maximizing Technical Efficiency Only
   b) Maximizing Social Relationships Only
   c) Balancing Technical Efficiency and Human Factors
   d) Ignoring Human Factors

Recommended Answer: C) Balancing Technical Efficiency and Human Factors

10) In a sociotechnical system, what can occur if human factors are ignored?
   a) Increased Efficiency
   b) Reduced Complexity
   c) Increased User Satisfaction
   d) Reduced System Effectiveness

Recommended Answer: D) Reduced System Effectiveness

11) What does the term 'E3 errors' refer to?
    a) Errors due to Emotional, Ethical, and Economic factors
    b) Errors due to Excessive reductionism, misplaced Emphasis, and oversimplification
    c) Errors due to External, Environmental, and Experiential factors
    d) Errors due to Execution, Evaluation, and Effectiveness

Recommended Answer: B) Errors due to Excessive reductionism, misplaced Emphasis, and oversimplification

12) Which of the following scenarios is most likely to result in an E3 error?
    a) Considering multiple factors when solving a complex problem
    b) Focusing only on the technical aspects of a social-technical system
    c) Employing a multidisciplinary approach to address an issue
    d) Analyzing the overall ecosystem to solve an ecological problem

Recommended Answer: B) Focusing only on the technical aspects of a social-technical system

13) In the context of systems thinking, how can one avoid making E3 errors?
    a) By reducing the problem to its simplest components
    b) By ignoring the interconnectedness of different system parts
    c) By focusing only on immediate problems
    d) By taking a holistic view of the system and its interdependencies

Recommended Answer: D) By taking a holistic view of the system and its interdependencies

14) Which of the following can be a consequence of E3 errors?
    a) Improved System Efficiency
    b) Reduced Unintended Consequences
    c) Increased Risk of Superficial Solutions
    d) Increased Interdisciplinary Collaboration

Recommended Answer: C) Increased Risk of Superficial Solutions

15) What does the 'E' in E3 errors stand for?
    a) Effective
    b) Errors
    c) Explanatory
    d) Engaging

Recommended Answer: B) Errors

Chapter 3
The Jungian Personality Framework (JPF)

ABSTRACT

The Jungian personality framework (JPF) was developed by Katherine Briggs and Isabelle Myer Brigg and is based on the pioneering work of the eminent Swiss psychiatrist/psychoanalyst Carl Jung. Jung observed that no matter what the field of human endeavor with which he was familiar—art, history, literature, psychology, etc.--the same basic differences in outlook emerged repeatedly. They represented the fundamental differences between how different people viewed any situation, field of human knowledge, and/or practice.

"People generally see what they look for, and hear what they listen for." Harper Lee, To Kill a Mockingbird

Learning Objectives

- List the four Personality Type Pairs
- Differentiate between Sensing and iNtuitive Types
- Contrast Extrovert from Introvert Personality Types
- Compare Thinking and Feeling Personality Types
- Describe the Judging and Perceiving Personality Types
- Illustrate an example of how the different Personality Types approach problems
- Describe the greatest impediment to effective problem solving

DOI: 10.4018/978-1-6684-6563-9.ch003

INTRODUCTION

Recognition of problems are greatly influenced by individual perspectives. The first and primary tool, the Jungian Personality Framework (JPF), is based on the pioneering work of the eminent Swiss Psychiatrist/Psychoanalyst Carl Jung. Jung observed that no matter what the particular field of human endeavour with which he was familiar—Art, History, Literature, Psychology, etc.--the same basic differences in outlook emerged repeatedly. They represented the fundamental differences between how different people viewed any situation, field of human knowledge, and/or practice. Jung was greatly supported in this work by two women; Katharine Briggs and her daughter Isabel Briggs Myers. During World War II they observed many people in the war effort were assigned tasks that were unsuited for their abilities (Kroeger, 2002). This prompted them to design a psychological instrument that would explain, in scientifically rigorous and reliable terms, differences according to Jung's theory of personality differences. This effort resulted in the Myers-Briggs Type Indicator instrument, whose aim is to establish individual preferences and then promote more constructive use of the differences between people (Kroeger, 2002).

There are four different preference pairs (Kroeger, 2002). The first has to do with where you get your energy: from outside yourself (Extroverted) or from within yourself (Introverted). The second addresses how you gather information: in a literal, sequential way (Sensing) or in a more holistic way (iNtuition). Third relates to the way decisions are made: objectively and impersonally (Thinking) or subjectively and personally (Feeling). Finally, the last pair addresses how you manage your day-to-day life: do you prefer to be decisive and planned (Judging) or flexible and spontaneous (Perceiving).

Table 1. Four different preference pairs

Extroverted (E)	Or	Introverted (I)
Sensing (S)	Or	iNtuitive (N)
Thinking (T)	Or	Feeling (F)
Judging (J)	Or	Perceiving (P)

Source: (Kroeger, 2002)

As shown in the Figure below, a juxtaposition between the Sensing/iNtuitive and Thinking/Feeling personality pairs are shown. The horizontal dimension refers to how one initially represents, structures, or views a complex entity. The vertical dimension refers to how one analyses, responds to, or the process one uses to make an important decision with regard to the entity.

Figure 1. Four quadrants of the Jungian personality framework (JPF) for SNTF types

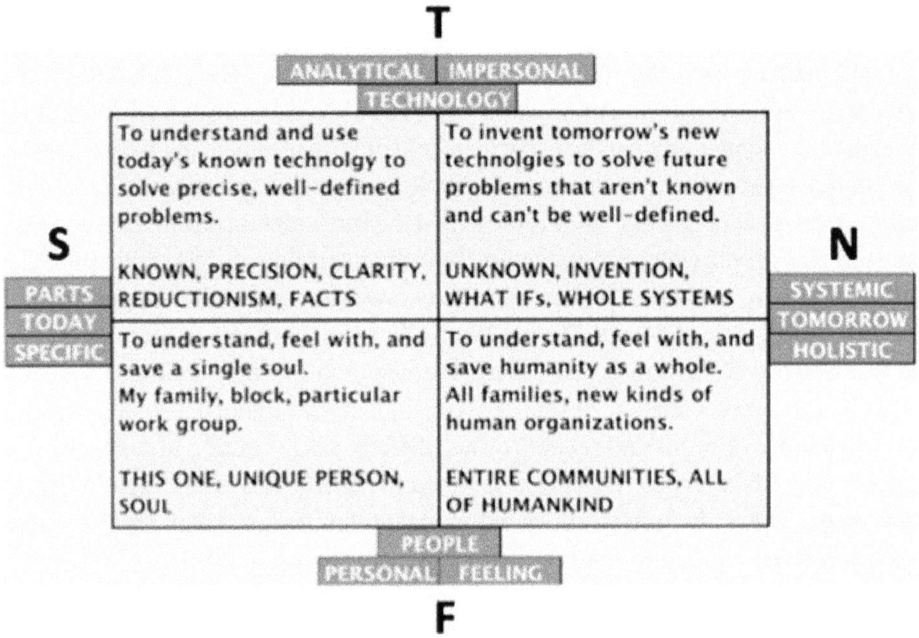

Figure 2. Four quadrants of the Jungian personality framework (JPF) for JPEI types

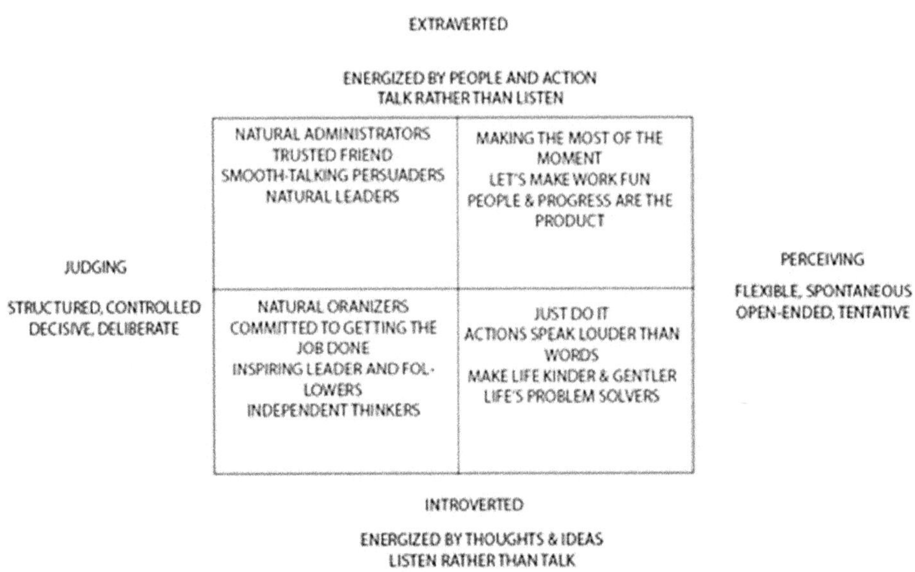

The left-hand side "Details Parts" refers to the fact that no matter what the particular entity or situation, there is always the perspective or point of view that instinctively breaks a complex whole (problem, situation, System, etc.) down into its so-called separate, individual parts and then analyses/studies the parts in isolation and independently of one another. In other words, some people are comfortable if and only if they can break a complex problem or whole down into its "separate, individual parts" so that they can focus solely on the parts alone. The left-hand side also represents those aspects of a system that can be understood in terms of established concepts, measures, and theories.

The left-hand side is called Sensing or S for short. Sensing Types—people whose S side of their personality is strongly developed--prefer to gather information in terms of their senses, or more generally, Scientific Data. In fact, anything that is not ultimately based on or reducible to "Hard Data" is not considered to be "valid information."

The right-hand side "Wholes" stands for those who instinctively prefer not to break something down into its so-called "separate, independent parts." Instead, they instinctively look at the whole of any entity or situation, i.e., the Big Picture. If they consider the "parts," it's not only to draw out all of the interconnections between them, but to create a whole whose value is greater than the "product" of the values of the individual parts. In other words, they don't look at anything in isolation. Finally, the right-hand side also represents the use of non-traditional concepts, innovative ideas, and measures to assess the performance of a system.

The term "product" is used deliberately. It's one of the key, defining properties of Systems. It reflects the basic fact that a System is the "product of the interactions" between all of its parts. In this sense, the common expression that a System is more than the "sum of its parts" does not fully capture the essence of what makes something a System.

The right-hand side is called Intuiting or N for short. (In JPF, the letter I is reserved for Introversion, and E for Extroversion, which is a whole other dimension altogether.) Intuiting type personalities—people whose N side is strongly developed--prefer to gather information in terms of their imagination. They focus on "possibilities," not "what currently is." In fact, anything that isn't ultimately based on imagination—"possibilities"-- isn't "informative," and hence "not information." In other words, so-called "hard facts" hem Ns in. It's not that facts don't matter, but that today's facts have a way of becoming the discarded realities of yesterday. In different terms, facts only matter in the aggregate, not in isolation.

The top of the vertical dimension, "Analytic," represents the use of impersonal means (Logic, Science, Statistics, etc.) of analysing entities and situations, and reaching key decisions. The bottom "People" represents the use of one's personal feelings to assess a person, organization, or situation. The bottom also represents looking at an organization, situation, etc. in intensely personal terms.

In terms of JPF, the top of the vertical dimension is called Thinking or T for short. Thinking type personalities—people whose T side is strongly developed--prefer to analyse situations impersonally. In sharp contrast, Feeling or F Types respond to every situation in intensely personal terms, e.g., in terms of "likes versus dislikes". It's not that one Type is "right" and the other is "wrong," but that both need and depend upon one another in order to pick up and respond appropriately to all of the facets that are involved in every situation.

It's also not the case that Feeling is strictly emotional for all of the Types can become highly emotional in defending their way of looking at the world.

Putting the horizontal and vertical dimensions together results in the four quadrants, or Personality Types, in the Figure.

In terms of the different types of problems we discussed in Chapter One, Type 1 problems are the province of ST; Type 2, NT; Type 3, NF; and Type 4, SF. One of the great redeeming features of JPF is that it makes abundantly clear why different Types of Personalities prefer different Types of problems. Indeed, it would seem that to be able to appreciate different kinds of problems, it requires that one be a specific Personality Type. Thus, the different diagonal Types have the most difficulty in getting along, and thus in appreciating their different perspectives. Whereas ST and NT share at least one dimension in common, namely T; NT and NF share N; NF and SF share F; and, ST and SF share S. In sharp contrast, NT and SF, and ST and NF, share nothing in common.

Ideally, an integrated Personality Type is best situated to appreciate all four Types of problems. This doesn't mean that all of the Types cannot learn to work together. It requires that one not only understand JPF, but appreciate why the different Types see the world differently. Most of all, it requires that one accept that they all have a fundamental role to play, and that by themselves, at best they only capture a part of the full nature of any problem.

PERSONALITY TYPES AND PROBLEM SOLVING

Each of the JPF personality types approach problem solving differently. A brief synopsis is presented below based on (Kroeger, 2002) and readers are encouraged to purchase the book for a more in-depth discussion and treatment of the topics. This is such a rich field; it is impossible to adequately cover the topic in full in this book. However, we do aim to provide a high-level overview to alert the reader to the importance of these topics.

Extraverts and Introverts

Extraverts prefer to solve problems by talking it through with someone else. They process reactions, both verbal and physical, from listeners. Even if the listener contributed nothing to the interaction, the Extraverts tend to feel that the experience was very helpful and aided them in reaching resolution.

Introverts are more comfortable when they can gather information and process in a private space where they can reflect and contemplate internally. Introverts tend to contribute listening skills and the ability to step back and more carefully consider the problem before jumping to a conclusion.

Sensors and iNtuitives

Sensors tend to approach problem solving by trusting the facts and evidence. Their focus is on moving towards practical and tangible results and spending too much time designing a solution or theorizing about alternatives is deemed a waste of time. Strategies to get Sensors to not get stuck on specifics include (Kroeger, 2002):

- Think of a bottom-line reason for the change
- Remember the sensory origins of the idea
- Find a short, memorable way to say it
- Make up an action plan
- Look around for something already in existence that is similar
- Run it by Sensors informally to find the practical pitfalls

The iNtuitive will avoid confronting a problem unless all the alternatives have been considered and various approaches developed to address every aspect of the problem. Problems are best solved when they are set in a context that gives perspective to the bigger picture. Approaches one can use to avoid iNtuitives from not being indecisive include (Kroeger, 2002):

- Before giving them the details, let them talk about their personal vision and tie the details into that
- Trace the details back to when they were a new and exciting idea
- Give them the Christmas tree before the ornaments, the framework before the details
- Don't judge their progress by the number of tangibles produced. Look instead at how the concept has progressed.

- Don't listen for your agenda when iNtuitives are imagining possibilities. Just try to identify the dream.
- To get them grounded, don't shoot them down. Throw them a line instead.

Thinkers and Feelers

Thinkers assume the role of alerting everyone to the potential consequences of any given action associated with the problem-solving venture. They see problem solving as a model in which elements can be moved and strategized, with a careful evaluation of cause and effect of each action. This allows Thinkers to maintain some 'separation' from the problem-solving process so they don't become overly involved with the personal aspects of the issues at hand, but may have difficulties staying objective.

Feelers ensure the problem-solving process addresses how people are affected. In problem-solving, the Feeler is the Barometer of what the interpersonal reaction to the solution will look like. Feelers can help question the perception of the potential solution. If the potential solution is not well-perceived, it is doomed for failure.

Judgers and Perceivers

The Judger's strength of being solution-oriented allows for a fairly rapid and streamlined process by which to arrive at a solution. However, this can lead to circumstances where not all potential viable options have been identified and evaluated and, as a result, the quality of the solution may not be as great as it could have been given more inquiry.

Perceivers can continue to massage a problem and generate new problems even after a course of action has been decided. Thus, this is both a strength and a weakness. Perceivers may actually interrupt themselves mid-solution and try alternatives to the alternatives and as a result, avoiding implementation/action. In the ideal world, there would be enough Perceivers to keep the Judgers from coming to premature solutions and enough Judgers to keep the Perceivers from overworking solutions (Kroeger, 2002).

Solving Problems

The Jungian framework leads to the appreciation that something is a global problem if and only if it has significant aspects in the four Jungian quadrants: Sensing, iNtuition, Thinking, and Feeling. If the significant aspects appear in only one or two of the Jungian quadrants, the problem may not be perceived as a problem across the larger group.

There is no doubt that on their surface and when they are first presented, many problems do not appear to involve all of the Jungian quadrants. Thus, it appears that many technical problems do not involve all of the quadrants. Nonetheless, from our experience, we have never seen a "problem" in the true sense of the term that does not have important aspects in all four quadrants. For instance, every problem has technical aspects of some kind (ST/NT). But given that it is humans who perceive what is and is not a "problem," every "problem" impacts human behavior and thereby has important NF and SF components.

To reiterate, something is a problem if and only if it has significant aspects in all of the quadrants. The danger is that the aspects we neglect or downplay often come back to haunt us in the form of major crises, a topic about which we say more later.

This leads to the following series of questions that everyone can use to assess him or herself:

1. How well do you do in managing the key issues that affect you in terms of the four Jungian quadrants? For instance, are your finances well managed in terms of ST concerns/metrics, i.e., in terms of impersonal, analytic details? In terms of NT, do you think and plan strategically? In terms of NF, do you feel that you are part of a larger community? In terms of SF, are you part of a small, tightknit community? Do you rely primarily on one of the quadrants to guide you in making key decisions?
2. In which quadrants are you especially strong and/or weak? Why?
3. Do you define/treat important problems from an integrated Jungian perspective? That is, do you strive to produce integrated (ST, NT, NF, and SF) definitions of important problems before working on them? Why, why not?
4. Do you seek out people who can help integrate the different Types of perspectives that constitute the Jungian quadrants?
5. Would you like to participate in on-going educational programs so that you can learn to integrate the Jungian quadrants? Why, why not?
6. Can you at least learn to speak the language of the different Jungian Types so that even if you can't be like them, you can better appreciate them?
7. Who do you know personally that serve as models with regard to JPF? What can you learn from them?

In sum, in terms of ST, we need the best models we can build that will not only help explain the nature of the problem, but will help us contain and ultimately defeat it. But to do it requires the intense cooperation of NT, NF, and SF.

Figure 3 shows a mapping of the four Jungian quadrants onto the Diamond Model presented in Chapter 1. In the Problem Identification quadrant, which focuses on recognizing and defining challenges, INTJ or INFJ types, with their intuitive and analytical abilities, would be particularly effective. For the Solution Design quadrant, where creative and practical solutions are crafted, the innovative thinking of ENTP or INTP personalities would shine. In the Implementation phase, requiring organized execution and management, ESTJ or ENTJ types, known for their leadership and systematic approach, would excel. Lastly, the Evaluation quadrant, emphasizing the assessment of outcomes against objectives, would benefit from meticulous scrutiny and attention to detail of ISTJ or ISFJ types.

Figure 3. Mapping of the four Jungian quadrants onto the diamond model

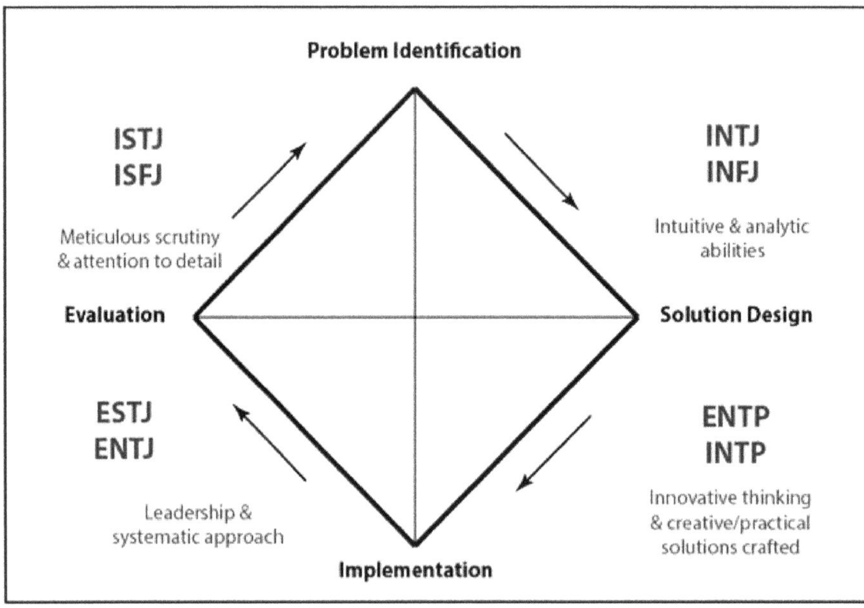

Sameness: Greatest Impediment to Problem Solving

The greatest impediment and major vulnerability to effective problem solving is not diversity, rather, sameness (Kroeger, 2002). Organizational hierarchies tend to be populated with groups of individuals with similar personality types. This leads to situations of 'groupthink' and typically results in partially defined problems and associated solutions and failed implementation attempts.

Groupthink is a psychological phenomenon where conformity and cohesiveness within a group can lead to poor decision-making. Research focuses on conditions fostering groupthink, symptoms, and prevention. The key factors are strong group cohesion, isolated environments, directive leadership, and high stress situations. Critics argue that the concept lacks empirical support and theoretical clarity, calling for more nuanced models. Example instances where groupthink may occur such as a CEO making unilateral decisions without consulting the team; a government agency adhering rigidly to set protocols, ignoring innovative solutions; a town hall meeting where community members vote on local issues; or a startup where team members pursue projects autonomously, without centralized control.

Figure 4. Five ways to avoid groupthink

Five Ways to Avoid Groupthink

1. **Encourage Dissent:** Create a culture where differing opinions are welcomed. Assign a "devil's advocate" to challenge prevailing viewpoints during meetings.
2. **Diverse Team Composition:** Include members with varied backgrounds, expertise, and perspectives to broaden the group's cognitive horizon.
3. **Structured Decision-Making:** Employ systematic approaches like SWOT analysis, pros-and-cons lists, or decision trees to evaluate options objectively.
4. **Seek External Input:** Consult experts, stakeholders, or even junior team members outside the core decision-making group to gain fresh perspectives.
5. **Leadership Neutrality:** Leaders should withhold their opinions until later in the discussion to avoid influencing team members unduly, allowing for a freer flow of ideas.

To overcome this vulnerability, problem-solving teams are strongly encouraged to assemble representatives from each of the four Jungian quadrants: Sensing, iNtuition, Thinking, and Feeling. Isabel Brigg Myers developed the "Z Model" which consists of the following steps (Kroeger, 2002):

Gather the facts: use Sensing (S) to look at the details of the problem at hand;
Brainstorm possibilities: use iNtuition (N) to develop possible causes and solutions to the problem;
Analyze objectively: use Thinking (T) to consider the cause and effect of each potential solution to the problem; and
Weigh the impact: use Feeling (F) to consider how people involved in the problem will be affected by the suggested solutions.

One can group the Sensing-Thinking (STs) into one group and all the iNtuitive-Feeling (NFs) into another and then ask each group to uncover and list a larger suite of problems (both implicit and explicit) associated with a messy topic or within a system, such as an organization, family unit, etc. In order for the approaches to be viable, the individuals and/or organizations must first be willing to not only take a brief psychological instrument or test (such as through taking the Myers Brigg personality test), but to have some belief in the framework as well (Barabba & Ian, 2014). The participants must also be willing to spend at least half a day working together in the personality type groups to gather valuable light and insight on themselves and the system being evaluated. Unless individuals and organizations are willing to spend time, unfortunately, dysfunctional systems are likely to continue unabated (Barabba & Ian, 2014).

This approach of acknowledging and leveraging personality types to problem-solving is robust in that it acknowledges and incorporates different perspectives in both the formulation of the problem statement as well as the configuration of potential solutions. Its breadth and depth will more responsibly confront the problem at hand and will be far more comprehensive in its configuration of effective solutions. This also highlights that it can be very challenging for any one person (with one personality type perspective) to tackle a complex messy problem. Don't go it alone...find your problem-solving team (SNTF)!

Illustrative Example One: Optimizing Supply Chain Management With Myers-Briggs and Systems Thinking

TechCorp Inc. faced a complex issue in its supply chain management that led to delays and increased operational costs. They decided to use both Myers-Briggs Personality Types (MBTI) and systems thinking to solve the problem.

The Problem:

Supply Chain Bottlenecks: Slowdowns at various points in the supply chain were causing delivery delays.

Steps Taken:

1. **MBTI Assessment**: Team members underwent MBTI testing to identify their personality types.
2. **Team Composition**: An INTJ for analytical problem-solving, an ENFP for creative solutions, an ISTJ for detailed analysis, and an ESFJ for team cohesion were selected.
3. **Identify System Components**: Using systems thinking, the team mapped out the entire supply chain network, identifying bottlenecks.
4. **Brainstorm Solutions**:

- INTJ proposed data analytics to predict and avoid bottlenecks.
- ENFP suggested liaising with suppliers for more flexible scheduling.
- ISTJ recommended internal audits to ensure compliance and efficiency.
- ESFJ focused on improving internal communication.

5. **Feedback Loops**: The team considered how changes would affect other parts of the system, recognizing interdependencies.

Outcomes:

1. **Balanced Solutions**: Combining the strengths of different MBTI types led to a multifaceted solution.
2. **Reduced Bottlenecks**: By employing data analytics and improving supplier relationships, bottlenecks decreased by 40%.
3. **Operational Efficiency**: Internal audits and communication improvements led to a 20% increase in operational efficiency.
4. **Stakeholder Satisfaction**: Addressing the ethical and logistical sides of the issue, thanks to the Feeling and Thinking types, led to increased stakeholder satisfaction.

Conclusion

Using Myers-Briggs along with systems thinking, TechCorp Inc. not only identified the root causes of their supply chain bottlenecks but also implemented a balanced and effective solution. The approach showcased how diverse personality types can enrich problem-solving in a complex system. Following the implementation of a strategy that melded Myers-Briggs personality types with systems thinking, TechCorp Inc. achieved remarkable gains in its supply chain efficiency. The initiative led to a 40% reduction in bottlenecks and a 20% boost in operational efficiency. These improvements not only expedited product delivery but also significantly cut down on storage and late-delivery costs. By optimizing the supply chain, the company also minimized the risk of stockouts or overstocking, reducing inventory costs. Overall, the initiative enhanced the reliability and cost-effectiveness of the supply chain, contributing positively to TechCorp Inc.'s profitability.

Illustrative Example Two: Enhancing Safety Culture with Myers-Briggs and Systems Thinking

SafeChem Industries, a chemical manufacturing company, faced rising safety incidents, affecting both employees and operational efficiency. Utilizing Myers-

Briggs Personality Types (MBTI) and systems thinking, the organization aimed to overhaul its safety culture.

The Problem:

- **Safety Incidents:** Increase in workplace accidents, leading to injuries and production halts.

Steps Taken:

1. **MBTI Assessment:** Employees across different departments underwent MBTI testing to identify their personality types.
2. **Team Formation:** A diverse team was created, including an ISTJ for procedural integrity, an ENFJ for interpersonal sensitivity, an INTJ for strategic planning, and an ESFP for adaptability and hands-on problem-solving.
3. **System Mapping:** Employing systems thinking, the team mapped the company's safety protocols and identified weak links leading to incidents.
4. **Brainstorming and Strategy Formation:**
   - ISTJ outlined stricter adherence to safety protocols.
   - ENFJ suggested training sessions focused on empathy and interpersonal communication for safety.
   - INTJ introduced a long-term strategy for integrating safety measures into the corporate culture.
   - ESFP devised quick, adaptable solutions for immediate safety concerns.
5. **Feedback Mechanism:** Established a loop for continuous feedback from employees to identify new areas of concern and adapt the strategies accordingly.

Outcomes:

1. **Comprehensive Approach:** The diverse MBTI types contributed to a multifaceted safety strategy that catered to both immediate and long-term concerns.
2. **Accident Reduction:** Implementation of stricter protocols and better communication led to a 50% reduction in safety incidents.
3. **Cultural Shift:** Training sessions aimed at understanding the systemic importance of individual actions contributed to a stronger safety culture.
4. **Employee Engagement:** Utilizing continuous feedback, employees felt more involved in safety processes, increasing overall satisfaction and compliance.

Conclusion

Integrating Myers-Briggs and systems thinking enabled SafeChem Industries to implement a comprehensive, adaptive safety culture. The different personality types enriched the problem-solving process, resulting in a safer and more efficient work environment. After implementing a strategy that combined Myers-Briggs personality insights with systems thinking, SafeChem Industries saw substantial improvements in its safety culture. The tailored approach led to a 50% reduction in workplace accidents, enhancing both employee well-being and operational efficiency. Moreover, this reduction in incidents translated into significant cost savings for the company. Streamlined safety protocols and heightened employee engagement not only minimized downtime but also reduced expenses related to accident-related litigation and medical care. Overall, the multifaceted strategy produced a safer, more efficient work environment while contributing to the company's bottom line.

Illustrative Example Three: Offshore Shipping Optimization with Myers-Briggs and Systems Thinking

SeaPath Logistics, an offshore shipping company, grappled with logistical delays, increased fuel consumption, and safety concerns. Utilizing both Myers-Briggs Personality Types (MBTI) and systems thinking, they aimed to revamp their offshore operations.

The Problem:

- **Operational Delays**: Unpredictable delays led to missed delivery windows and contractual penalties.
- **Safety Concerns**: A rising number of near-miss incidents and minor accidents.

Steps Taken:

1. **MBTI Assessment**: Crew members, logistics staff, and executive teams underwent MBTI testing.
2. **Team Composition**: A diversified team was assembled, consisting of an ESTJ for logistical structuring, an INFP for ethical and safety considerations, an ENTJ for strategic oversight, and an ISFP for practical, on-ground inputs.
3. **System Mapping**: Employed systems thinking to map out the entire offshore shipping process, from planning to execution, identifying weak points in logistics and safety.
4. **Strategic Planning**:

- ESTJ optimized route planning and cargo organization.
- INFP introduced safety checks emphasizing the human element.
- ENTJ formulated a strategic vision for long-term operational excellence.
- ISFP recommended real-time solutions for common on-board issues.

5. **Feedback Loops**: Established regular reporting and review mechanisms to continually update strategies based on performance and incident reports.

Outcomes:

1. **Enhanced Coordination**: The diverse perspectives contributed to a well-rounded approach, optimizing both logistics and safety.
2. **Reduced Delays**: Route optimization and better cargo organization led to a 30% reduction in operational delays.
3. **Safety Improvements**: Incorporation of human-centric safety checks resulted in a 25% decrease in near-miss incidents and minor accidents.
4. **Cost Savings**: Improved efficiency and safety led to reduced fuel consumption and fewer contractual penalties, contributing to an estimated 15% cost savings.

Conclusion

By integrating Myers-Briggs and systems thinking, SeaPath Logistics transformed its offshore shipping operations. The multi-dimensional approach not only streamlined logistics but also enhanced safety measures, leading to significant cost savings and operational improvements. After integrating Myers-Briggs and systems thinking into their strategy, SeaPath Logistics achieved marked improvements in both safety and efficiency for their offshore shipping operations. Operational delays were reduced by 30%, owing to optimized route planning and cargo organization. In terms of safety, a human-centric approach led to a 25% decrease in near-miss incidents and minor accidents. These operational and safety enhancements translated into substantial cost savings for the company, estimated at 15%. Reduced fuel consumption, fewer contractual penalties, and improved safety collectively contributed to a more cost-effective and reliable shipping process.

CONCLUSION

Myers-Briggs personality types offer valuable insights into human behavior, aiding systems thinking and problem-solving. Different types bring unique approaches to analytical reasoning, creative thinking, and social dynamics. For instance, a Thinking type excels in logical analysis, while a Feeling type adds ethical considerations. Together, they can formulate holistic solutions that account for a system's multiple facets.

Different MBTI types perceive and tackle problems through distinct lenses. Sensing types prefer concrete data and direct experience. Intuitive types, on the other hand, favor abstract concepts and big-picture thinking. Thinking types prioritize objectivity and logical reasoning, while Feeling types weigh emotional and ethical factors. These varied approaches can be harnessed to analyze and solve complex issues from multiple perspectives.

Groupthink poses a significant barrier to effective problem-solving. It stifles innovation and hampers critical thinking by pushing for conformity and discouraging dissent. Diverse perspectives get overshadowed, leading to poor decision-making. In a system-focused setting, this lack of diversity can result in solutions that fail to consider all variables, ultimately weakening the integrity of the system.

When Myers-Briggs and systems thinking are jointly employed, the result is often a more comprehensive and effective problem-solving approach. The synergy enables teams to analyze issues from multiple angles, balancing logical reasoning with ethical considerations and practical constraints. This multi-dimensional approach often yields solutions that are both innovative and robust, optimizing various aspects of a system while minimizing unintended negative impacts. In essence, the combination enhances both the depth and breadth of problem analysis, leading to more sustainable outcomes.

The reader is strongly urged to take the Myers-Briggs Personality Assessment (MBTI) online, The MBTI gives a comprehensive evaluation of one's Personality Type.

COMPREHENSION EXERCISES

1) How many personality types are there in the Myers-Briggs Type Indicator (MBTI)?
   a) 4
   b) 8
   c) 12
   d) 16
2) Which dimension of MBTI focuses on how people gather information?
   a) Extraversion/Introversion
   b) Sensing/Intuition
   c) Thinking/Feeling
   d) Judging/Perceiving

3) What does the 'T' in INTJ stand for?
   a) Thinking
   b) Typing
   c) Tactful
   d) Temperate
4) Which of the following types is considered an introverted type?
   a) ESFJ
   b) INFP
   c) ENTP
   d) ESTP
5) What does the Judging/Perceiving dimension primarily assess?
   a) Decision-making style
   b) Information gathering
   c) Orientation to the outer world
   d) Social interaction
6) Who are the original creators of the MBTI?
   a) Carl Jung and Sigmund Freud
   b) Isabel Briggs Myers and Katharine Cook Briggs
   c) Albert Bandura and Erik Erikson
   d) B.F. Skinner and John Watson
7) What is the opposite of 'Extraversion' in MBTI?
   a) Sensing
   b) Introversion
   c) Thinking
   d) Judging
8) Which dimension is concerned with how individuals make decisions?
   a) Extraversion/Introversion
   b) Sensing/Intuition
   c) Thinking/Feeling
   d) Judging/Perceiving
9) What does the MBTI primarily aim to assess?
   a) Intelligence
   b) Skills
   c) Personality Preferences
   d) Emotional Stability
10) Which of these is NOT one of the four dimensions of MBTI?
   a) Sensing/Intuition
   b) Extraversion/Introversion
   c) Optimistic/Pessimistic
   d) Thinking/Feeling

11) What is the primary characteristic of groupthink?
    a) Open debate and discussion
    b) Conformity and poor decision-making
    c) Diversity of opinions
    d) Effective problem-solving
12) Which of the following is NOT a symptom of groupthink?
    a) Belief in inherent group morality
    b) Collective rationalization
    c) Encouragement of dissent
    d) Illusion of unanimity
13) What is 'sameness' often associated with in the context of groupthink?
    a) Diversity
    b) Homogeneity
    c) Complexity
    d) Randomness
14) How can a leader prevent groupthink?
    a) By making decisions quickly
    b) By suppressing dissenting opinions
    c) By promoting open dialogue and encouraging different viewpoints
    d) By being strongly directive
15) What is a common outcome of groupthink?
    a) High-quality decision-making
    b) Exposure to diverse perspectives
    c) Poor risk assessment
    d) Incremental innovation

REFERENCES

Barabba, V. P., & Ian, I. M. (2014). *Business Strategies for a Messy World - Tools for Systemic Problem Solving*. Palgrave Macmillan. doi:10.1057/9781137386403

Kroeger, O. w. (2002). *Type Talk at Work - How the 16 Personality Types Determine Your Success on the Job (Revised and Updated)*. Dell Publishing.

ADDITIONAL READING

Bayne, R. (1995). *The Myers-Briggs Type Indicator: A Critical Review and Practical Guide*. Chapman & Hall.

Capraro, M. V., & Capraro, R. M. (2002). Myers-Briggs Type Indicator Score Reliability Across: Studies a Meta-Analytic Reliability Generalization Study. *Educational and Psychological Measurement*, *62*(4), 590–602.

Carskadon, T. G. (1985). *MBTI Manual (A guide to the development and use of the Myers Briggs type indicator)*. Consulting Psychologists Press.

Esser, J. K. (1998). Alive and Well after 25 Years: A Review of Groupthink Research. *Organizational Behavior and Human Decision Processes*, *73*(2-3), 116–141.

Hammer, A. L. (1996). *MBTI Applications: A Decade of Research on the Myers-Briggs Type Indicator*. Consulting Psychologists Press.

Janis, I. L. (1982). *Groupthink: Psychological Studies of Policy Decisions and Fiascoes*. Houghton Mifflin.

Janis, I. L. (1972). *Victims of Groupthink: A Psychological Study of Foreign-policy Decisions and Fiascoes*. Houghton Mifflin.

Jung, C. G. (1921). *Psychological Types*. Routledge.

Keirsey, D., & Bates, M. (1984). *Please Understand Me: Character and Temperament Types*. Prometheus Nemesis Book Co.

Kroeger, O., & Thuesen, J. M. (1988). *Type Talk: The 16 Personality Types That Determine How We Live, Love, and Work*. Delacorte Press.

Kroeger, O., Thuesen, J. M., & Rutledge, H. (2002). *Type Talk at Work (Revised): How the 16 Personality Types Determine Your Success on the Job*. Delta.

Lawrence, G. D. (1982). *People Types and Tiger Stripes: Using Psychological Type to Help Students Discover Their Unique Potential*. Center for Applications of Psychological Type.

McCrae, R. R., & Costa, P. T. Jr. (1987). Validation of the Five-Factor Model of Personality Across Instruments and Observers. *Journal of Personality and Social Psychology*, *52*(1), 81–90.

Myers, I. B., & McCaulley, M. H. (1985). *Manual: A Guide to the Development and Use of the Myers-Briggs Type Indicator*. Consulting Psychologists Press.

Myers, I. B. (1980). *Gifts Differing: Understanding Personality Type.* Davies-Black Publishing.

Paul, A. M., & Clifford, G. T. D. (2012). Diverse Groups Are More Productive But Less Cohesive, and Vice Versa, Right? Not Exactly. *Harvard Business Review.*

Pittenger, D. J. (1993). The Utility of the Myers-Briggs Type Indicator. *Review of Educational Research, 63*(4), 467–488.

Quenk, N. L. (2000). *In the Grip: Our Hidden Personality.* Consulting Psychologists Press.

Thompson, H., & Kummerow, J. M. (2000). *Introduction to Type and Teams.* CPP, Inc.

Tieger, P. D., & Barron-Tieger, B. (2001). *Do What You Are: Discover the Perfect Career for You Through the Secrets of Personality Type.* Little, Brown and Company.

Turner, M. E., & Pratkanis, A. R. (1998). Twenty-Five Years of Groupthink Theory and Research: Lessons from the Evaluation of a Theory. *Organizational Behavior and Human Decision Processes, 73*(2-3), 105–115.

APPENDIX - COMPREHENSION EXERCISES: SOLUTIONS

1) How many personality types are there in the Myers-Briggs Type Indicator (MBTI)?
   a) 4
   b) 8
   c) 12
   d) 16
   Recommended Answer: d)
2) Which dimension of MBTI focuses on how people gather information?
   a) Extraversion/Introversion
   b) Sensing/Intuition
   c) Thinking/Feeling
   d) Judging/Perceiving
   Recommended Answer: b) Sensing/Intuition
3) What does the 'T' in INTJ stand for?
   a) Thinking
   b) Typing
   c) Tactful
   d) Temperate
   Recommended Answer: a) Thinking
4) Which of the following types is considered an introverted type?
   a) ESFJ
   b) INFP
   c) ENTP
   d) ESTP
   Recommended Answer: b) INFP
5) What does the Judging/Perceiving dimension primarily assess?
   a) Decision-making style
   b) Information gathering
   c) Orientation to the outer world
   d) Social interaction
   Recommended Answer: c) Orientation to the outer world
6) Who are the original creators of the MBTI?
   a) Carl Jung and Sigmund Freud
   b) Isabel Briggs Myers and Katharine Cook Briggs
   c) Albert Bandura and Erik Erikson
   d) B.F. Skinner and John Watson

Recommended Answer: b) Isabel Briggs Myers and Katharine Cook Briggs

7) What is the opposite of 'Extraversion' in MBTI?
   a) Sensing
   b) Introversion
   c) Thinking
   d) Judging

   Recommended Answer: b) Introversion

8) Which dimension is concerned with how individuals make decisions?
   a) Extraversion/Introversion
   b) Sensing/Intuition
   c) Thinking/Feeling
   d) Judging/Perceiving

   Recommended Answer: c) Thinking/Feeling

9) What does the MBTI primarily aim to assess?
   a) Intelligence
   b) Skills
   c) Personality Preferences
   d) Emotional Stability

   Recommended Answer: c) Personality Preferences

10) Which of these is NOT one of the four dimensions of MBTI?
   a) Sensing/Intuition
   b) Extraversion/Introversion
   c) Optimistic/Pessimistic
   d) Thinking/Feeling

   Recommended Answer: c) Optimistic/Pessimistic

11) What is the primary characteristic of groupthink?
   a) Open debate and discussion
   b) Conformity and poor decision-making
   c) Diversity of opinions
   d) Effective problem-solving

   Recommended Answer: b) Conformity and poor decision-making

12) Which of the following is NOT a symptom of groupthink?
   a) Belief in inherent group morality
   b) Collective rationalization
   c) Encouragement of dissent
   d) Illusion of unanimity

   Recommended Answer: c) Encouragement of dissent

13) What is 'sameness' often associated with in the context of groupthink?
   a) Diversity

b) Homogeneity
c) Complexity
d) Randomness
Recommended Answer: b) Homogeneity

14) How can a leader prevent groupthink?
a) By making decisions quickly
b) By suppressing dissenting opinions
c) By promoting open dialogue and encouraging different viewpoints
d) By being strongly directive
Recommended Answer: c) By promoting open dialogue and encouraging different viewpoints

15) What is a common outcome of groupthink?
a) High-quality decision-making
b) Exposure to diverse perspectives
c) Poor risk assessment
d) Incremental innovation
Recommended Answer: c) Poor risk assessment

Chapter 4
Inquiry Systems

ABSTRACT

This tool is concerned with the different kinds of knowledge that are best suited for different kinds of problems. (1) Expert agreement—something is objective if and only if it's based on "hard Data, facts, or observations" and the "tight agreement" between different observers as to the data, etc. (2) True formula—something is objective if, and only if, it's based on logical reasoning from self-evident first principles or premises. (3) Multiple perspectives—something is objective if and only if it's the product and the result of multiple points of view. (4) Expert disagreement—something is objective if and only if it's the product and the result of (that is, it survives) the most intense debate between the most disparate points of view. And finally, (5) Systems thinking—something is objective if and only if it's the product and the result of the most intense effort of sweeping in knowledge from the arts, humanities, professions, philosophy, sciences, etc.

"The right question is usually more important than the right answer." –Plato

Learning Objectives

- List the five Inquiry Systems
- Differentiate between Expert Consensus/Empiricism and Analytic Modeling/Rationalism
- Explain the Multiple Models/Kantian Inquiry System
- Identify an example of the Dialectic Inquiry System
- Summarize the Systemic/Pragmatic Inquiry System
- Describe how Inquiry Systems impact Problem Solving

DOI: 10.4018/978-1-6684-6563-9.ch004

INTRODUCTION

Inquiry systems, rooted in philosophy, systems theory, and cognitive science, study the methodologies and processes of gaining knowledge. Major ideas include types of inquiry like deductive, inductive, and abductive reasoning, and systems based on dialogue, consensus, or scientific methods. Key figures like John Dewey, Karl Popper, and C. West Churchman have significantly impacted the field. Recent trends focus on integrating technology, handling complex information, and interdisciplinary approaches. Research from the mid-20th century to now marks the most active period in this academic discourse.

Ian Mitroff has extended these ideas from philosophy and systems theory to organizational behavior and decision-making (Mitroff & Linstone, 1993). Mitroff's work emphasizes the role of human values and ethics in shaping inquiry. He argues for "mixed-scanning approaches" that combine empirical data and subjective interpretation for holistic problem-solving. His contributions have deepened understanding of complex, interrelated systems and have influenced disciplines from management science to public policy.

Mitroff (Mitroff & Linstone, 1993) identifies five types of inquiry systems:

1. **Expert Consensus** aims for single, consensual answers through simple data collection and are often used for straightforward problems. Example applications include:
    a. **Public Opinion Polls**: Collecting opinions from a sample to gauge public sentiment on an issue.
    b. **Market Research**: Gathering consumer preferences for new product development.
    c. **Medical Diagnosis**: Using symptoms to identify a single likely illness.
    d. **Student Grading**: Using test scores and assignments to determine a final grade.
    e. **Employee Satisfaction Surveys**: Collecting feedback from employees to identify overall workplace satisfaction.
    f. **Safety Audits**: Conducting regular checks to collect data on compliance with safety standards, aiming for a single measure of safety levels.
2. **Analytic-Deductive** relies on formal models and algorithms, serving well-defined problems that require precise, quantitative solutions. Example applications include:
    a. **Financial Forecasting:** Using algorithms to predict stock market trends.
    b. **Climate Modeling:** Employing complex simulations to predict weather or climate changes.

c. **Supply Chain Optimization:** Utilizing data and algorithms to streamline operations.
d. **Pharmaceutical Testing:** Conducting controlled experiments to validate a drug's efficacy.
e. **Route Optimization:** Using algorithms to determine the most efficient delivery routes for logistics companies.
f. **Accident Modeling:** Using algorithms and statistical models to predict and prevent workplace accidents based on historical data.

3. <u>**Multiple Models**</u> acknowledges that different perspectives can co-exist, offering multiple, even conflicting solutions for complex issues. Example applications include:
   a. **Mental Health Treatment:** Tailoring therapy based on different psychological models.
   b. **Crisis Management:** Employing multiple strategies to handle various aspects of a crisis.
   c. **Ecological Studies:** Analyzing an ecosystem through the lenses of various scientific disciplines.
   d. **Art Interpretation:** Applying different critical theories to interpret a work of art.
   e. **Cultural Anthropology:** Investigating social norms and beliefs from the perspectives of different cultural frameworks.
   f. **Cross-Departmental Safety Assessments:** Reviewing safety protocols from the perspectives of different departments like engineering, HR, and operations to gain a multifaceted understanding.
4. <u>**Dialectical**</u> employs opposing viewpoints to uncover the complexities of an issue and are ideal for problems with inherent conflicts. Example applications include:
   a. **Political Debates:** Pitting different viewpoints against each other to scrutinize policies.
   b. **Ethics Committees:** Discussing moral implications of scientific research.
   c. **Legal Systems:** Using adversarial processes to arrive at a verdict.
   d. **Urban Planning:** Balancing community needs and commercial interests in development projects.
   e. **Conflict Resolution:** Utilizing mediation to explore opposing viewpoints and arrive at a mutual agreement.
   f. **Safety Committee Discussions:** Facilitating dialogue between management and employees to address opposing views on safety measures, aiming to find a balanced approach.

5. **Systemic** integrates these different methods, advocating for a holistic approach that accounts for complex interrelationships, values, and ethics. Example applications include:
    a. **Sustainable Development:** Balancing economic growth, social inclusion, and environmental sustainability.
    b. **Healthcare Policy:** Integrating medical research, economics, and social factors to guide policy.
    c. **Organizational Strategy:** Combining internal data analysis, market trends, and stakeholder inputs to make long-term plans.
    d. **National Security:** Using multi-faceted approaches, including intelligence gathering, diplomacy, and military strategy, for national defense.
    e. **Smart Cities:** Integrating technological solutions, urban planning, and community engagement to create sustainable and efficient urban environments.
    f. **Integrated Safety Management:** Combining employee training, risk assessment, equipment checks, and emergency response planning to create a comprehensive safety culture.

Mitroff's taxonomy provides a comprehensive framework for tackling problems across various disciplines. The array of examples presented illustrate how Mitroff's inquiry systems can be applied across a range of disciplines and problem-solving contexts.

AN EXAMPLE: HEALTHY BARS

Healthy Bars Inc. makes healthy food energy bars. Its goal is not only to be the number one company in its industry in terms of market share, but it wants to be the company that consumers think of first when they think of an environmentally responsible and Ethical company.

In order to increase awareness of its products and thus to boost sales, Healthy Bars Inc. decided to hold a worldwide contest. They invited consumers to send in recipes on "how to make the perfect dish with fruit bars."[1] The only restriction was that the recipes had to use one of Healthy Bars Inc.'s products. Other than this, consumers were free to add any ingredients they wished, providing of course that they were safe, environmentally friendly, and legal. The contest winner not only received free health bars for a year, but more importantly, the honorific title of "Master Chef."

The First Way of Deciding: Expert Consensus

Like most organizations, Healthy Bars Inc. appointed a small committee to judge the entries it received. To its chagrin, the committee soon found that it was literally drowning in entries. Thousands poured in from all over the world.

The committee was completely stymied. There was no way that a small group could sift through thousands of submissions.

Besides, what was the meaning of "perfect?" They hadn't even considered that a definition of what they were looking for might be important before they started the contest. Rather naively, they thought that it would just emerge. Recall from Chapter One that it's only in Type 1 problems--that is, problems that are Bounded and Well-Structured--do we start with a clear definition of the problem at the beginning of an inquiry. Further, the initial definition does not vary over the course of the process.

One of the committee members suggested tabulating all the entries by putting them into a PC. The particular recipe receiving the most votes or the one that had the most in common with all the individual recipes--the "average"--would be declared the winner, in this case, the "perfect dish." The member pointed out that this was a convenient way of bypassing the definition of "perfect." "Perfect" would in effect emerge from the process itself. As one of the members of the committee said, "Why get hung up on definitions?" (Notice that by doing so, they were bypassing the first critical step of Problem Solving, i.e., Problem Definition.)

However, as soon as this was suggested, it raised more concerns and issues than it settled. Most of the committee members felt that it was a complete copout.

Why was the "average" in any sense the definition of "perfect?" Couldn't it lead to the selection of the most bland and inoffensive entry? Besides, what did it mean to "average" entries from around the world? Were all entries equal? Was everyone who submitted an entry a "master chef?" Were all "chefs" of equal standing?

In effect, the committee couldn't agree among themselves to use the Method of Agreement to settle the contest! Thus, this particular method was rejected before it even got started. In other words, the taken-for-granted and implicit assumption that the problem was Bounded and Well-Structured was false.

Even if they polled "experts" for their opinions, there would be still problems. For instance, how would they define an expert? If an "expert" was defined as the "community" of "distinguished chefs" worldwide, say all those working in Two-Star Michelin restaurants or better, the committee still felt that this way of choosing the winner would be inadequate, for it would privilege a certain group of experts over all others. In using experts, one is not only dependent on the consensus between them for producing "Truth" in the first place—in this case "'Truth' is the 'perfect' dish'" — but one is also assuming that the more Agreement there is between the experts, the stronger, and therefore, the "better," the "Truth." [2] The distinguishing feature of this System is that "Truth" is that with which a group of reputable experts agrees strongly.

Appropriately enough, this approach is known as the Expert Consensus Way of Knowing or of Producing Knowledge. "Truth" is both the product of and the outcome of the Agreement between the judgments, observations, or opinions of different experts.

In Science, the Expert Consensus Way of Knowing or of Producing Knowledge takes the form of "tight agreement" between the Data, facts, or observations produced by independent qualified experts and observers. Global Warming is one of the most important examples. The "body of 'reputable Climate Scientists worldwide'" is now in substantial agreement that human activities are a significant factor responsible for Global Warming. This "fact" is taken as "strong, if not conclusive, evidence" that the debate whether humans are or are not responsible for Global Warming is essentially over even if all the mechanisms for it are not understood completely.

The point is that Agreement is no less important in Science than in any field of human activity. One could in fact argue that Agreement is even more important in Science where so much is riding on the outcome of Scientific Knowledge.

Consider the critical role that Agreement plays with regard to the Coronavirus. The Scientific Community is in strong Agreement that absent a vaccine, the wearing of masks, social distancing, and even isolation are key in preventing the spread of the Pandemic. Indeed, even with a vaccine, we still have to practice the wearing of masks, etc. The point is that at its best, the Method of Agreement is a fundamental part of Science.

For short, we refer to it as Expert Agreement.

The Second Way of Deciding: "The One True Formula!"

One of the members on the committee had a PhD in Chemistry from a top university. She argued that Chemistry should be used to derive the ingredients and the recipe for the perfect dish. The winner of the contest would be that person or persons whose submission matched the recipe derived from this procedure.

In the second system or model of inquiry, the perfect recipe is based on the theoretical principles and laws of some "hard science" such as Chemistry and that particular Science alone. Thus, in this System, we see even more directly the explicit linkage with Science. Science is in fact The Model for inquiry and "Truth" is equivalent to a formula.

The reasoning behind this model is that "the perfect dish"—Truth itself—should not be based on anything so crass as the mere opinions of a group of experts no matter how distinguished they are. Truth shouldn't even be based on what a particular set of experts regard as the "facts" because the "facts" of one group and of one age have an uncanny way of becoming the falsehoods of another. After all, it was once a "fact" that the Earth was flat, and the heavens revolved around it.

Truth should be based on the established principles—the laws—of hard science. In fact, proceeding from firmly established scientific first principles, one should be able to derive a single formula. For instance, in the case of a falling body, the distance D that it covers in time T is given by the familiar formula, $D = ½ G T^2$ where G equals the acceleration due to gravity. That is, the formula is familiar to those who have taken a basic course in Physics. Since the formula for falling bodies can be derived directly from Newton's laws of gravitation—one of the first principles of Physical Science—the formula is akin to a "hard law of Nature." (Those that understand the differential calculus can indeed derive it.) The important point is that this system seeks to produce a single abstract formula that it regards as "the Truth."

Appropriately enough, this system is known as the Pure Theory Way of Knowing. For short, we refer to it as The One True Formula. Alternately, it also goes by the name of Analytic Modeling.

This system is actually much broader than mathematics or science alone. Much more basic is the idea that the Pure Theory Way of Knowing is a coherent belief system—a framework of basic, presumably rational, first principles. In this broader sense, it does not always appear in the form of a formula.

Needless to say, the committee didn't buy this way of choosing the winner as well. Why should the winner be decided by a single Scientific discipline, let alone something so ridiculous as a single formula? Why was Chemistry superior to any other Science, or for that matter, any nonscientific discipline or profession such as being a Chef? If one was restricted to choosing a single discipline, why shouldn't it be Psychology? Weren't the attitudes of the contestants just as important as the physical ingredients themselves?

Since the committee couldn't answer their own questions based on their own First Principles (pun intended), they rejected the Method of First Principles in choosing the winner.

The Third Way: Multiple Perspectives, Multiple Formulas

One of the committee members suggested an approach with which all of the members agreed instantly. For the first time, they felt that they were making progress.

Notice that in agreeing so readily, they were buying into the first method, Expert Agreement. In effect, they were using the first way of producing knowledge to select another way of producing it.[3] There is nothing inherently wrong with combining ISs. This is in fact an important way of getting around the limitations of any single System. The "Truth" no longer depends or rests upon a single System.

Instead of lumping all of the entries together and averaging them, suppose that one grouped them initially by countries or regions of the world. Or, suppose that one first grouped them by different schools or philosophies of baking. Then, from each group, one could select a winner by using the first way of knowing, that is, Expert Agreement.[4]

Another way to put it is to say that instead of their being a single, best formula for all of the entries, suppose that each group of entries had its own special formula. Using each formula, one would determine the winners of each group, and from these, one would select an overall winner.

The third system is a combination of the first two: Expert Agreement and The One True Formula. In this approach, backed up by whatever Data and facts they have to support their judgments, one samples the opinions, of different regions or schools of cooking. Presumably, each region or school has its own distinct recipe or formula.

This System allows a decision-maker to witness explicitly how the outcome, "the perfect fruit dish," varies as one changes the underlying method or formula (recipe) for producing it. It thus allows a decision maker, in this case, the committee, who may not be an expert in, or a proponent of, any particular school of cooking to better understand the reasoning behind each school by seeing how they each approach the "same problem."

This System allows one to see explicitly the differences between various approaches. In other words, it does not leave variety to chance. Unlike the first two ways, it does not believe that there is one best answer to complex problems or questions. To the contrary!

The third way believes that on any problem of importance, one must produce at least two different views of the problem so that one can even begin to ascertain whether one is committing what we referred to earlier as Type Three Errors, Solving the Wrong Problems Precisely. Unless we have two or more different formulations of a problem, we cannot possibly know whether we are solving the "wrong" or the "right" problems. And in fact, without two or more views to compare, the terms "right" and "wrong" have no meaning, unless of course one believes in unequivocally the "Truth" of a single System or way of looking at the world.

In short, this System is a minimal requirement for ascertaining whether we are committing Type Three Errors.

One can also begin to understand why the Third Way of Knowing is the basis of Critical Thinking. It forces one to examine the assumptions that underlie any particular formulation of a problem by explicitly comparing different versions of it.

After one has witnessed the differences between different approaches, one can then pick and choose--blend if need be--between them to form one's own unique recipe.

Appropriately enough, this system is known as the Multiple Perspective or the Multiple Formula Approach to Knowledge. It argues that complex problems are too important to be left to the reasoning of any single approach no matter how appealing it is. Indeed, all the more that a particular approach is alluring, the more one needs to resist the temptation to fall under its sway.

This system is also known as Multidisciplinary Inquiry. The end result of this form of inquiry is a conclusion or recommendation that is the product of two or more Scientific disciplines or professions. But since the disciplines or professions that are involved in Multidisciplinary Inquiry are not necessarily affected by one another—they remain separate and distinct--this system is not Interdisciplinary. The basic disciplines and the professions themselves do not change as a result of their being involved in the Third Way of Knowing. They remain unaffected and undisturbed.

As we shall see, we have to reach the level of the Fifth System, Systems Thinking, before we can say that we are engaged in an inquiry that is Interdisciplinary.

Finally, there is another aspect of this system that is most important to note. The first two Systems assume that Data (expert judgments, facts, observations, etc.) and theories are independent of one another. Expert Agreement assumes that one can gather Data, facts, and observations on an issue or phenomenon without having to presuppose any prior theory with regard to it. In other words, it assumes that Data, facts, and observations are theory and value-free.

In contrast, The One Best Formula assumes that theories are free or independent of Data, facts, and observations. In principle, the formulation of theories is dependent only upon pure thought or Logic alone.

In contrast, the Third System assumes that our prior beliefs whether in the form of The One True Formula or not, affect what we decide is important to collect or to observe. Every observation we make presumes that we have made a decision about what is worth observing. This "decision," certainly the assumptions upon which it is based, may be regarded as a form of "theory," however informal it may be. In this sense, every observation presupposes some prior theory. Data, facts, and observations are not theory free. They certainly are not value free.

Indeed, ever since the great Prussian Philosopher Immanuel Kant, philosophers have recognized that Data are not theory and/or value-free. Our theories and values not only underlie what we observe, but we cannot make any observations without them.

Since values are involved, this means that, whether we acknowledge it or not, Ethics is an important part of every inquiry. In fact, the less we acknowledge it, the more important it is, because instead of examining and debating our Ethical assumptions, the more we take them for granted.

The Fourth Way: Expert Disagreement

Someone in the committee had another idea. Instead of depending upon the Agreement between experts, suppose they used Disagreement. The winner of the debate between experts would then be the winner of the contest.

The Fourth Approach is the direct opposite of the First. Whereas Expert Consensus is the Guarantor of the perfect fruit dish, and the way to produce it in the First Approach to Truth, intense conflict is the Guarantor, and the way to obtain it, in the Fourth Model. (The Guarantor is one of the most important and critical parts of an IS. The Guarantor is the part that "guarantees" that starting with the "right" initial building blocks of knowledge [basic assumptions, elemental or fundamental "truths," Data, facts, observations, etc.] and combing them in the "right ways," then one will arrive at "the Truth.")

In the Fourth Approach, one picks two schools of cooking that disagree the most. One then arranges a knockdown, no-holds-barred, debate between them. The recipe that emerges from (survives) the debate, which may be neither of the original two recipes, is then dubbed the "Truth." Appropriately, this model is known as The Dialectical Theory or Model of Knowledge. It is also known as The Conflict Theory of Truth, or Expert Disagreement for short.

To show how the Fourth Approach applies more generally, and therefore in essence to all professions, consider the following: Alfred P. Sloan, Chairman of General Motors from 1937 to 1956, is one of the very few executives who not only understood the importance of the Fourth Way implicitly, but actually used it when he had an important decision to make. (Of course, this doesn't mean that he necessarily understood it at a deep Philosophical level.) When his top executives agreed too quickly and too readily with his ideas, Sloan is reputed to have said, "Gentlemen, I propose we postpone further discussion until our next meeting to give ourselves time to develop disagreement and perhaps gain some understanding of what the decision is all about."[5]

It should be noted that as was characteristic of his times, there were apparently no women who were key members of Sloan's top executive group, a condition that wouldn't and shouldn't be tolerated today.

A particularly instructive example of the fourth approach is the different definitions of death that are found in different cultures.[6] In the U.S., death is defined as "brain death." Partially, this is because in the West, the essence of a person—the

Self-- is thought to lie in the brain, not in the body. The West thus subscribes to a "body/mind dualism" that dates back as least as far as Descartes. For another, it makes the criterion of death relatively easy to determine. (In effect, it makes the determination of death into an exercise.) We only have to have one "organ" fail in order to determine death (shades of the first two ways of knowing). When the brain "dies," the person dies as well even though his body may not have died. However, in Japan, a person's soul is thought to reside in the body. Therefore, it is only when the body dies that the person has died.

These differences are not just those of semantics alone. They have profound consequences for serious issues such as organ donation and transplantation, and hence for medical science. In the West, and the U.S. in particular, organ transplantation is a huge business.[7] If death is defined as "brain death," and the body's organs can be kept viable through machines, then the body can be "harvested" for its remaining "parts." In the West, it is quite common to have cases of brain death, but where blood is still pumped through the body by the heart so that all of the remaining organs are in some sense still "alive." This certainly makes organ transplantation much more acceptable. However, because of a differing definition of death and a differing concept of the body, organ transplantation is generally much less acceptable in Japan, and the East in general.

No wonder why the differences between different cultures are often so profound.

The Fifth Way: Pragmatism—Systems Thinking

The committee still wasn't satisfied. They still felt that something fundamental was missing, but they didn't know exactly what it was. Someone finally exclaimed, "We need help."

With this, another person added, "We're thinking too narrowly. We need to expand our thinking." This led her to say, "We need to bring in someone who can help us to think more broadly. Isn't this what Systems Thinking is all about? Why don't we call in a Systems expert?"

The last way of knowing is the most comprehensive of all. It is known as the Systems Way of Thinking, or simply, Systems Thinking.

In this model, one sweeps in considerations that are typically overlooked in the first four models. For instance, Ethical and Aesthetic considerations are given center stage. Using the "right," i.e., "Ethical," ingredients that are not harmful to the environment are central in this approach. For another, the Ambience or the Aesthetic design of the kitchen in which a fruit dish is produced is as important as the actual physical recipe itself. In fact, anything that affects the mental state and the well-being of the cook is potentially an essential part of the "recipe," for example, the lighting and the color of the walls of the kitchen, etc.

This helped to put some of the entries in a special light (pun intended). A few of the entries described the setting in which they prepared their submissions. They felt that the kitchen in which the fruit dishes were prepared was as important as the raw ingredients themselves. For this reason, they included pictures of their kitchens along with their recipes.

The Essence of Systems Thinking

The last way of knowing is based on the work of C. West Churchman, and his Philosophical mentor E.A. Singer Jr.[8] (As a side note, Churchman was Mitroff's primary mentor in the Philosophy of Science, which was his minor field of study for his PhD in Engineering Science at UC Berkeley.) In turn, Singer was one of the best students of the eminent American Philosopher/Psychologist William James. Singer emphasized repeatedly that there are no "basic disciplines." For Singer and Churchman, no particular branch of Science, no profession or field of knowledge, was more basic or superior to any other. This idea is so important that it is one of the fundamental cornerstones of Systems Thinking.

In Systems Thinking, the Physical Sciences, certainly knowledge about the physical world, are inseparable from the Social Sciences and knowledge about the social world. The Physical and the Social Sciences are not only inseparable, but they presuppose one another. Neither is possible without the other. After all, whether we admit it or not, Physical Science is done by all-too-human beings that not only have a "Psychology" but operate within a "Social Context." The Psychology and the Sociology of the investigator not only affect the production of Physical Knowledge but its very existence.[9]

Nonetheless, we have to say that for all its brilliance, in terms of the Jungian Personality Framework, it's a pure Intuitive Thinking, i.e., NT, account of Systems. Accordingly, it needs to be modified to consider how the other Jungian Types view them.

From the perspective of NT, a System is an intentionally designed, systematically organized, whole entity (e.g., an automobile, computer, smart building, etc.) that has one or more essential functions so that an individual and/or groups of people are thereby able to accomplish a set of important purposes. Furthermore, the functions, not the parts, are critical in defining a System.

Notice immediately how the different Types define purposes. For STs, purposes are akin to "measurable objectives" one wishes to accomplish. For NFs, purposes are deep expressions of the fundamental feelings and values of a community. For SFs, they are the intensely personal values that both define and unite one's immediate families and friends. The point is that for Feeling Types, purpose are not impersonal aims and/or objectives.

From the perspective of NT, an automobile is defined primarily by its functions, not its parts. Of course the parts are critical for without them, the functions cannot be realized

A car's function is to allow people to accomplish specific purposes, e.g., move to a desired set of locations by a preferred set of routes in specific times. Cars also have additional functions such as to enable people to engage in a form of entertainment and relaxation, thereby satisfying NF and SF concerns and needs. Driving a car also allows people to "blow off steam" under "semi controlled conditions" even though it can very easily lead to road rage, which can be deadly.

By means of their functions, the parts exist to allow people to accomplish significant purposes, not the other way around. That is, people do not exist for the parts or the System(s) in which they are embedded, although the parts can certainly give rise to new functions and purposes than the System's designers anticipated or intended. This is increasingly true of Technology where the unintended consequences produce effects that negate its positive benefits.

A critical distinction is that a System's parts have functions while only humans as purposive individuals have purposes. Thus, a car has major functions (e.g., transportation, the ability to change direction and speed when directed by a purposeful individual, etc.) that allow humans to satisfy purposes in the form of desired outcomes.

Only humans purposefully create specific means to accomplish intended outcomes or ends. In brief, humans (and of course certain other animals) are purposeful beings and thus exhibit purposive behavior even if they are not completely self-contained, i.e., autonomous.

Individual humans are not autonomous because they only exist by virtue of being members of even larger Systems, e.g., families, organizations, and societies. For one, infants do not have the innate ability to survive on their own. In short, the lines between individuals and the society of which they are members is thin at best. In fact, neither exists without the other. In a word, Systems cannot exist without NF and SF.

To take another example, the heart and lungs have essential functions, but they don't have independent purposes, let alone an existence of their own apart from the entire human body. Similarly, the engine in a car obviously has an important function, but it doesn't have a purpose of its own independently of the combined human-machine system, i.e., NT. But once again, it wouldn't function without the necessary support of NF and SF. By themselves, wheels do not exhibit purposeful motion. They only carry out their intended function by being part of the car as a whole System that not only includes but is directed by a purposeful being.

In addition, a System also consists of at least two or more essential parts that satisfy three conditions. If something only has one part, then it is not a system. In terms of NF, a system consists of at least two or more persons, not just impersonal parts alone.

The first condition is that a System cannot accomplish its defining function(s) without its essential parts, and people. An engine is an essential part for locomotion, but a cigarette lighter is not. Similarly, the brain, heart, and lungs are essential parts of humans, but as Ackoff notes, the appendix is not. This is in fact why it is termed an "appendix."

The second condition is that by itself an essential part cannot affect a System independently of at least one other essential part. The essential parts are not only interconnected, but they interact. Thus, the heart affects the lungs and vice versa. Indeed, they don't exist without the other. In other words, without interactions and interdependencies, there is no System.

The third condition is that no group of a System's essential parts—that is, no subsystem—has an independent effect on the whole System. Once again, the nervous and metabolic subsystems of humans do not have independent effects on the whole human body as a System.

These definitions and conditions have important consequences for the performance of Systems and thus illuminate additional properties.

Improvement in the parts taken separately does not improve a System overall as a whole. Indeed, it often leads to its failure and complete destruction. Merely improving an engine without the careful coordination of and simultaneous improvements in the suspension and transmission does not improve the overall performance of a car. If anything, it can cause a car to spin dangerously out of control.

Thus, attempts to improve the overall costs of Medical Care by lowering the costs of the individual parts of the System have failed. In fact, they have done just the opposite.[10]

Lastly, a System has defining properties that none of its parts have. Thus, purposeful motion is a property of the combined (i.e., interactive) human-machine System that is a car. It is not a function of the engine or wheels alone. Indeed, without a driver or human interaction of some kind, NF and SF, e.g., remote control, a car cannot exhibit purposeful motion. Similarly, no amount of analysis of the parts would reveal a car's property as a social status symbol, i.e., clearly NF and SF.

Objectivity

Our discussion of different ISs helps to make clear why the admonition to be "Objective" is in most cases laughable, if not meaningless. Which kind of Objectivity for the problem at hand is the proper response.

According to Expert Agreement, something is Objective if and only if it's based on "hard Data, facts, or observations" and the "tight agreement" between different observers as to the data, etc.

According to the One True Formula, something is Objective if and only if it's based on logical reasoning from self-evident first principles or premises. The trouble is that as the American humorist Ambrose Bierce observed, "self-evident means evident to one's self and to no one else."

According to Multiple Perspectives, something is Objective if and only if it's the product and the result of multiple points of view.

According to Expert Disagreement, something is Objective if and only if it's the product and the result of (that is, it survives) the most intense debate between the most disparate points of view.

And finally, in Systems Thinking, something is Objective if and only if it's the product and the result of the most intense effort of sweeping in knowledge from the Arts, Humanities, Professions, Philosophy, Sciences, etc.

What then does it mean to be "Objective?" To be "Objective" is to "choose" the "'correct' mode of Inquiry depending upon the purposes of one's study." And, to "choose" means to debate which mode of Inquiry is "best" in the light of knowledge of all the various modes.

Notice that this same analysis applies to "right" and "wrong" with respect to problems, and hence, to Type Three Errors. For example, according to Expert Agreement, something is "right" if and only if it's based on "hard Data, facts, or observations" and the "tight agreement" between different observers as to the Data, etc. For another, according to the One True Formula, something is "right" if and only if it's based on logical reasoning from self-evident premises, and so forth.

The Problem With Traditional Education

Traditional Education primarily stresses the First Two Ways of Knowing or ISs: Expert Agreement and the One Best or True Formula. Educators pound "well-accepted facts" based on the First Way of Knowing, Expert Agreement, into our heads, and they stress knowledge of "well-accepted theories"—The One Best Formula—in solving problems. Anything that cannot be reduced to hard Data, facts, or observations--the First Way--or represented in terms of accepted theories--the Second Way--is false, dangerous, and misleading.

The First and the Second Ways are historically the foundations of education and of knowledge for a traditional world. But they are seriously deficient and inadequate for a world that is global and increasingly interconnected along every conceivable dimension. For one, they are too restrictive. They assume that the problems we need to solve are already well-known and well-defined. But as we have stressed, the "problem" with most problems is "to define what the problem(s) is (are) in the first place." That is, the Semantic Phase is critical.

The first two ways are not well suited for complex problems. Once again, as we write, the world is undergoing a Global Pandemic the likes of which that has not been seen in years. The definition, let alone the resolution, of the crisis is as difficult and as messy as any we've ever faced. This is precisely where the Third (Multiple Formulas), the Fourth (Expert Disagreement), and the Fifth (Systems Thinking) ways are required.

The Third Way, Multiple Perspectives, says that we explicitly need to see multiple definitions of a problem so that we can do our best to avoid Type Three Errors. Again, how can we even begin to assess, let alone know, if we are "solving the 'wrong problem' " if we don't have more than one formulation of a problem for our explicit consideration? We can't.

Notice that comparing two or more different formulations of a problem is no iron-glad guarantee that we will solve the right problems precisely. At best, it is a minimal Guarantor. But, we can say that without examining explicitly two or more different formulations of a problem, the probability of committing Type Three Errors goes up considerably.

The Third, Fourth, and Fifth Ways require us to exercise judgment, and an even more precious commodity, Wisdom.

The Moral

The moral of the story is not that we should never use the First Two Ways of Knowing, but that we should use them only after we have assured ourselves that, by using the Third, Fourth, and Fifth Ways, we are working on the "right problem(s)" to begin with. The Third, Fourth, and Fifth Ways are best suited for problem formulation (the Semantic Phase); in contrast, the First Two Ways are best suited for problem solving (the Syntactic and Solution Phases), once we have assured ourselves that we have defined the "right problem(s)."

A complex, globally interconnected world requires that we manage problems not solve them exactly them as we attempted to do in a simpler, fragmented world. A complex, globally interconnected world also requires that we acknowledge that the predominant Philosophical bases of a simpler, fragmented world--the First Two Ways of Knowing—do not apply in their entirety. They apply only in the sense that we still collect Data when we can and we still apply accepted Scientific thinking, but we both acknowledge and accept their limitations.

In the end, one of the most essential aspects of Systems Thinking is the realization that we only get out of Inquiry what we put into it initially. And, what we fundamentally put into every Inquiry is "us" through our collective Psychology and Sociology.

In far too many cases, we are obsessed with what John Dewey referred to as The Quest for Certainty.[11] The First Two Ways differ only in where they locate the certainty we so desperately seek. The first way, Expert Agreement, attempts to find certainty in hard Data and expert consensus, supposedly the "facts" on which everyone can agree. The second way, The One Best Formula, attempts to find it in the "indisputable scientific laws of nature, pure thought, or abstract logic." For Dewey, both were neurotic attempts on the part of humankind to manage the anxiety brought about by a dangerous and uncertain world into which all of us are thrust. Notice carefully that Dewey did not say that "basic facts" or "elemental truths" were neurotic in and of themselves. What was neurotic was our obsessive need for certainty.

The danger is not that we will agree, but that we will agree too readily by being pressured to go along with crowd.

Leveraging Inquiry Systems in Problem Solving

So how do these Inquiry Systems help us with problem solving? If we overlay the Inquiry Systems on the Diamond Model, we can graphically illustrate that these Inquiry Systems play different roles at different phases of the problem-solving process. Additionally, the problem-solving process utilizes ALL of the Inquiry Systems, there is no reliance on a single technique. Use of a single technique will certainly lead to "failure" (where failure is the instance where the intended outcome is greatly (well beyond 20%) different than the actual outcome) within the context of complex systems.

Figure 1. Mapping the inquiry systems onto the Diamond Model

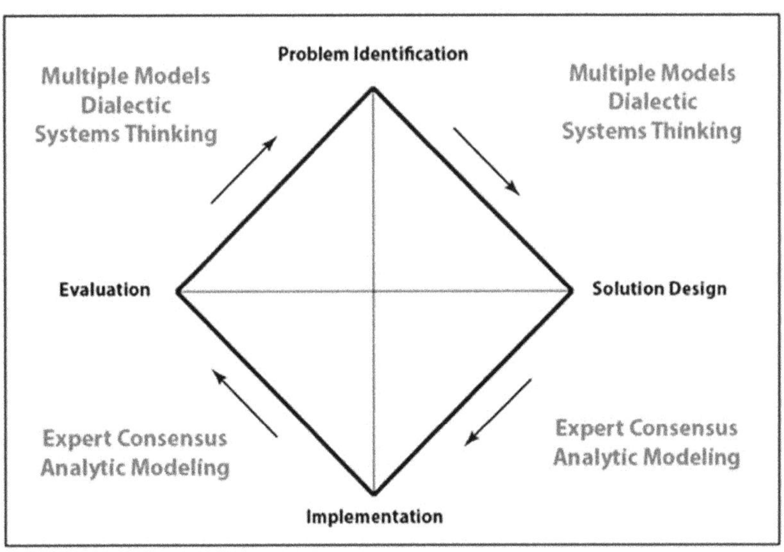

CONCLUSION

Mitroff's work on inquiry systems draws upon philosophy, systems theory, and organizational studies. He presents a taxonomy of five inquiry systems—Expert Consensus, Analytic-Deductive, Dialectic, Multiple Realities, and Systemic—to better understand problem-solving approaches. Mitroff's work stresses the importance of human values and ethical considerations in inquiry, and advocates for integrating various methods, especially when tackling complex, multifaceted issues.

Applications of Mitroff's inquiry systems are broad, extending from business and public policy to ethics and scientific research. Expert Consensus systems are suitable for generating single, agreed-upon solutions and are commonly used in settings like market research or medical diagnosis. Analytic-Deductive systems excel in well-defined problems that require precise answers, such as financial forecasting or pharmaceutical testing. Dialectic systems are designed for situations with inherent conflicts and are often used in legal frameworks or ethical committees. Multiple Realities systems accept the co-existence of different viewpoints and are employed in complex analyses like ecological studies. Lastly, Systemic inquiry aims for holistic solutions by combining multiple methods and is used in integrative fields like sustainable development or healthcare policy.

In the realm of problem-solving, Mitroff's Inquiry Systems offer a structured framework to understand and approach a wide range of issues. By identifying the most appropriate Inquiry System or combination of systems, individuals and organizations can tailor their problem-solving methods to the specific nature of the problem at hand. Whether the challenge is straightforward or highly complex, the choice of Inquiry System can significantly impact the effectiveness of the solution, thereby reinforcing the practical value and adaptability of Mitroff's contributions to the field.

COMPREHENSION EXERCISES

1) Which inquiry system aims for single, consensual answers through simple data collection?
   a) Dialectic
   b) Analytic-Deductive
   c) Expert Consensus
   d) Multiple Realities

2) Which system employs formal models and algorithms to solve well-defined problems?
   a) Expert Consensus
   b) Analytic-Deductive
   c) Dialectic
   d) Systemic
3) In which inquiry system are opposing viewpoints considered to understand the complexities of an issue?
   a) Dialectic
   b) Analytic-Deductive
   c) Multiple Realities
   d) Expert Consensus
4) Which inquiry system is ideal for problems where different perspectives can co-exist?
   a) Dialectic
   b) Multiple Realities
   c) Expert Consensus
   d) Systemic
5) Which system offers a holistic approach, integrating methods from different inquiry systems?
   a) Systemic
   b) Dialectic
   c) Expert Consensus
   d) Analytic-Deductive
6) Which inquiry system is commonly used for financial forecasting?
   a) Dialectic
   b) Expert Consensus
   c) Analytic-Deductive
   d) Systemic
7) In which system would a safety audit most likely be conducted?
   a) Expert Consensus
   b) Analytic-Deductive
   c) Dialectic
   d) Multiple Realities
8) Which inquiry system would be most useful for conflict resolution?
   a) Dialectic
   b) Analytic-Deductive
   c) Expert Consensus
   d) Systemic

9) Which system would likely be employed in cross-departmental safety assessments?
   a) Dialectic
   b) Multiple Realities
   c) Expert Consensus
   d) Systemic
10) Which inquiry system combines multiple methods and considers human values and ethics?
   a) Analytic-Deductive
   b) Dialectic
   c) Multiple Realities
   d) Systemic
11) What is the main focus of Expert Consensus systems?
   a) Complexity
   b) Precision
   c) Consensus
   d) Conflict
12) What kind of problems is the Analytic-Deductive system best suited for?
   a) Well-defined
   b) Ambiguous
   c) Conflict-ridden
   d) Diverse
13) Which inquiry system acknowledges that different solutions can be simultaneously valid?
   a) Expert Consensus
   b) Analytic-Deductive
   c) Multiple Realities
   d) Dialectic
14) Which inquiry system is most likely to be used in ethical committee discussions?
   a) Expert Consensus
   b) Analytic-Deductive
   c) Dialectic
   d) Systemic
15) In which inquiry system would integrated safety management be most likely implemented?
   a) Expert Consensus
   b) Analytic-Deductive
   c) Dialectic
   d) Systemic

REFERENCES

Ackoff, R. L. (1981). *Creating the Corporate Future: Plan or be Planned For*. John Wiley & Sons.

Ackoff, R. L. (1999). *Ackoff's Best: His Classic Writings on Management*. John Wiley & Sons.

Argyris, C. (1982). *Reasoning, Learning, and Action: Individual and Organizational*. Jossey-Bass.

Banathy, B. H. (1991). Systems Design of Education: A Journey to Create the Future. *Educational Technology*.

Checkland, P. (1981). *Systems Thinking, Systems Practice*. John Wiley & Sons.

Churchman, C. W. (1971). *The Design of Inquiring Systems: Basic Concepts of Systems and Organization*. Basic Books.

Flood, R. L., & Jackson, M. C. (1991). *Creative Problem Solving: Total Systems Intervention*. John Wiley & Sons.

Forrester, J. W. (1968). *Principles of Systems*. Productivity Press.

Gharajedaghi, J. (2005). *Systems Thinking: Managing Chaos and Complexity - A Platform for Designing Business Architecture*. Butterworth-Heinemann.

Linstone, H. A. (1999). *Decision Making for Technology Executives: Using Multiple Perspectives to Improved Performance*. Artech House.

Mason, R. O., & Mitroff, I. I. (1981). *Challenging Strategic Planning Assumptions: Theory, Cases, and Techniques*. John Wiley & Sons.

Midgley, G. (2000). *Systemic Intervention: Philosophy, Methodology, and Practice*. Kluwer Academic/Plenum Publishers. doi:10.1007/978-1-4615-4201-8

Mitroff, I. I., & Linstone, H. A. (1993). *The Unbounded Mind: Breaking the Chains of Traditional Business Thinking*. Oxford University Press.

Senge, P. M. (1990). *The Fifth Discipline: The Art & Practice of The Learning Organization*. Doubleday.

Ulrich, W. (1983). *Critical Heuristics of Social Planning: A New Approach to Practical Philosophy*. Haupt.

ENDNOTES

1 This example is taken from several student papers from Mitroff's classes.

2 An Inquiry System consists of: Inputs, an Operator that transforms the Inputs into Outputs, which are then regarded as the "truth." One of the most critical features of an Inquiry System is what Churchman labels the "guarantor." The guarantor is that feature of an inquiry system that "guarantees" that if one starts with the "right kind of Inputs," Operates on them in the "right way," then the Output(s) of the system will be the "truth." In the first model, the tighter the agreement between experts, i.e., the stronger the agreement between them, supposedly the "more" that the agreement is or approaches the truth. Thus, in the first model, the guarantor is the agreement between independent experts. Notice that the guarantor and the operator are confounded. That is, they are not independent. Agreement is the operator—it is used to manufacture or to produce the output--and agreement is also the guarantor of the system as well. For this reason, one is well advised to be suspicious of how agreement is obtained, e.g., whether it is forced or not.

3 There is nothing wrong per se in using one method initially to select another method of reaching an important decision. Once we have all of the various methods at our disposal, we can use them in various combinations. The important point is the pure methods, systems, or models themselves are rarely discussed in the arena of business, let alone their combinations.

4 See the previous footnote.

5 Quoted in David Marcum and Steven Smith, *Egonomics* (Simon and Schuster, 2007), 132.

6 Lesley A. Sharp, *Strange Harvest* (Berkeley, CA: University of California Press, 2006.)

7 Ibid.

8 See Churchman and Singer, Op cit.

9 Mitroff, Op cit, 1974.

10 Mitroff, Ian I., and Silvers, Abe, Dirty *Rotten Strategies: How We Trick Ourselves and Others into Solving the Wrong Problems Precisely*, Stanfornd University Press, Palo Alto, CA., 2009.

11 John Dewey, *The Quest for Certainty* (New York: Putnam, 1960.)

APPENDIX - COMPREHENSION EXERCISES: SOLUTIONS

1) Which inquiry system aims for single, consensual answers through simple data collection?
   a) Dialectic
   b) Analytic-Deductive
   c) Expert Consensus
   d) Multiple Realities

Recommended Answer: C) Expert Consensus

2) Which system employs formal models and algorithms to solve well-defined problems?
   a) Expert Consensus
   b) Analytic-Deductive
   c) Dialectic
   d) Systemic

Recommended Answer: B) Analytic-Deductive

3) In which inquiry system are opposing viewpoints considered to understand the complexities of an issue?
   a) Dialectic
   b) Analytic-Deductive
   c) Multiple Realities
   d) Expert Consensus

Recommended Answer: A) Dialectic

4) Which inquiry system is ideal for problems where different perspectives can co-exist?
   a) Dialectic
   b) Multiple Realities
   c) Expert Consensus
   d) Systemic

Recommended Answer: B) Multiple Realities

5) Which system offers a holistic approach, integrating methods from different inquiry systems?
   a) Systemic
   b) Dialectic
   c) Expert Consensus
   d) Analytic-Deductive

Recommended Answer: A) Systemic

6) Which inquiry system is commonly used for financial forecasting?
   a) Dialectic
   b) Expert Consensus
   c) Analytic-Deductive
   d) Systemic

Recommended Answer: C) Analytic-Deductive

7) In which system would a safety audit most likely be conducted?
   a) Expert Consensus
   b) Analytic-Deductive
   c) Dialectic
   d) Multiple Realities

Recommended Answer: A) Expert Consensus

8) Which inquiry system would be most useful for conflict resolution?
   a) Dialectic
   b) Analytic-Deductive
   c) Expert Consensus
   d) Systemic

Recommended Answer: A) Dialectic

9) Which system would likely be employed in cross-departmental safety assessments?
   a) Dialectic
   b) Multiple Realities
   c) Expert Consensus
   d) Systemic

Recommended Answer: B) Multiple Realities

10) Which inquiry system combines multiple methods and considers human values and ethics?
   a) Analytic-Deductive
   b) Dialectic
   c) Multiple Realities
   d) Systemic

Recommended Answer: D) Systemic

11) What is the main focus of Expert Consensus systems?
    a) Complexity
    b) Precision
    c) Consensus
    d) Conflict

Recommended Answer: C) Consensus

12) What kind of problems is the Analytic-Deductive system best suited for?
    a) Well-defined
    b) Ambiguous
    c) Conflict-ridden
    d) Diverse

Recommended Answer: A) Well-defined

13) Which inquiry system acknowledges that different solutions can be simultaneously valid?
    a) Expert Consensus
    b) Analytic-Deductive
    c) Multiple Realities
    d) Dialectic

Recommended Answer: C) Multiple Realities

14) Which inquiry system is most likely to be used in ethical committee discussions?
    a) Expert Consensus
    b) Analytic-Deductive
    c) Dialectic
    d) Systemic

Recommended Answer: C) Dialectic

15) In which inquiry system would integrated safety management be most likely implemented?
    a) Expert Consensus
    b) Analytic-Deductive
    c) Dialectic
    d) Systemic

Recommended Answer: D) Systemic

Chapter 5
Assumptional Analysis:
The Key Role of Assumptions

ABSTRACT

The authors present a general method known as assumptional analysis for uncovering and analyzing key assumptions. Assumptions are plotted on a two-dimensional chart. The horizontal dimension ranged from those assumptions on the left that were relatively unimportant to those on the right that were extremely important to a strategy's success. The vertical dimension ranged from those assumptions on the top that were felt to be certain to those on the bottom that were felt to be uncertain. They were as likely to be false as they were to be true.

"Your assumptions are your windows on the world. Scrub them off every once in a while, or the light won't come in." — Isaac Asimov

Learning Objectives

- Define Assumptions
- List the steps for Assumptional Analysis
- Describe an approach to challenge an assumption
- Identify three common false assumptions
- Describe what the letters SWOT stand for
- Explain the inherent differences between SWOT and SAST

DOI: 10.4018/978-1-6684-6563-9.ch005

INTRODUCTION

The Strategic Assumption Surfacing Technique (SAST) was pioneered by James Emshoff, who was then at Wharton School at the University of Pennsylvania, serves to identify and assess assumptions underlying organizational strategies. Subsequently, it's been developed further by Mitroff and his colleagues.

SAST facilitates dialogue among team members, helping them uncover implicit beliefs that could affect decision-making. By bringing hidden assumptions to surface, organizations can analyze their validity, reduce conflicts, and align their teams for more effective execution of strategies.

In SAST, participants are divided into groups, each of which is assigned a specific aspect of the strategic issue at hand. Groups identify key assumptions and then present them for collective examination. Assumptions may be categorized as either "taken-for-granted," which are often unconscious but widely accepted, or as "contingent," which are conditional on certain events or circumstances. This process exposes discrepancies, contradictions, or gaps in the strategy, which can then be addressed or tested.

A successful application of SAST can yield transformative results for an organization, strengthening its strategic footing and enhancing team alignment. By surfacing hidden assumptions, the team becomes more aware of potential blind spots or vulnerabilities in their planning, allowing for the design of more resilient strategies. The process also fosters open dialogue and critical thinking, thereby enriching the organizational culture with a deeper sense of collaboration and accountability. Moreover, SAST serves as a preemptive measure against conflicts or misunderstandings that could arise later due to unexamined assumptions. As a result, the organization not only gains a robust, adaptable strategy but also nurtures an environment of transparency and collective problem-solving, equipping it to navigate future complexities with greater agility and confidence. Examples of implementation include:

Mergers and Acquisitions: During the planning stages of a merger or acquisition, SAST can be used to uncover assumptions about corporate culture, potential synergies, and expected financial outcomes. By identifying these assumptions, companies can develop more robust integration strategies, pre-empt potential cultural clashes, and set realistic financial goals.

Product Development: In the tech industry or any fast-paced sector, SAST can help teams uncover assumptions about market demand, technological feasibility, and competitor behavior. Doing so can lead to a more well-rounded understanding of risks and opportunities, aiding in the development of a product that addresses actual market needs rather than perceived ones.

Healthcare Policy: When governments or organizations are designing new healthcare policies or interventions, SAST can assist in surfacing assumptions about public behavior, efficacy of treatments, and resource allocation. This ensures that the policies are built on a sound basis and are more likely to achieve their intended outcomes.

Educational Reform: School boards and educational policymakers can use SAST to scrutinize assumptions regarding student learning, teacher effectiveness, and resource allocation. By challenging such assumptions, they can design reforms that are better aligned with the needs of students and educators, ultimately improving educational outcomes.

Supply Chain Management: Businesses dealing with complex supply chains can use SAST to uncover assumptions about supplier reliability, shipping times, or material quality. This helps in creating a more resilient and flexible supply chain strategy, better prepared for disruptions or changes in market conditions.

Organizational Safety Culture: In industries like manufacturing, construction, or energy, where safety is a paramount concern, SAST can be used to examine assumptions about employee behavior, equipment reliability, and safety protocols. Often, organizations operate under the assumption that existing safety measures are sufficient, or that employees are fully compliant with safety guidelines. By surfacing these assumptions, a dialogue opens up that may lead to the identification of overlooked risks or the development of enhanced safety training and procedures. This proactive approach fosters a more robust safety culture, minimizing the potential for accidents or mishaps.

EXAMPLE: MCNEIL PHARMACEUTICALS

Assumptions are critically important! For this reason, we describe the Strategic Assumptions and Surfacing Technique, SAST, for uncovering and analyzing key assumptions in terms of an important case with which Mitroff was involved. The case involved McNeil Pharmaceuticals, an important subsidiary of Johnson and Johnson. Indeed, Assumptional Analysis owes its origin to it.

The case concerned the fact that a major painkiller that was a financial mainstay of the company was threatened by the onslaught of cheaper generic drugs. If they were successful, generics would in effect destroy the market for the company's painkillers, thereby threatening its entire financial standing and well-being.

Since the company was threatened as a whole, all of the top executives were involved in responding to the situation. At the heart of the matter was the fact that they split themselves into three equally powerful sub-groups that recommended three very different ways of responding to the threat. One group wanted the lower the price of their drugs thereby in effect to "out-generic the generics." Another wanted to raise the price thereby sending a clear signal to consumers that they had supreme confidence in the fact that their drug was vastly superior to generics. The third wanted to hedge their bets by setting the price midway between the first two groups. Since all three groups were of equal standing, none of them could force through their individual strategy without the full consent of the others.

In effect, all three groups were making very different assumptions about the key Stakeholders who were at the heart of each strategy. Among them were Patients, Pharmacists, and Physicians. The difficulty was the fact that all of the groups were only barely aware of the assumptions and how they influenced their strategies.

This was the situation when James Emshoff, a researcher at the Wharton School at the University of Pennsylvania, and Mitroff entered as external consultants. Mitroff, who by then was a Full Professor at the Graduate School of Business at the University of Pittsburgh, was a Visiting Professor at Penn for the year 1978-79.

To get at the assumptions, Emshoff began by asking what each Stakeholder needed to be like for a particular strategy to work. Next, the assumptions were then plotted on a two-dimensional chart that showed how they interacted to form three very different, but equally coherent, Belief Systems.

The horizontal dimension ranged from those assumptions on the Left that were Relatively Unimportant to those on the Right that were Extremely Important to a strategy's success. The Vertical dimension ranged from those assumptions on the Top that were felt to be Certain to those on the Bottom that were felt to be Uncertain. They were as likely to be False as they were to be True.

All of the groups felt that the key assumptions with regard to Patients were both Certain and Very Important. Namely, Patients wanted high quality, low-priced drugs. At the same time, they would go along with whatever their Primary Care Physician recommended. They also felt that Pharmacists would go along as well with whatever a Physician recommended, but they were less Certain for in some States, Pharmacists were mandated by law to recommend a lower price generic drug if it was available. But the biggest difference by far was with regard to Physicians.

The group that wanted to lower the price of the drug was assuming that because of the rising costs of Health Care, Physicians were increasingly Price-Sensitive. In sharp contrast, the group that wanted to raise the price of the drug was assuming that Physicians were Price-Insensitive. If a Physician felt that a particular drug was absolutely necessary to the health and well-being of a Patient, then he or she would prescribe it regardless of the cost. But once the various assumptions were stated, neither group had the Data to prove its case beyond all doubt. Were all Physicians everywhere Price Sensitive or Insensitive to the same degree? They didn't know because they never had to test their assumptions before. Again, they were largely unaware of them.

Figure 1. Importance and certainty matrix for the generic drug example

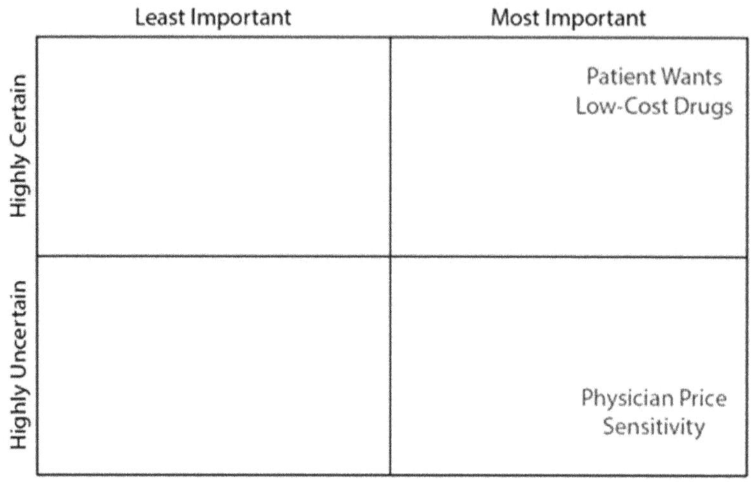

Even though they couldn't agree on a final strategy, as a result of the process, they decided to carefully raise the price of the drug in certain key test markets to see what the responses were. They reasoned that if they lowered the price of the drug, then they wouldn't find out if they could have raised it for who would push back against a lower-price drug.

We will not burden the reader with further details except to mention the name of the drug, Extra-Strength Tylenol.

Implementing SAST

SAST was developed to reveal the critical assumptions underlying questions at hand (problems, strategic plans and policies, etc.) and to create explicit visual maps for exploring those assumptions. To achieve these ends, SAST consists of the following key principles as described in (Barabba & Mitroff, 2014):

- **Adversarial:** SAST is based on the underlying premise that the best way to test an assumption is by making the strongest case one can for the strongest opposing assumptions one is able to envision;
- **Participative:** SAST is based on the premise that the knowledge and resources necessary to solve and implement a solution to a complex problem are distributed among a group of individuals. In other words, no single individual no matter how well placed he or she is in an organization has all the relevant knowledge or even power to address a problem or issue adequately;

- **Integrative:** SAST is based on the premise that a unified set of assumptions and action plans are needed to guide decision-making and that what comes out of the adversarial and participative elements of the process can be integrated;
- **Supportive:** SAST is based on the premise that the ability to expose and examine assumptions deepens insight into an organization, its policies, planning processes, and strategic thinking.

The detailed steps of SAST include (Barabba & Mitroff, 2014):

1. Group formation
   a. Key individuals from functional areas in an organization are formed into small six to eight person groups. In a private-sector organization, these include the CEO, Heads of Finance, Information Technology, Legal, Public Affairs, Security, etc.
   b. To minimize conflict, ideally the groups should consist of those individuals who get on relatively well with one another.
   c. To maximize differences, the groups should differ in their particular knowledge and perspectives of important issues or problems. Each group should have a different orientation, perspective, or policy option from which to approach an issue.
2. Assumption surfacing and rating
   a. Each group meets separately, and from it's own viewpoint, identifies the key assumptions that are inherent in an issue and especially in its own approach to it. All of the assumptions generated are then listed.
3. Debate within groups
   a. The debate involves three key activities:
      i. By means of eliminating irrelevant assumptions, each group determines which assumptions need to be accepted as strategic premises. To accomplish this, each group asks itself, "If the opposite of a particular assumption is true, does it have any significant bearing on the issue?" If the answer is "No," then the assumption is judged "not relevant" to the group's position. That is, neither the truth nor falsify of a particular assumption is relevant. Of course, this may not only change over time, but another group may not accept it.
      ii. The group then ranks its assumptions with regard to their relative degrees of importance and certainty.
      iii. At this stage, individual data are then opened for discussion.
   b. Assumptions that are both important and certain to become the central assumptions of policy.

  c. Assumptions that are important but uncertain require monitoring and research.
  d. Assumptions in the other two quadrants may be dropped, but if the resource and time allow, these may be monitored as well.
  e. Using an Importance/Certainty graph, each group debates which assumptions are pivotal, that is, absolutely central to its position, and it prioritizes them.

4. Further debate activities
  a. The groups are brought together, and a spokesperson for each group presents their Importance/Certainty graph and concentrates on those assumptions that are central to the policy (important and certain, and important and uncertain). In order not to bog down presentations, only clarifying questions are permitted at this stage. When all of the groups have presented, all of the assumptions are combined in a single slide and thrown open for evaluation, debate, and, discussion.
  b. The assumptions that are central, in the sense that they are cross-cutting, are the basis for debate. The most contentious assumptions are special objects of debate.

5. Final synthesis
  a. Ideally, the debate leads to a set of modified assumptions or a new set of agreed upon assumptions. If agreement on an assumption is not reached, it warrants further investigation. Where the data are inadequate, activities are undertaken to acquire specific data necessary to resolve a strategic issue.
  b. A Planning Book can be created that consists of the following elements:
    i. A prioritized list of the most critical issues;
    ii. An assessment of the current state of knowledge with respect to the solution of the issues;
    iii. A list of current and future activities to produce information designed to improve the state of the knowledge relevant to the critical issues;
    iv. When a policy-decision must be made, the results of the information produced in accordance with SAST are collected and related to the issues for which they were undertaken. A final debate is held and judgment is made on the best set of assumptions that are known at the present time from which to proceed; and
    v. An appropriate policy is chosen, based on the new information and the synthesis that has hopefully emerged.

SAST can be a highly demanding process that requires a great deal of understanding, patience, and commitment of time by those individuals and organizations desiring to use it (Barabba & Mitroff, 2014). It is critical that there is a clear and explicit understanding that assumptions are the presumed properties of stakeholders and the decision-makers surface and debate the most critical assumptions, upon which all crucial decisions are made. Ideally, every organization should have a map of its most critical assumptions and needs to monitor, critique, and update these assumptions on a regular basis as conditions change and new information is obtained (Barabba & Mitroff, 2014).

Figure 2. Mapping of the SAST steps onto the Diamond Model described in chapter one

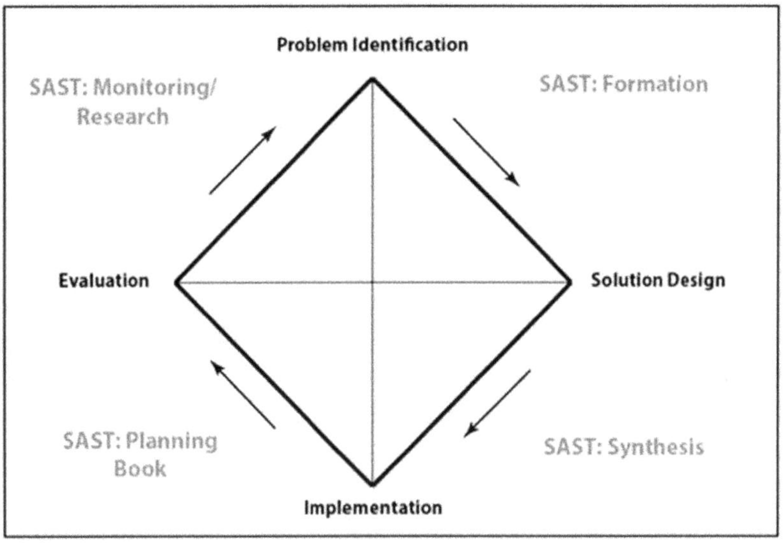

SAST ORGANIZATIONAL KEY PERFORMANCE METRICS (KPIs)

Key Performance Indicators (KPIs) are quantifiable metrics that organizations use to gauge the effectiveness and impact of their strategies, processes, and actions. These indicators serve as navigational beacons, offering insights into what's working well and what needs adjustment. When applied to a SAST process, KPIs help in objectively assessing the campaign's success in achieving its goals, such as improving strategic alignment, enhancing decision-making, or mitigating risks. Formulating KPIs for a SAST campaign involves identifying the specific outcomes you wish to measure, which should align with the broader objectives that led to employing SAST in the first place. These could range from internal metrics like team alignment and project success rates, to external metrics like market share and customer satisfaction. Once identified, these KPIs are tracked over time to evaluate the effectiveness of the SAST process, offering a data-driven foundation for ongoing refinement and improvement.

Examples of SAST-derived Key Performance Indicators (KPIs) might include:

1. **Strategic Alignment Score**: This KPI measures the degree to which team members' understanding of strategic objectives align before and after the SAST process. An increase in this score indicates improved alignment and shared understanding within the team.
2. **Decision-making Speed**: By removing ambiguities and clarifying assumptions, organizations can often expedite the decision-making process. A decrease in the time taken to make crucial decisions can be a positive indicator of SAST's effectiveness.
3. **Conflict Resolution Rate**: A trackable improvement in resolving internal conflicts or disagreements, especially those related to strategy execution, suggests that the SAST process has helped in clarifying underlying issues.
4. **Employee Engagement Metrics**: Surveys or interviews could reveal increased employee satisfaction and engagement post-SAST, as employees often feel more involved and clear about the organization's direction.
5. **Risk Mitigation Effectiveness**: The number of identified and mitigated risks pre- and post-SAST can demonstrate how the technique helps in proactively identifying vulnerabilities and taking action.
6. **Strategy Execution Success Rate**: This KPI tracks the percentage of strategic initiatives that meet or exceed their goals. A higher rate post-SAST indicates that strategies are more grounded and effective.
7. **Project Failure Rate**: A reduction in the number of projects that fail due to incorrect assumptions or lack of clarity can serve as a valuable KPI to gauge the effectiveness of a SAST application.
8. **Resource Utilization Efficiency**: Improved allocation and utilization of resources, both human and capital, can indicate that assumptions about resource needs and constraints were accurately identified and addressed.
9. **Market Share Growth**: An increase in market share could suggest that the organization's clarified and realigned strategy is more attuned to market needs and opportunities.
10. **Customer Satisfaction Scores**: If customer satisfaction rates rise after the implementation of a new, SAST-informed strategy, this would indicate that internal clarity may have translated to more effective external operations, benefiting the end-users or customers.

These KPIs collectively offer a comprehensive view of the organizational transformations that can result from a well-executed SAST campaign.

SWOT ANALYSIS

The SWOT analysis framework traces its origins back to the 1960s. It is attributed to Robert Franklin Stewart, who was a planner at Lockheed and later joined the Stanford Research Institute (Puyt et al, 2023). They initially introduced the SOFT analysis, focusing on “Satisfactory,” “Opportunity,” “Fault,” and “Threat,” which later evolved into the more universally recognized SWOT framework—Strengths, Weaknesses, Opportunities, and Threats. Though other researchers and business thinkers have since contributed to the refinement and popularization of the tool, Humphrey’s work is considered foundational. The timeline for its widespread adoption really took off in the 1980s and 1990s as it became a staple in business schools and corporate strategic planning activities.

Implementing a SWOT analysis involves a structured approach to evaluating both the internal and external environments affecting an organization or a specific project. Internally, strengths and weaknesses are assessed, usually focusing on assets, processes, and people. Externally, the organization looks at opportunities that can be exploited and threats that could adversely impact its objectives. Typically, a cross-functional team gathers to brainstorm and populate each quadrant of the SWOT matrix, combining various perspectives to create a comprehensive analysis. The output serves as a strategic foundation, often used in conjunction with other planning methods, to develop action plans and set priorities for achieving organizational goals.

Both SAST (Strategic Assumption Surfacing Technique) and SWOT (Strengths, Weaknesses, Opportunities, and Threats) are strategic planning tools designed to help organizations make better-informed decisions. They both encourage critical thinking and involve cross-functional teams to evaluate various aspects of an organization or a specific issue. However, their approaches and focuses differ significantly. SWOT is a more straightforward framework that categorizes internal and external factors affecting an organization into four quadrants—strengths, weaknesses, opportunities, and threats. It is often used for a broad analysis of the organization’s current state, but may not delve deeply into the underlying assumptions that influence strategic choices. On the other hand, SAST is focused specifically on uncovering and scrutinizing the implicit assumptions behind strategies. It goes beyond surface-level observations to explore the foundational beliefs that shape organizational decisions, thereby offering a deeper, more nuanced analysis. While SWOT provides a snapshot of the current landscape, SAST works to expose the hidden thought processes that could influence future strategic success or failure.

Table 1. SWOT vs. SAST

Aspect	SWOT	SAST
Origin	Developed by Albert Humphrey in the 1960s	Developed by Chris Argyris and Ian Mitroff
Focus	Broad analysis of internal and external factors	Deep dive into underlying assumptions behind strategies
Components	Strengths, Weaknesses, Opportunities, Threats	Taken-for-granted assumptions, Contingent assumptions
Methodology	Categorization into a four-quadrant matrix	Group discussions aimed at surfacing and analyzing assumptions
Team Involvement	Cross-functional teams populate the SWOT matrix	Teams divide into groups focusing on different aspects of the strategic issue
Application	General strategic planning, specific projects	Strategic planning, particularly for complex or high-stakes issues
Outcome	Identification of key factors for strategic planning	Uncover and scrutinize assumptions, align team, improve decision-making
Timeframe	Generally shorter, sometimes as quick as a single session	May require multiple sessions for deep analysis
Complexity	Less complex, often used as a preliminary step	More complex, designed for deeper, nuanced analysis
External Analysis	Includes an explicit focus on external opportunities and threats	Usually focuses internally but can be adapted to consider external assumptions
Integrative Potential	Often used in conjunction with other methods	Can also be used in conjunction with other methods, but less commonly so

SWOT Example One: Safety Culture in a Manufacturing Company

The need for implementing a SWOT analysis on safety culture arose after a series of minor incidents and one significant accident in the company's manufacturing facility over the past year. While no fatalities occurred, these incidents were a wake-up call for the management, triggering an immediate need to reevaluate and strengthen the existing safety protocols. Stakeholders felt the urgency to identify internal and external factors that could influence the safety culture positively or negatively. The company aimed to move beyond mere compliance with safety regulations and aspired to establish a culture where safety is an integral part of the operational ethos. The SWOT analysis served as a foundational tool to reassess the effectiveness of current safety measures and identify areas for strategic improvement. The findings of this fictional example are summarized in Table 2.

Table 2. SWOT analysis for safety culture in a manufacturing company

Strengths	- Comprehensive employee training on safety - Strong management commitment to safety - Regular safety audits - Advanced safety technology
Weaknesses	- Incomplete incident reporting system - Employee perception that productivity overrules safety - Limited employee participation in safety committees - Lapses in emergency response time
Opportunities	- Robust new safety technologies - Partnership opportunities with safety consultancies - Potential for a positive brand image - Government grants for safety improvement
Threats	- Rising industry accidents and insurance premiums - Regulatory changes requiring new safety measures - High turnover rates - Negative public perception due to safety incidents

Following the SWOT analysis on safety culture, the manufacturing company took several strategic actions. First, they revamped the incident reporting system to be more user-friendly, encouraging thorough reporting and learning from every safety event. Second, management introduced a performance metric that prioritized safety over speed, countering the prevailing culture that emphasized productivity at the expense of safety. Third, they expanded employee participation in safety committees and incentivized involvement through recognition and rewards. Fourth, emergency response drills were organized quarterly, and the findings were used to improve response times. Lastly, the company entered a partnership with a safety consultancy firm to stay abreast of the latest safety technologies and protocols, thereby aiming to become an industry leader in safety.

SWOT Example Two: A Company's Response to Climate Change

The initiative for a SWOT analysis in this fictitious example focused on climate change was sparked by increased stakeholder pressure, including from investors, customers, and regulatory bodies. With a growing global emphasis on sustainability, the company recognized that its response to climate change would significantly impact its long-term viability and brand reputation. There was also a need to comply with new and forthcoming environmental regulations to avoid legal and financial repercussions. Executives and key decision-makers used the SWOT analysis to gauge the company's current standing in terms of sustainability, uncover potential risks, and identify opportunities for becoming an industry leader in environmental responsibility.

This was also an attempt to align the company's climate initiatives with its broader business goals. The findings of this fictional example are summarized in Table 3.

After conducting the SWOT analysis on their climate change response, the company initiated five key actions. First, they created a dedicated sustainability unit staffed with experts to drive the company's climate initiatives. Second, they initiated a switch to renewable energy sources for at least 50% of their operations within the next two years. Third, a waste management system was designed to reduce landfill contributions by 30% within a year. Fourth, the company entered strategic partnerships with organizations focusing on circular economy solutions, aimed at recycling and reusing materials in the production process. Finally, an internal communication campaign was launched to keep all employees informed and engaged in the company's sustainability goals, thereby fostering a culture of environmental responsibility.

Table 3. SWOT analysis for a company's response to climate change

Strengths	- Established corporate sustainability team - Access to renewable energy - Strong brand reputation for eco-friendliness - Partnerships with environmental organizations
Weaknesses	- High dependency on fossil fuels - Lack of comprehensive waste management - Limited expertise in sustainable technologies - Inconsistent communication about climate initiatives
Opportunities	- Market demand for eco-friendly products - Tax incentives for sustainability - Strategic partnerships for circular economy - Employee engagement programs on sustainability
Threats	- Regulatory fines for emission standards - Rising costs of climate-sensitive raw materials - Public backlash against perceived inaction - Competitive disadvantage against more sustainable rivals

CONCLUSION

The Strategic Assumption Surfacing Technique (SAST) is used to identify and assess assumptions underlying organizational strategies. This method facilitates dialogue among team members, helping them uncover implicit beliefs that could affect decision-making. By bringing these hidden assumptions to light, organizations can analyze their validity, reduce conflicts, and align the team for more effective strategy execution.

In SAST, participants divide into groups, each assigned a specific aspect of the strategic issue at hand. Groups identify key assumptions and then present them for collective examination. Assumptions may be categorized as either "taken-for-granted," which are often unconscious but widely accepted, or as "contingent," which are conditional on certain events or circumstances. This process exposes discrepancies, contradictions, or gaps in the strategy, which can then be addressed or tested.

The technique enhances strategic planning by fostering critical thinking and open discussion. By revealing the foundational assumptions that influence strategy, teams can adapt plans to better suit the current environment or future uncertainties. This iterative process allows for more resilient and dynamic strategies, making organizations better equipped to navigate complexities and challenges.

The SWOT analysis is a strategic tool that serves as a cornerstone for organizational planning and decision-making. By mapping out Strengths, Weaknesses, Opportunities, and Threats, this framework offers a comprehensive view of both internal and external factors that can affect an entity's objectives. Strengths and weaknesses are intrinsic aspects that the organization can control and improve upon, whereas opportunities and threats are external elements that it must navigate. The utility of a SWOT analysis goes beyond mere identification of these factors; it drives actionable insights and helps prioritize initiatives. The analysis informs resource allocation, identifies areas requiring improvement or investment, and sets the foundation for constructing a more robust strategic plan. Overall, SWOT analysis provides valuable data to guide an organization toward its goals effectively and efficiently.

COMPREHENSION EXERCISES

1. What is the primary purpose of using the Strategic Assumption Surfacing Technique (SAST)?
    a) To conduct SWOT analysis
    b) To identify and assess underlying assumptions in organizational strategies
    c) To allocate resources efficiently
    d) To perform market research
2. Who are the primary developers of SAST?
    a) Peter Drucker and Michael Porter
    b) Chris Argyris and Ian Mitroff
    c) Henry Mintzberg and Gary Hamel
    d) John Kotter and Edgar Schein

3. In SAST, what does the term "taken-for-granted assumptions" refer to?
   a) Assumptions that are conditional
   b) Assumptions that are widely accepted and often unconscious
   c) Assumptions that are easily changed
   d) Assumptions that are subject to frequent testing
4. Which of the following best describes the "contingent assumptions" in SAST?
   a) Widely accepted beliefs
   b) Assumptions dependent on certain conditions or events
   c) Easily modifiable beliefs
   d) None of the above
5. How does SAST contribute to strategic planning?
   a) By identifying target customers
   b) By specifying marketing channels
   c) By fostering critical thinking and open discussion
   d) By focusing only on financial outcomes
6. What is a key outcome of successfully employing SAST in an organization?
   a) Faster product development
   b) Elimination of all risks
   c) Improved strategic alignment and decision-making
   d) Doubling of profits
7. During a SAST session, what is the primary role of team members?
   a) To critique company policies
   b) To uncover and present assumptions for collective examination
   c) To finalize strategic goals
   d) To analyze financial reports
8. Which sector could benefit from SAST in the context of policy development?
   a) Healthcare
   b) Fast-food industry
   c) Fashion
   d) Entertainment
9. What type of assumptions do SAST sessions usually focus on surfacing?
   a) Obvious
   b) Irrelevant
   c) Hidden or implicit
   d) None of the above
10. Which of the following KPIs could effectively measure the impact of a SAST campaign?
    a) Employee turnover rate
    b) Decision-making speed
    c) Number of social media followers
    d) Customer age demographics

11. What does the acronym SWOT stand for?
    a) Strengths, Weaknesses, Opportunities, Technologies
    b) Strengths, Weaknesses, Objectives, Threats
    c) Strengths, Weaknesses, Opportunities, Threats
    d) Systems, Weaknesses, Objectives, Tactics
12. Which of the following components of SWOT are considered internal factors?
    a) Strengths and Weaknesses
    b) Opportunities and Threats
    c) Strengths and Opportunities
    d) Weaknesses and Threats
13. Which component of SWOT would include an analysis of competitors?
    a) Strengths
    b) Weaknesses
    c) Opportunities
    d) Threats
14. What is the primary purpose of a SWOT analysis?
    a) To analyze financial statements
    b) To create a business plan
    c) To understand internal and external factors affecting an organization
    d) To conduct market research
15. If a company has a well-established brand and customer loyalty, under which section would this be classified in a SWOT analysis?
    a) Strengths
    b) Weaknesses
    c) Opportunities
    d) Threats

REFERENCES

Ackermann, F., & Eden, C. (2011). Strategic Management of Stakeholders: Theory and Practice. *Long Range Planning*, *44*(3), 179–196. doi:10.1016/j.lrp.2010.08.001

Ackoff, R. L. (1981). The Art and Science of Mess Management. *Interfaces*, *11*(1), 20–26. doi:10.1287/inte.11.1.20

Argyris, C. (1964). *Integrating the Individual and the Organization*. Transaction Publishers.

Argyris, C. (1982). *Reasoning, Learning, and Action: Individual and Organizational*. Jossey-Bass.

Argyris, C. (1990). *Overcoming Organizational Defenses: Facilitating Organizational Learning*. Allyn & Bacon.

Argyris, C. (1993). *Knowledge for Action: A Guide to Overcoming Barriers to Organizational Change*. Jossey-Bass.

Argyris, C. (1999). *On Organizational Learning*. Blackwell.

Argyris, C., & Schön, D. A. (1978). *Organizational Learning: A Theory of Action Perspective*. Addison-Wesley.

Argyris, C., & Schön, D. A. (1996). *Organizational Learning II: Theory, Method, and Practice*. Addison-Wesley.

Barabba, V. P., & Ian, I. Mitroff. (2014). Business Strategies for a Messy World - Tools for Systemic Problem Solving. New York: Palgrave Macmillan.

Checkland, P. (1999). *Soft systems methodology: a 30-year retrospective*. John Wiley & Sons.

Courtney, J. F. (2001). Decision making and knowledge management in inquiring organizations: Toward a new decision-making paradigm for DSS. *Decision Support Systems*, *31*(1), 17–38. doi:10.1016/S0167-9236(00)00117-2

Eden, C., & Huxham, C. (1996). Action research for management research. *British Journal of Management*, *7*(1), 75–86. doi:10.1111/j.1467-8551.1996.tb00107.x

Emery, F. E. (1959). *Characteristics of socio-technical systems*. Tavistock Institute.

Flood, R. L., & Jackson, M. C. (1993). Total systems intervention: A practical face to critical systems thinking. *Systems Practice*, *6*(4), 341–355.

Mason, R. O., & Mitroff, I. I. (1973). A Program for Research on Management Information Systems. *Management Science*, *19*(5), 475–487. doi:10.1287/mnsc.19.5.475

Mason, R. O., & Mitroff, I. I. (1981). *Challenging Strategic Planning Assumptions: Theory, Cases, and Techniques*. John Wiley & Sons.

Mitroff, I. I. (1983). *Stakeholders of the Organizational Mind*. Jossey-Bass.

Mitroff, I. I. (2018). *The Essential Guide to Managing Corporate Crises: A Step-by-Step Handbook for Surviving Major Catastrophes*. Oxford University Press.

Mitroff, I. I., & Denton, E. A. (1999). A study of spirituality in the workplace. *MIT Sloan Management Review*, *40*(4), 83–92.

Mitroff, I. I., & Kilmann, R. H. (1978). *Methodological approaches to social science: Integrating divergent concepts and theories*. Brooks/Cole Publishing Company.

Mitroff, I. I., & Linstone, H. A. (1993). *The Unbounded Mind: Breaking the Chains of Traditional Business Thinking*. Oxford University Press.

Mitroff, I. I., & Mason, R. O. (1976). Business Policy and Metaphysics. *Academy of Management Review*, *1*(2), 67–74.

Mitroff, I. I., & Pauchant, T. C. (1990). Strategic Assumption Surfacing and Testing. In *We're So Big and Powerful Nothing Bad Can Happen to Us: An Investigation of America's Crisis Prone Corporations*. Birch Lane Press.

Mitroff, I. I., & Pauchant, T. C. (1992). *Transforming the Crisis-Prone Organization: Preventing Individual, Organizational, and Environmental Tragedies*. Jossey-Bass.

Puyt, R. W., Lie, F. B., & Wilderom, C. P. M. (2023). The origins of SWOT analysis. *Long Range Planning, 56*(3), 102304–. doi:10.1016/j.lrp.2023.102304

Ramage, M., & Shipp, K. (2009). *Systems Thinkers*. Springer. doi:10.1007/978-1-84882-525-3

Schwaninger, M. (2002). Methodologies in conflict: Achieving synergies between system dynamics and organizational cybernetics. *Systems Research and Behavioral Science*, *19*(4), 341–358.

Ulrich, W. (1983). *Critical heuristics of social planning: A new approach to practical philosophy*. Haupt.

APPENDIX - COMPREHENSION EXERCISES: SOLUTIONS

1. What is the primary purpose of using the Strategic Assumption Surfacing Technique (SAST)?
    a) To conduct SWOT analysis
    b) To identify and assess underlying assumptions in organizational strategies
    c) To allocate resources efficiently
    d) To perform market research

Recommended Answer: B. To identify and assess underlying assumptions in organizational strategies

2. Who are the primary developers of SAST?
    a) Peter Drucker and Michael Porter
    b) Chris Argyris and Ian Mitroff
    c) Henry Mintzberg and Gary Hamel
    d) John Kotter and Edgar Schein

Recommended Answer: B. Chris Argyris and Ian Mitroff

3. In SAST, what does the term "taken-for-granted assumptions" refer to?
    a) Assumptions that are conditional
    b) Assumptions that are widely accepted and often unconscious
    c) Assumptions that are easily changed
    d) Assumptions that are subject to frequent testing

Recommended Answer: B. Assumptions that are widely accepted and often unconscious

4. Which of the following best describes the "contingent assumptions" in SAST?
    a) Widely accepted beliefs
    b) Assumptions dependent on certain conditions or events
    c) Easily modifiable beliefs
    d) None of the above

Recommended Answer: B. Assumptions dependent on certain conditions or events

5. How does SAST contribute to strategic planning?
    a) By identifying target customers
    b) By specifying marketing channels
    c) By fostering critical thinking and open discussion
    d) By focusing only on financial outcomes

Recommended Answer: C. By fostering critical thinking and open discussion

6. What is a key outcome of successfully employing SAST in an organization?
    a) Faster product development
    b) Elimination of all risks
    c) Improved strategic alignment and decision-making
    d) Doubling of profits

Recommended Answer: C. Improved strategic alignment and decision-making

7. During a SAST session, what is the primary role of team members?
    a) To critique company policies
    b) To uncover and present assumptions for collective examination
    c) To finalize strategic goals
    d) To analyze financial reports

Recommended Answer: B. To uncover and present assumptions for collective examination

8. Which sector could benefit from SAST in the context of policy development?
    a) Healthcare
    b) Fast-food industry
    c) Fashion
    d) Entertainment

Recommended Answer: A. Healthcare

9. What type of assumptions do SAST sessions usually focus on surfacing?
    a) Obvious
    b) Irrelevant
    c) Hidden or implicit
    d) None of the above

Recommended Answer: C. Hidden or implicit

10. Which of the following KPIs could effectively measure the impact of a SAST campaign?
    a) Employee turnover rate
    b) Decision-making speed
    c) Number of social media followers
    d) Customer age demographics

Recommended Answer: B. Decision-making speed

16. What does the acronym SWOT stand for?
    a) Strengths, Weaknesses, Opportunities, Technologies
    b) Strengths, Weaknesses, Objectives, Threats
    c) Strengths, Weaknesses, Opportunities, Threats
    d) Systems, Weaknesses, Objectives, Tactics

Recommended Answer: C. Strengths, Weaknesses, Opportunities, Threats

17. Which of the following components of SWOT are considered internal factors?
    a) Strengths and Weaknesses
    b) Opportunities and Threats
    c) Strengths and Opportunities
    d) Weaknesses and Threats

Recommended Answer: A. Strengths and Weaknesses

18. Which component of SWOT would include an analysis of competitors?
    a) Strengths
    b) Weaknesses
    c) Opportunities
    d) Threats

Recommended Answer: D. Threats

19. What is the primary purpose of a SWOT analysis?
    a) To analyze financial statements
    b) To create a business plan
    c) To understand internal and external factors affecting an organization
    d) To conduct market research

Recommended Answer: C. To understand internal and external factors affecting an organization

20. If a company has a well-established brand and customer loyalty, under which section would this be classified in a SWOT analysis?
    a) Strengths
    b) Weaknesses
    c) Opportunities
    d) Threats

Recommended Answer: A. Strengths

Chapter 6
Conflict Modes

ABSTRACT

There are basically five different ways or modes of handling conflict. Two underlying dimensions are at the basis of the model: assertiveness and cooperativeness. The first dimension, assertiveness, is the extent to which a person tries to satisfy his or her needs or concerns irrespective of those of others. The second dimension, cooperativeness, is the extent to which a person tries to satisfy another person's needs or concerns irrespective of his or hers. Combining the two dimensions in all ways results in five basic modes: Competing (high in assertiveness and low in cooperativeness), accommodating (low in assertiveness and high in cooperativeness), compromising (moderate in both assertiveness and cooperativeness), avoiding (low on both dimensions), and collaborating (high on both dimensions).

"10% of conflict is due to difference in opinion and 90% is due to delivery and tone of voice." – Unknown

Learning Objectives

- Identify the five different modes of handling conflict
- Summarize Assertiveness
- Describe Cooperativness
- List key attributes of a conflict situation

DOI: 10.4018/978-1-6684-6563-9.ch006

INTRODUCTION

The Jungian Personality Framework does not of course exhaust all of the relevant attributes of a person's personality. Indeed, no single framework ever could. One of the most important aspects is how a person handles and responds to conflict. In this regard, the Thomas-Kilmann Conflict Model (Kilman, 2021)is particularly relevant. For this reason, the student is especially encouraged to go online and take the Thomas-Kilmann Conflict Assessment Instrument. Current academic discourse notes that the model is valuable for self-awareness and team dynamics but raises questions about its oversimplification of complex human interactions. Critics argue that cultural, gender, and power dynamics are not fully captured. Overall, the TKI remains a foundational tool, albeit with limitations recognized by the academic community.

Essentially, there are basically five different ways or modes of handling conflict. Two underlying dimensions are at the basis of the Model: Assertiveness and Cooperativeness. The first dimension, Assertiveness, is the extent to which a person tries to satisfy *his or her* needs or concerns irrespective of those of others. The second dimension, Cooperativeness, is the extent to which a person tries to satisfy *another* person's needs or concerns irrespective of his or hers.

Figure 1. The two dimensions of the TKI conflict model: Assertiveness and cooperativeness
(Kilman, 2021)

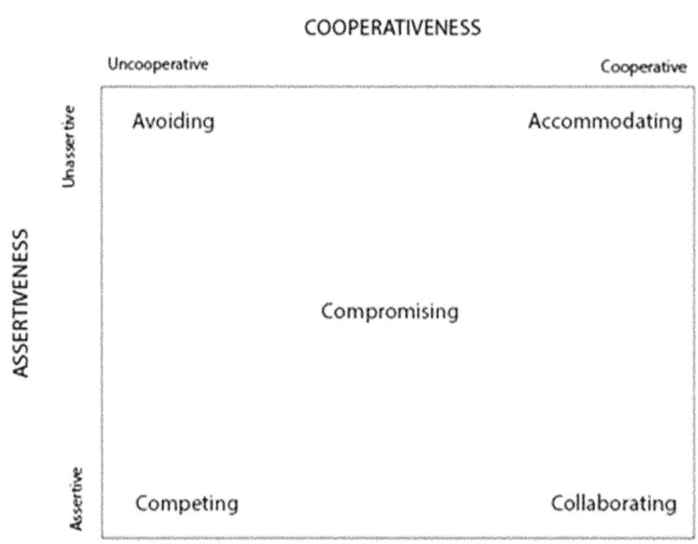

Combining the two dimensions in all ways results in five basic modes: Competing (high in Assertiveness and low in Cooperativeness), Accommodating (low in Assertiveness and high in Cooperativeness), Compromising (moderate in both Assertiveness and Cooperativeness), Avoiding (low on both dimensions), and Collaborating (high on both dimensions).

Think of it in terms of a pie. If one is high in Competing, then one wants the whole pie for him or herself. If one is high in Accommodating, then one gives the whole pie to the other person, thereby getting nothing for oneself. If one is high in Avoiding, then neither person gets any of the pie. In effect, both withdraw from a conflict situation. Conversely, if one is high in Collaborating, then one expands the pie such that both parties get a whole pie. And, finally, if one is high in Compromising, then each party gets half of the pie.

Obviously, Collaborating and Compromising take time and trust to achieve. However, if one is in a dangerous situation such as a burning house, then Competing is best in that he or she who knows the best way out to safety is to be followed without any discussion. This of course requires Accommodating on the part of others.

Based on extensive research with the Conflict Model Instrument (TKI), it's been found that at best people typically rely on only one or two of the five modes. As a result, they tend not to use the remaining ones. Nonetheless, all five modes are applicable to virtually all situations. Each is helpful in addressing and resolving different needs and perspectives. The key is whether a particular mode matches the key attributes and/or requirements of a situation.

For this reason, we strongly urge everyone not to use a mode purely out of habit or based on their underlying personality. Instead, depending on one's answers to the following questions, one needs to choose one or more of the five modes as they are appropriate:

The Eight Key Attributes of a Conflict Situation

1. How stressful is the situation?
2. Is it simple or complex?
3. How important is the topic to each person?
4. Is there ample time to discuss the issues?
5. Is there sufficient trust to openly share needs and concerns?
6. Do people have good listening and communication skills?
7. Do the Culture and Reward Systems of an organization actively encourage people to share their true needs and concerns?
8. How important are the relationships to each person in the situation?

Depending on one's responses to the questions, one ideally chooses the particular mode that has the best chance of incorporating their perspective along with the opposing perspectives of others. One especially needs to practice using those modes that one typically doesn't. At the same time, one also needs to reduce one's use of those with which one is most comfortable. To emphasize a key point: *The first step for managing a conflict is correctly assessing the immediate situation before selecting a particular mode of behavior so that the chances of having a constructive debate and thereby integrating opposing viewpoints are maximized.* Notice that "correctly assessing a situation" demands at the very least that we use a Multiple Realities IS.

If there is high, or worse yet, overwhelming stress in a situation, then the five ways of handling a conflict quickly collapse to three defensive reactions: Fight, Flight, or Freeze. Ideally, as much as possible, all discussions or debates need to take place under conditions of low to moderate stress so that those involved in will be able to choose that mode that is best suited to the situation. At the same time, one is hopefully able to switch modes as the situation changes.

Fight, Flight, or Freeze are wired into as it were by evolution. Thus, when faced with a serious threat, our autonomous nervous systems make an instant decision as to whether to Fight, Flee, or Freeze. If we feel we have both the capability and power to overcome an adversary or threat, then we stay and Fight. If we feel we don't have either the capability or the power, then we Flee, but only if we have the means to Bolt. However, if we have neither the power or the means to escape, then we Freeze.

Figure 2. Overwhelming stress results in 'fight, flight, or freeze'
(Kilman, 2021)

Table 1. Summary of when to use various TKI conflict modes (Kilman, 2021)

When to use	Competing	Collaborating	Compromising	Avoiding	Accommodating
Stress	High/moderate	Stimulating	High/moderate	Overwhelming	High/moderate
Problem Complexity	Simple/unidimensional	Complex/multidimensional	Simple/unidimensional	Simple/unidimensional	Simple/unidimensional
Importance	More important to you than others	Equally important to all	Moderately important to all	Not important	More important to others
Time	Little time for discussion	Much time for discussion	Little time for discussion	Little time for discussion	Little time for discussion
Trust	Low or moderate	High levels	Low or moderate	Low levels	Low or moderate
Interactions	People can communicate their views	Effective interactions	Respectful	Ineffective interactions	Ineffective interactions
Reward System	Supports win/lose	Actively encourages exploration, cooperation, teamwork	Encourages quick fixes	Discourages confrontation	Encourages compliance
Relationships	Not concerned with sustaining relationships	Lasting relationships	Indifferent on lasting relationships	Don't particularly care about relationships	Eager to please others to maintain relationships

It's also important to stress that Fight, Flight, and Freeze have different connotations. Thus, Fight does not necessarily mean Physical. Most often, it means standing up for an action or idea in which one believes strongly. Thus, in the case of Crisis Management, it means doing everything one can to get one's organization to be Crisis Prepared. In a similar fashion, Flight does not always mean Fleeing Physically, but in accepting that the conditions are not right for pushing an idea. In the same way, Freezing can mean taking a "timeout." One accepts that things will have to "Unfreeze" before one can move ahead.

APPLICATION EXAMPLES

Three separate fictitious application examples have been developed to illustrate the five different conflict modes. Each of the three application areas (Healthcare, Academic Faculty, and Corporate Critical Project Funding) are presented from each of the five conflict mode perspectives.

Competing Conflict Mode

Competing Example One: Healthcare

In a healthcare setting, two surgeons, Emily and David, are competing for the opportunity to lead a groundbreaking surgical procedure. The stakes are high, given the procedure's potential to revolutionize treatment in a particular medical field. The stress is intense, given the surgery's complexity and the looming decision deadline. Both surgeons have extensive experience, but Emily opts for a Competing mode, leaning on her track record and leveraging relationships with hospital administration. The reward system in the hospital generally favors high-profile cases as a measure of a surgeon's skill and contributions, making the opportunity highly coveted.

Emily successfully secures the lead role in the surgery, achieving her immediate goal. While this serves her career and aligns with the hospital's reward system, it strains her professional relationship with David and other colleagues who were also interested in the opportunity. The single-minded pursuit begins to tarnish trust within the surgical team, with future interactions tinged with a sense of rivalry. As people become more protective of their opportunities for fear of being overshadowed, the team's overall ability to collaborate and share knowledge suffers. The longer-term impact potentially compromises patient care quality, as the focus shifts subtly from collective success to individual recognition.

Competing Example Two: Academic Faculty

In an academic context, two professors, Sarah and Mark, are both aiming for a prestigious research grant that is only awarded annually. The stress is high; both have invested years into their respective research fields. The problem is complex, as both are contributing valuable knowledge but in differing disciplines. The grant is crucial for laboratory funding and research assistants. With a tight deadline for applications, Sarah adopts a Competing conflict mode, using her substantial publication record and network to lobby department heads and influential committee members, aligning with a reward system that often recognizes individual achievement over collaborative efforts.

While Sarah wins the grant, the aggressive approach has nuanced effects. In the short term, it ensures that her research continues uninterrupted. However, it also sets a precedent for future interactions with Mark, eroding mutual trust and contributing to an atmosphere of internal competition rather than collaboration. Furthermore, the department now faces a skewed reward system that places significant importance on aggressive pursuit of limited opportunities, affecting future relationships and collaborations. Colleagues become more guarded, fearing that information sharing might jeopardize their own chances for rewards, thereby negatively affecting the department's overall cohesion and productivity.

Competing Example Three: Corporate Critical Project Funding

In a corporate setting, a project manager named Alex employs the Competing mode to secure funding for a critical project. This occurs in a high-stress environment with multiple teams vying for limited resources. The problem is complex, involving multiple stakeholders and high organizational impact. The importance of securing the budget is paramount for the project's success. Alex leverages existing trust and credibility to convince senior management, emphasizing the short time frame and the urgency. The reward system in place is designed to favor those who can deliver results under tight deadlines. Although the approach alienates some colleagues who feel their projects are equally deserving, Alex's competing style achieves the immediate goal.

However, this competitive approach has longer-term repercussions. Although effective in the short term due to the high-stress nature and limited time, this style erodes trust among peers and fosters a zero-sum mentality. Interactions become transactional, influenced by a reward system that values competition over collaboration. Team relationships suffer, as colleagues now view each other as obstacles to their own project success rather than as partners in organizational success. Alex's behavior signals to others that aggressive tactics get results, potentially creating a toxic culture in the long run.

Collaborating Conflict Mode

Collaborating Example One: Healthcare

In the healthcare context, Emily and David choose the Collaborating mode in their quest to lead the groundbreaking surgical procedure. The problem is complex, time-sensitive, and stressful, making it all the more crucial to involve multiple perspectives. Instead of leveraging their individual credentials, they jointly present a proposal to hospital administration that leverages both of their strengths. Given that the reward system also recognizes collaborative advancements in medical science, this seems a fitting approach.

By choosing collaboration, Emily and David not only share the responsibilities and rewards but also enhance team dynamics and trust. Colleagues notice this shift and are encouraged to adopt similar collaborative strategies in their own professional endeavors. The long-term impact is a more cohesive, open, and effective healthcare team that places collective patient care above individual accolades. This nuanced shift significantly influences future interactions, making for a more effective, trusting team capable of tackling complex medical challenges collaboratively.

Collaborating Example Two: Academic Faculty

In the academic setting, Sarah and Mark opt for a Collaborative approach towards the prestigious research grant. Both acknowledge the stress and complexity of the situation, but also realize the potential for synergies in their research. They decide to combine their efforts and submit a joint application, highlighting the interdisciplinary nature of their work. They work together to convince department heads that this innovative approach aligns with the long-term academic goals, leveraging the trust they've built over years of collaboration. The department's reward system, although often focused on individual accomplishments, also values groundbreaking interdisciplinary work.

As a result of this collaboration, not only do Sarah and Mark secure the grant, but they also pave the way for a more collaborative culture within the department. Relationships among faculty members improve as they see the value in pooling resources and expertise. Future academic endeavors are more easily supported due to this shift in interactions and trust, providing a counterbalance to the typically competitive nature of academia.

Collaborating Example Three: Corporate Critical Project Funding

In the corporate scenario, project manager Alex chooses the Collaborating mode when vying for limited project resources. Recognizing the high stress and complexity of the situation, Alex approaches colleagues to explore mutual interests and brainstorm solutions that benefit multiple teams. The problem's importance and tight timeline demand swift action, but Alex believes that a collaborative solution could be more sustainable and less divisive. Trusting that others also aim for the organization's success, Alex taps into that mutual goodwill. The company's reward system, while often favoring quick results, also has mechanisms for recognizing teamwork and innovation.

By using the Collaborating approach, Alex fosters an environment where colleagues willingly share ideas and resources. While it takes more time upfront, this approach reinforces trust and encourages more open interaction among team members. In the long run, this makes it easier to navigate future conflicts and complex problems, improving the overall company culture. The reward system starts to evolve as well, recognizing the value of collective achievements over individual triumphs.

Compromising Conflict Mode

Compromising Example One: Healthcare

In healthcare, Emily and David choose a Compromising approach when competing for the chance to lead the groundbreaking surgical procedure. Given the high stakes, they propose co-leading the surgery, each taking responsibility for different components where they have specialized expertise. They present this idea to hospital administration, pointing out that the procedure's complexity and high importance warrant a shared leadership role. Though the hospital's reward system usually recognizes individual achievements, Emily and David argue that patient outcomes are the ultimate measure of success.

The Compromising approach results in both sharing the leadership of the surgery, each contributing their unique skills and expertise. While neither gains exclusive recognition, the relationships within the surgical team remain strong, and the level of trust even increases. The team learns that compromise can be an effective approach to solving complex, high-stakes problems. Future interactions among team members are marked by a greater willingness to find middle-ground solutions, ultimately benefiting patient care and team cohesion.

Compromising Example Two: Academic Faculty

In academia, Sarah and Mark decide to adopt a Compromising approach regarding the prestigious research grant. Both realize the stress and competitive nature of the situation but agree that they have overlapping research interests. Instead of competing, they submit separate but complementary grant applications, advocating for a portion of the grant money to be allocated for joint research initiatives. They both tap into the trust they have built among department members and propose this as a solution that can yield collective benefits, even though the reward system is generally more attuned to individual achievements.

The compromise results in both receiving a portion of the grant, allowing them to progress in their individual projects while also pooling resources for a joint initiative. Although neither gets the full grant, the relationships among faculty are preserved, and an atmosphere of collaboration is encouraged. This partial victory ensures that both can continue their work, changing future interactions in the department to include more openness to compromise and co-funding opportunities.

Compromising Example Three: Corporate Critical Project Funding

In the corporate setting, Alex adopts a Compromising approach to secure funding for his project. Recognizing the stress and complexity due to multiple teams seeking limited resources, Alex proposes splitting the available budget among several high-impact projects. Despite the urgency and the reward system favoring decisive action, Alex believes that partial funding can still yield substantial progress for all involved. He leverages the mutual trust within the team to advocate for this middle-ground solution, expecting that this compromise will satisfy the immediate needs without deeply affecting team relationships.

The outcome is a more equitable distribution of resources, relieving some of the immediate stress. Although no team gets full funding, relationships remain intact, and trust within the team isn't eroded. The compromise also leads to more cooperative interactions in future projects, even if it doesn't entirely align with a reward system that usually applauds individual success. Team members become more open to shared solutions in subsequent conflicts, promoting a more balanced organizational culture.

Avoiding Conflict Mode

Avoiding Example One: Healthcare

In the healthcare setting, Emily and David choose an Avoiding approach when the opportunity to lead the groundbreaking surgical procedure arises. Understanding the stress and high stakes involved, both decide that the risk of strained relations and a competitive atmosphere isn't worth it. Even though the hospital's reward system tends to favor high-profile cases, they place more value on team cohesion and trust.

By choosing to avoid the competition, Emily and David maintain a harmonious team environment. However, a third surgeon ends up leading the procedure, which affects Emily's and David's professional growth opportunities. Though the avoiding approach keeps team dynamics stable in the short term, it fails to address the long-term issue of career advancement and the opportunity to participate in groundbreaking medical work.

Avoiding Example Two: Academic Faculty

In academia, both Sarah and Mark choose an Avoiding strategy when it comes to the coveted research grant. Acknowledging the stress, complexity, and potential for a damaged relationship, both decide not to apply for the grant this year. They maintain their focus on ongoing projects and look for alternative funding sources, believing that the department's typical reward system of individual achievements isn't worth disrupting their long-term academic relationships and collaborative potential.

By both avoiding the competition for the grant, Sarah and Mark preserve their professional relationship and the collaborative atmosphere within the department. However, the downside is that both miss out on a significant funding opportunity, which may slow down their research progress. Although avoiding the conflict mitigates immediate stress, it doesn't offer a solution to the challenge of securing necessary resources for their work.

Avoiding Example Three: Corporate Critical Project Funding

In the corporate scenario, project manager Alex opts for an Avoiding approach in the competitive environment for limited resources. Faced with high stress, a complex problem, and a short time frame, Alex decides not to engage in open competition or negotiations for the budget. Although the project is important, Alex assesses that the tension and potential for conflict outweigh the benefits of securing immediate funding. Trust and long-term relationships are considered more valuable, given that the company's reward system can sometimes favor cutthroat competition at the expense of teamwork.

By avoiding direct confrontation, Alex maintains team relationships and keeps trust intact. However, his project doesn't receive immediate funding, creating delays and challenges for future progress. While the Avoiding approach reduces tension and conflict in the short term, it doesn't resolve the underlying issue of resource allocation. This tactic also sidelines Alex in organizational politics, potentially limiting his influence in future endeavors.

Accommodating Conflict Mode

Accommodating Example One: Healthcare

In healthcare, Emily takes an Accommodating approach when the opportunity arises to lead a revolutionary surgical procedure. Recognizing the high-stress, competitive environment, she steps back to allow David the chance to lead, believing that preserving team unity is more critical than individual recognition. Although the hospital's reward system generally favors individual accomplishments, Emily sees greater value in maintaining a supportive, collaborative work environment.

By stepping back, Emily preserves the team's dynamics and mutual trust. Her act enhances her reputation as a team player, which could positively influence future collaborations. However, she misses out on a significant professional opportunity, and the decision may affect her career advancement in a system that often rewards high-profile leadership roles. While her accommodating approach maintains team harmony, it doesn't address her own professional development needs.

Accommodating Example Two: Academic Faculty

In academia, Sarah opts for an Accommodating strategy regarding the prestigious research grant. Aware of the stress and competitiveness, she withdraws her application in favor of Mark's, judging that maintaining a collaborative relationship is more valuable than winning the grant. This move is somewhat counter to the department's typical reward system, which leans heavily toward individual achievements.

By accommodating, Sarah preserves her relationship with Mark and promotes a culture of collegiality within the department. However, she misses out on substantial research funding, potentially slowing down her work. While her relationship with Mark and other colleagues is strengthened, her personal research goals take a hit. This approach avoids immediate conflict but may create challenges in securing resources for her future academic pursuits.

Accommodating Example Three: Corporate Critical Project Funding

In the corporate environment, Alex adopts an Accommodating approach, conceding the funding battle to other teams even though he believes his project is critical. Given the high-stress situation and complex nature of the problem, Alex prioritizes maintaining good relationships and team harmony. He trusts that his project will eventually gain recognition and support without having to engage in a direct struggle for resources. The company's reward system usually encourages aggressive competition, but Alex places higher value on interpersonal relationships.

Alex's Accommodating approach preserves trust and good will among team members. His team appreciates his cooperative demeanor, which in turn fosters a more congenial working environment. However, the downside is that his project goes unfunded, impacting its progress and potentially its ultimate success. While immediate tensions are diffused, Alex's accommodating stance does not solve the fundamental issue of resource allocation, and it might set a precedent that his projects can be easily sidelined in the future.

CONCLUSION

The Thomas-Kilmann Instrument (TKI) identifies five primary conflict resolution modes: Competing, Collaborating, Compromising, Avoiding, and Accommodating. Each mode has distinct characteristics and is appropriate for specific situations. Competing is assertive and uncooperative, focusing on individual goals. Collaborating seeks win-win solutions, involving both assertiveness and cooperation. Compromising aims for quick, middle-ground solutions, requiring moderate levels of both assertiveness and cooperation.

Avoiding is unassertive and uncooperative, dodging conflict rather than addressing it. Accommodating is cooperative but unassertive, often yielding to the other party to maintain harmony. Each mode's effectiveness depends on factors like the complexity of the problem, the importance of the issue, time constraints, and the existing level of trust among participants.

While the TKI framework offers valuable insights into conflict resolution, it isn't without critiques. Critics argue that the modes may be overly simplistic, failing to account for cultural differences or the fluidity of human interaction. Nonetheless, the TKI remains a widely used tool for understanding and navigating conflict in various settings, from corporate environments to personal relationships.

COMPREHENSION EXERCISES

1. Which TKI mode is considered both assertive and cooperative?
   a) Competing
   b) Collaborating
   c) Compromising
   d) Avoiding
2. In which mode do individuals focus solely on their own concerns at the expense of others?
   a) Competing
   b) Collaborating
   c) Compromising
   d) Accommodating
3. Which mode is best suited for situations where the issue is of low importance?
   a) Competing
   b) Avoiding
   c) Collaborating
   d) Compromising
4. Which mode seeks to find a middle-ground solution?
   a) Competing
   b) Collaborating
   c) Compromising
   d) Avoiding
5. Which mode is often used to maintain harmony and avoid conflict?
   a) Competing
   b) Collaborating
   c) Compromising
   d) Accommodating
6. Which mode involves high levels of both assertiveness and cooperation?
   a) Collaborating
   b) Compromising
   c) Accommodating
   d) Competing
7. Which mode is least effective when quick, decisive action is required?
   a) Competing
   b) Collaborating
   c) Compromising
   d) Avoiding

8. Which mode could potentially result in a lose-lose situation?
    a) Avoiding
    b) Collaborating
    c) Competing
    d) Accommodating
9. Which mode often results in a win-lose outcome?
    a) Competing
    b) Collaborating
    c) Compromising
    d) Avoiding
10. Which mode is ideal when preserving relationships is a top priority?
    a) Competing
    b) Collaborating
    c) Accommodating
    d) Avoiding
11. Which mode is most time-consuming?
    a) Competing
    b) Collaborating
    c) Compromising
    d) Avoiding
12. Which mode is characterized by moderate levels of both assertiveness and cooperation?
    a) Competing
    b) Collaborating
    c) Compromising
    d) Accommodating
13. Which mode is best for complex problems that require innovative solutions?
    a) Competing
    b) Collaborating
    c) Compromising
    d) Accommodating
14. Which mode is most likely to lead to short-term solutions?
    a) Competing
    b) Collaborating
    c) Compromising
    d) Avoiding

15. Which mode is often employed to maintain peace in the short term, but may lead to unresolved issues?
    a) Competing
    b) Collaborating
    c) Compromising
    d) Avoiding

COMPREHENSION EXERCISES: SOLUTIONS

1. Which TKI mode is considered both assertive and cooperative?
    a) Competing
    b) Collaborating
    c) Compromising
    d) Avoiding

Recommended Answer: B) Collaborating

2. In which mode do individuals focus solely on their own concerns at the expense of others?
    a) Competing
    b) Collaborating
    c) Compromising
    d) Accommodating

Recommended Answer: A) Competing

3. Which mode is best suited for situations where the issue is of low importance?
    a) Competing
    b) Avoiding
    c) Collaborating
    d) Compromising

Recommended Answer: B) Avoiding

4. Which mode seeks to find a middle-ground solution?
    a) Competing
    b) Collaborating
    c) Compromising
    d) Avoiding

Recommended Answer: C) Compromising

5. Which mode is often used to maintain harmony and avoid conflict?
   a) Competing
   b) Collaborating
   c) Compromising
   d) Accommodating

Recommended Answer: D) Accommodating

6. Which mode involves high levels of both assertiveness and cooperation?
   a) Collaborating
   b) Compromising
   c) Accommodating
   d) Competing

Recommended Answer: A) Collaborating

7. Which mode is least effective when quick, decisive action is required?
   a) Competing
   b) Collaborating
   c) Compromising
   d) Avoiding

Recommended Answer: D) Avoiding

8. Which mode could potentially result in a lose-lose situation?
   a) Avoiding
   b) Collaborating
   c) Competing
   d) Accommodating

Recommended Answer: A) Avoiding

9. Which mode often results in a win-lose outcome?
   a) Competing
   b) Collaborating
   c) Compromising
   d) Avoiding

Recommended Answer: A) Competing

10. Which mode is ideal when preserving relationships is a top priority?
    a) Competing
    b) Collaborating
    c) Accommodating
    d) Avoiding

Recommended Answer: C) Accommodating

11. Which mode is most time-consuming?
    a) Competing
    b) Collaborating
    c) Compromising
    d) Avoiding

Recommended Answer: B) Collaborating

12. Which mode is characterized by moderate levels of both assertiveness and cooperation?
    a) Competing
    b) Collaborating
    c) Compromising
    d) Accommodating

Recommended Answer: C) Compromising

13. Which mode is best for complex problems that require innovative solutions?
    a) Competing
    b) Collaborating
    c) Compromising
    d) Accommodating

Recommended Answer: B) Collaborating

14. Which mode is most likely to lead to short-term solutions?
    a) Competing
    b) Collaborating
    c) Compromising
    d) Avoiding

Recommended Answer: C) Compromising

15. Which mode is often employed to maintain peace in the short term, but may lead to unresolved issues?
    a) Competing
    b) Collaborating
    c) Compromising
    d) Avoiding

Recommended Answer: D) Avoiding

REFERENCES

Blake, R. R., & Mouton, J. S. (1964). *The Managerial Grid: The Key to Leadership Excellence*. Gulf Publishing Co.

Dreu, D. (1997). Using conflict in organizations. Sage.

Fisher, R., Ury, W., & Patton, B. (1981). *Getting to Yes: Negotiating Agreement Without Giving In*. Penguin.

Folger, J. P., Poole, M. S., & Stutman, R. K. (1997). *Working through conflict: Strategies for relationships, groups, and organizations*. HarperCollins College Publishers.

Jehn, K. A. (1995). A Multimethod Examination of the Benefits and Detriments of Intragroup Conflict. *Administrative Science Quarterly*, *40*(2), 256–282. doi:10.2307/2393638

Kilman, R. H. (2021). *Creating a Quantum Organization, The Whys and Hows of Implementing Eight Tracks for Long-Term Success*. Newport Coast: Kilman Diagnostics LLC.

Kilmann, R. H. (1975). Quantifying a Theoretical Model of Managerial Conflict. *Decision Sciences*, *6*(1), 57–67.

Kilmann, R. H. (1982). Conflict and Negotiations. In *Handbook of Industrial and Organizational Psychology* (pp. 771–826). Consulting Psychologists Press.

Kilmann, R. H., & Thomas, K. W. (1977). Developing a Forced-Choice Measure of Conflict-Handling Behavior: The 'MODE' Instrument. *Educational and Psychological Measurement*, *37*(2), 309–325. doi:10.1177/001316447703700204

Kolb, D. M., & Williams, J. (2000). Breakthrough Bargaining. *Harvard Business Review*, *78*(1), 130–137. PMID:11213701

Pruitt, D. G., & Carnevale, P. J. (1993). *Negotiation in Social Conflict*. Brooks/Cole.

Putnam, L. L., & Wilson, J. M. (1988). Communicative Strategies in Organizational Conflicts: Reliability and Validity of a Measurement Scale. *Communication Yearbook 11. Sage.*

Rahim, M. A. (1983). A Measure of Styles of Handling Interpersonal Conflict. *Academy of Management Journal*, *26*(2), 368–376. doi:10.2307/255985 PMID:10263067

Rubin, J. Z., Pruitt, D. G., & Kim, S. H. (1994). *Social Conflict: Escalation, Stalemate, and Settlement*. McGraw-Hill.

Thomas, K. W. (1976). Conflict and Conflict Management. In *Handbook of Industrial and Organizational Psychology*. Rand McNally.

Thomas, K. W. (1992). Conflict and Conflict Management: Reflections and Update. *Journal of Organizational Behavior, 13*(3), 265–274. doi:10.1002/job.4030130307

Thomas, K. W. (1996). The Social Construction of Conflict. *The Social Construction of Difference and Inequality*. Mayfield Publishing.

Thomas, K. W. (2000). *Intrinsic Motivation at Work: Building Energy & Commitment*. Berrett-Koehler Publishers.

Thomas, K. W., & Kilmann, R. H. (1974). *Thomas-Kilmann Conflict Mode Instrument*. Xicom.

Tjosvold, D. (1986). Effects of Approach to Controversy on Superiors' Incorporation of Subordinates' Information in Decision Making. *Academy of Management Journal, 29*(2), 233–246.

Wall, J. A. Jr, & Callister, R. J. (1995). Conflict and its management. *Journal of Management, 21*(3), 515–558. doi:10.1177/014920639502100306

Chapter 7
The Toulmin Argumentation Framework

ABSTRACT

The authors present Stephen Toulmin's incredibly powerful framework for analyzing the structure of arguments: the Toulmin argumentation framework, or TAF for short. Every argument terminates in a claim, the end conclusion of an argument. Every argument also makes use of evidence of some kind. In short, the evidence is the evidentiary support upon which an argument is built. The warrant, which is the because part of an argument, is the bridge between the evidence and the claim. The backing is the deeper set of background reasons why the warrant should be accepted. Finally, every argument has a rebuttal. The rebuttal is the full set of counter-arguments against every part of the main argument, for example, why the claim is dubious and makes no sense at all, why the evidence is flawed and therefore doesn't support the claim, why the warrant is deficient, and why the backing doesn't support the warrant.

"If you can't explain it simply, you don't understand it well enough." –Albert Einstein

Learning Objectives

- List the five components of the Toulmin Argumentation Framework (TAF)
- Differentiate between a 'claim' and a 'rebuttal'
- Illustrate an example of a 'warrant'
- Recognize the 'backing' for a 'warrant'

DOI: 10.4018/978-1-6684-6563-9.ch007

INTRODUCTION

In The Uses of Argument, the distinguished Philosopher Stephen Toulmin laid out an incredibly powerful framework for analyzing the structure of arguments. The Toulmin Argumentation Framework offers a practical approach to analyzing and constructing arguments. The framework consists of six elements (Figure 1): claim, data, warrant, backing, qualifier, and rebuttal. The claim is the main point or thesis, supported by data or evidence. The warrant links the data to the claim, while the backing strengthens the warrant. Qualifiers add nuance, specifying the conditions under which the claim holds true. Rebuttals anticipate counterarguments, offering responses to weaken them.

In practice, the framework provides a blueprint for constructing persuasive arguments. It starts with asserting a Claim, then offering Data or Evidence to support it. The Data or Evidences needs to be validated by a Warrant, which itself may require additional Backing. Once the core Claim-Data-Warrant structure is solid, the argument can be fine-tuned by adding Qualifiers and Rebuttals. Qualifiers make the argument more nuanced, avoiding overgeneralizations. Rebuttals address potential criticisms, making the argument more robust and persuasive.

The Toulmin framework is versatile, applicable to many fields including Law, Journalism, and Academia. It promotes clarity by breaking down arguments into their constituent elements. This approach allows for easy identification of the weaknesses in an argument, fostering more effective communication and debate. By using this structured mode of TAFl, individuals can create well-supported, nuanced arguments that can withstand scrutiny.

Every argument terminates in a Claim, the End Conclusion of an argument. Every argument also makes use of Data or Evidence of some kind. In short, the Evidence is the Evidentiary support upon which an argument is built. The Warrant, which is the Because part of an argument, is the Bridge between the Evidence and the Claim. That is, given the Evidence, the Warrant asserts why the Claim directly follows from it. Every argument also has a Backing. The Backing is the Deeper set of Background Reasons why the Warrant should be accepted. Finally, every argument has a Rebuttal. The Rebuttal is the full set of Counter-Arguments against every part of the main argument, for example, why the Claim is dubious and makes no sense at all, why the Evidence is flawed and therefore doesn't support the Claim, why the Warrant is deficient, and why the Backing doesn't support the Warrant.

An important example—which is also a classic type of argument—is the Claim that humans are mainly responsible for Global Warming. The Evidence is the Fact that based on their rigorous scientific studies—and thereby not on mere opinion alone--97% of Reputable Climate Scientists worldwide are in strong Agreement that humans are the Primary Cause of Global Warming. Thus, the Evidence is a mixture of Solid Scientific Evidence and the Substantial Agreement between a group of Reputable Experts. Notice that the Evidence itself is also the result, and thus the Claim, of a prior argument, namely the validity of the methods used in its production. The Warrant is the assertion that the Claim follows because it's based on the proper use of Scientific Method. The Backing is in fact the great body of Science itself, i.e., Scientific Reasoning, the Community of Scientists, etc. The Backing also consists of the Fact that all of the other causes that could account for Global Warming such as Natural Fluctuations in the Earth's Temperature have been eliminated and therefore humans remain as the primary cause. The Backing also asserts that there are no effective Rebuttals. They are the result of those who don't believe in Science or scientists, and therefore, the Claims of scientists are always to be treated with deep skepticism. The Counter Rebuttal, which is an integral part of the Backing, is that "Science has proved time and again to be the most reliable basis of Knowledge that humans have ever devised. Furthermore, Science is its own best Rebuttal in that it is self-correcting. Its results are always subject to revision. Indeed, Science constantly challenges itself more than any of its doubters could ever do."

Figure 1. Overview of the Toulmin argumentation framework

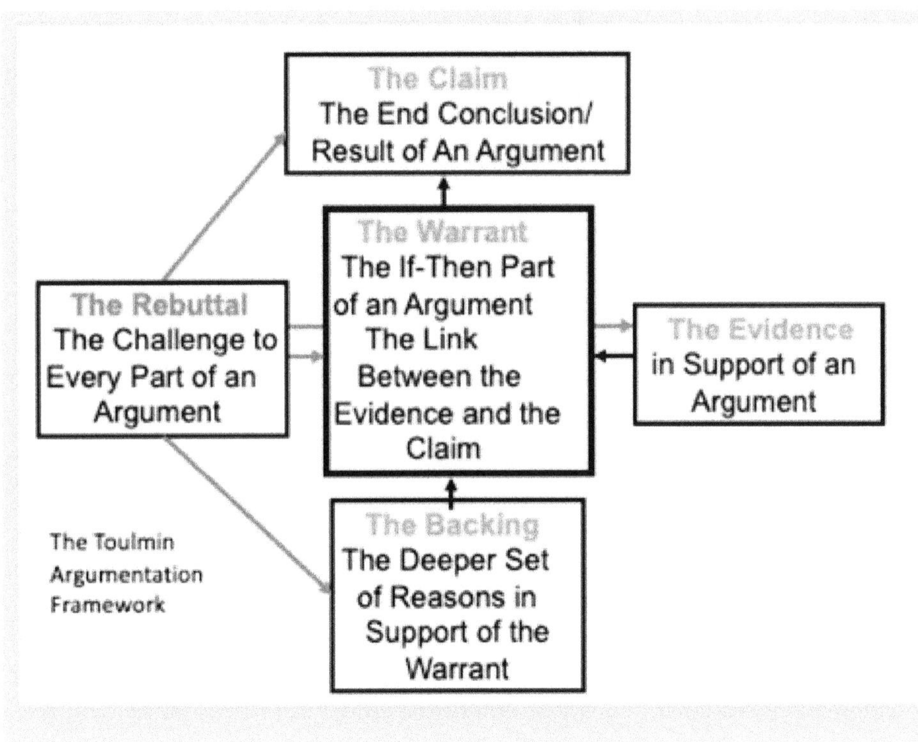

Of course, many, if not most, arguments do not follow the demanding standards of scientific reasoning. Indeed, its common to start with a favored Claim and then work backwards to justify it by deliberating concocting or finding Evidence and a Warrant that supports it. In this way, one makes it appear that one is following the proper procedures of argumentation when one is not. The Rebuttal to this is that we're always working backwards and forwards from a Claim so that there's nothing wrong with this per se.

By far, the most pernicious arguments are those for conspiracy theories. The Figure below outlines the essence of such arguments, if they can be dignified by calling them that. Every part is dubious which in fact is the Rebuttal.

Figure 2. TAF construct for conspiracy theories

APPLICATION TO "MESSY" PROBLEMS

Russell Ackoff's concept of "messy problems", as discussed in Chapter 1, refers to complex, interrelated issues that don't have straightforward solutions. In these situations, where the problem is multifaceted and involves various stakeholders with conflicting interests, the Toulmin Argumentation Framework can be particularly useful. The framework's structured approach helps dissect a messy problem into individual claims, supporting data, and warrants. By breaking down the complexity into manageable components, stakeholders can analyze the underlying assumptions, evidence, and logic that go into various proposed solutions. This methodical breakdown aids in spotting gaps in reasoning, unsupported assumptions, or areas requiring further evidence.

Qualifiers and rebuttals, two key elements of the Toulmin framework, can also bring clarity to messy problems. Qualifiers allow stakeholders to recognize the limitations or specific conditions under which a particular solution may work. This can lead to more realistic and nuanced proposals that consider the complexity of the issue. Rebuttals help in pre-emptively identifying objections or counterarguments, ensuring that solutions aren't blindsided by overlooked considerations. By using qualifiers and rebuttals, stakeholders can proactively address uncertainties and ambiguities, making their solutions more robust.

The Toulmin Argumentation Framework offers a systematic way to approach Ackoff's messy problems. The framework encourages clear reasoning by compartmentalizing an argument's elements, thereby simplifying complex issues for easier analysis and discussion. Qualifiers and rebuttals add layers of nuance and counter-argument, fostering solutions that are both comprehensive and resilient. The result is a more thoughtful, well-supported approach to tackling the inherent complexities of messy problems.

Example One: Wildfire Hazard Management

In the context of wildfire management, controlled burns are presented as an effective preventative measure. A 25% decrease in large wildfires in areas using this technique serves as the supporting data. The rationale is that controlled burns eliminate the dry vegetation that fuels larger fires, a point backed by fire ecologists. The method's effectiveness is acknowledged to depend on professional execution and weather conditions, and the risk of burns getting out of control is considered but deemed manageable with proper oversight. In this fictional example, we would construct something like this:

- **Claim**: Controlled burns are an effective method to reduce the risk of larger wildfires.
- **Data**: Regions that have implemented controlled burns show a 25% decrease in large wildfires.
- **Warrant**: Controlled burns eliminate dry vegetation that serves as fuel for larger fires.

- **Backing**: Forest service studies and fire ecologists provide empirical evidence supporting controlled burns.
- **Qualifier**: This method is effective when executed by trained professionals and under specific weather conditions.
- **Rebuttal**: Some may argue that controlled burns are risky and can get out of control, but protocols and expert oversight minimize this risk.

The claim here advocates for controlled burns as a preventive measure against larger wildfires. Data supporting a 25% decrease in large wildfires serves as the Evidence, and the Warrant explains that these burns eliminate the dry vegetation that fuels large fires. The argument is further reinforced by Backing from forest service studies and fire ecologists. The Qualifier outlines the conditions under which the method is effective, while the Rebuttal addresses the counter-argument that controlled burns can go awry, arguing that proper oversight minimizes this risk.

Supported by Data and Expert Opinion, the argument for controlled burns is robust and highlights proactive Risk Mitigation. The argument would be weakened if not carried out under specific conditions by trained professionals, and it doesn't fully address potential ecological impact. Most people would probably find the argument sound, but some may have concerns about the risks of controlled burns going awry or affecting local ecosystems.

Wildfire management is a complicated issue that involves ecology, public safety, and resource allocation. The argument for using controlled burns focuses this complexity by presenting a clear claim, supported by data and expert backing. Qualifiers about proper execution and weather conditions, as well as rebuttals addressing the risks, provide limitations and boundaries to the issue. This structured approach helps stakeholders understand the parameters of effective wildfire management, allowing for a more targeted and informed discussion in an otherwise messy problem area.

Example Two: Artificial Intelligence in Medicine

The argument in the medical field advocates for the use of AI algorithms for more accurate diagnoses. Clinical trials showing 10% higher accuracy rates for AI-backed diagnoses support the claim. The central reasoning is that AI can analyze more data and recognize patterns that may escape human experts. While peer-reviewed studies back this up, it is noted that the algorithm's effectiveness depends on quality data and its applicability varies across medical specializations. In this fictional example, we would construct something like this:

- **Claim**: AI algorithms can improve the accuracy of medical diagnoses.
- **Data**: In clinical trials, AI algorithms have shown a 10% higher diagnostic accuracy compared to experienced doctors.
- **Warrant**: Algorithms can analyze more data points and recognize patterns that humans might overlook.
- **Backing**: Peer-reviewed scientific papers support the efficacy of AI in medical diagnosis.
- **Qualifier**: The effectiveness of AI depends on the quality of data and the specific medical field.
- **Rebuttal**: Critics might argue that AI lacks the human touch in medicine, but this claim focuses solely on diagnostic accuracy.

The claim that AI algorithms can improve diagnostic accuracy is supported by Data from clinical trials. The Warrant explains why AI can be more accurate—it can process more data points and patterns than a human. Scientific papers back up this point, giving the argument more weight. The Qualifier addresses the limitations relating to data quality and field-specific applicability. The Rebuttal preempts the argument that AI cannot replace human intuition or empathy in medicine but refocuses the discussion on diagnostic accuracy.

The argument benefits from clinical trial Data and Scientific Backing, making it persuasive in terms of diagnostic accuracy. The argument could be stronger if it addressed Ethical considerations or the "human touch" that AI lacks. The general public might find the potential for improved diagnosis compelling but could have reservations about over-reliance on technology in healthcare.

Medical diagnosis is a complicated field involving various expertise, patient variables, and ethical concerns. By arguing that AI can improve diagnostic accuracy, the Toulmin framework simplifies this intricate issue. Data from clinical trials serves as compelling evidence, while Qualifiers ensure the technology's limitations are considered. Rebuttals acknowledge potential criticisms about the lack of a human touch, offering a more balanced perspective. This gives stakeholders a structured way to evaluate the potential and limits of AI in medicine, making the messy problem more navigable.

Example Three: Autonomous Vehicles

The debate around autonomous vehicles centers on their potential to reduce traffic fatalities. Citing human error as the cause of 94% of road accidents, the argument posits that autonomous vehicles, engineered to obey traffic laws, will reduce fatalities. Preliminary studies affirm this, but the Claim is Qualified by the technology's maturity and thorough testing. Potential machine failures are acknowledged as a counterpoint but considered less frequent than human errors. In this fictional example, we would construct something like this:

- **Claim**: Widespread adoption of autonomous vehicles will reduce traffic-related fatalities.
- **Data**: Research indicates that 94% of road accidents are caused by human error, which autonomous vehicles can eliminate.
- **Warrant**: Autonomous vehicles are designed to follow traffic rules consistently, without the influence of human factors like fatigue or distraction.
- **Backing**: Preliminary studies on autonomous vehicles show fewer instances of traffic violations compared to human drivers.
- **Qualifier**: The claim is true assuming the technology is mature and has undergone rigorous testing for all driving conditions.
- **Rebuttal**: Skeptics may argue that machine failures can still cause accidents, but the rate would be lower than human-caused incidents.

The Claim here focuses on the potential for autonomous vehicles to reduce traffic fatalities, backed by compelling Data regarding human error in accidents. The Warrant connects this data to the autonomous vehicles' engineered reliability, and this point is further backed by studies comparing human and autonomous driving. The Qualifier adds a layer of caution by mentioning the need for mature technology and rigorous testing. Finally, the Rebuttal addresses concerns about machine failure but argues that such events are expected to be less frequent than human errors.

The Claim is substantiated by compelling statistics attributing the vast majority of accidents to human error, an element removed by autonomous driving. The argument may lose ground if autonomous vehicle technology is not yet sufficiently mature or fails to consider various driving conditions. Many would find the promise of safer roads appealing but could be skeptical about the technology's readiness and potential glitches.

Traffic safety is a multifaceted issue that involves human behavior, vehicle design, and regulatory considerations. The argument that autonomous vehicles can reduce traffic-related fatalities distills this complexity into a focused Claim supported by Data and Warrants. By setting Qualifiers about the technology's maturity and Rebutting concerns about machine failures, the argument provides boundaries to the messy problem. This helps policymakers and the public identify where further research or regulation might be needed, making the debate more structured and productive.

Example Four: Safety Culture in Manufacturing

In a manufacturing setting grappling with rising accidents, the argument posits that increased safety training will lower incidents. Supported by data showing a 30% reduction in accidents in similar scenarios, the reasoning hinges on the idea that training improves risk awareness and prevention. The argument gains strength from expert endorsement but acknowledges that the quality and mandatory nature of training are crucial. It also anticipates the Counterclaim that equipment upgrades are also essential but argues that training is a significant first step. In this fictional example, we would construct something like this:

- **Claim**: Investing in more safety training for employees will reduce the number of workplace accidents.
- **Data**: Studies show that companies with robust safety training programs report 30% fewer incidents compared to those without such programs.
- **Warrant**: Safety training educates employees about risks and preventative measures, thereby increasing their ability to avoid accidents.
- **Backing**: Safety experts and occupational health research support the effectiveness of training in reducing workplace accidents.
- **Qualifier**: This claim holds true if the training programs are up-to-date, comprehensive, and mandatory for all employees.
- **Rebuttal**: Critics may argue that training alone is insufficient and must be combined with equipment upgrades.

In this example, the Claim is that investing in safety training will reduce accidents. The Data from studies serves as the Evidence supporting the Claim, while the Warrant provides the logical connection between the Data and the Claim. The Backing from safety experts lends additional credibility to the Warrant. The Qualifier acknowledges that the quality and mandatory nature of the training are critical for the argument to hold. Finally, the Rebuttal anticipates and addresses a potential counterargument—that equipment upgrades are also necessary—by acknowledging it but not allowing it to invalidate the primary Claim.

The argument's strength lies in its evidence-based approach, using Data that correlates safety training with a reduction in workplace incidents. Expert backing adds credibility. The argument could be weakened if the quality of training is not considered, or if it overlooks other contributing factors like outdated machinery. A regular person might find this argument compelling but may question whether training alone is sufficient without considering equipment and environmental factors.

The Toulmin Argumentation Framework brings order to the inherently messy problem of workplace safety by identifying a clear Claim—increased safety training reduces accidents—and supporting it with concrete Data. By using Warrants and Backing from experts, the argument builds credibility and navigates the complexities surrounding safety measures. Qualifiers and Rebuttals add nuance, acknowledging that while training is crucial, it isn't the sole factor in enhancing workplace safety. This structured approach helps stakeholders pinpoint specific areas of agreement and contention, aiding in more focused, evidence-based discussions.

Example Five: Banking Industry

The discussion in the banking sector focuses on combating online fraud through implementing two-factor authentication (2FA). Reports of a 40% reduction in fraud cases in banks using 2FA bolster the argument. The logic lies in the added security layer that 2FA provides, endorsed by cybersecurity experts. However, the argument is contingent on customers having the means for secondary authentication and acknowledges the inconvenience factor as a minor trade-off for enhanced security. In this fictional example, we would construct something like this:

- **Claim**: Implementing two-factor authentication (2FA) will significantly reduce instances of online banking fraud.
- **Data**: Financial institutions using 2FA have reported a 40% reduction in online fraud cases.
- **Warrant**: 2FA adds an extra layer of security that makes it harder for unauthorized users to access accounts.
- **Backing**: Cybersecurity experts and academic research endorse 2FA as an effective method to deter fraud.
- **Qualifier**: This claim is valid assuming that customers have access to secondary authentication methods like smartphones.
- **Rebuttal**: Critics may argue that 2FA can be cumbersome for users, but the security benefits outweigh the inconvenience.

In this argument, the Claim is clearly stated: 2FA will reduce fraud. The Data, a 40% reduction in fraud cases, serves as empirical support, and the Warrant makes a logical link between 2FA and increased security. The Backing comes from expert opinions in cybersecurity, reinforcing the argument's credibility. Qualifiers indicate that the Claim assumes customers can perform secondary authentication, and the Rebuttal deals with the inconvenience aspect by stating that the benefits are significant enough to warrant the inconvenience.

The argument is strong due to the concrete data showing a 40% reduction in fraud cases with 2FA, backed by cybersecurity experts. It doesn't fully address potential implementation challenges or the inconvenience to older or less tech-savvy customers. Most people would likely view this as a reasonable trade-off for enhanced security, although some might find the extra authentication step cumbersome.

The discussion in the banking sector focuses on combating online fraud through implementing two-factor authentication (2FA). Reports of a 40% reduction in fraud cases in banks using 2FA bolster the argument. The logic lies in the added security layer that 2FA provides, endorsed by cybersecurity experts. However, the argument is contingent on customers having the means for secondary authentication and acknowledges the inconvenience factor as a minor trade-off for enhanced security.

MORAL ARGUMENTS

We note that some of the most important arguments are clearly Moral. (Notice that this statement is itself an important argument.) They fall into two general types, ST/NT versus SF/NF. ST/NT are based on Formal Theories of Ethics. For example, Utilitarianism, which is the basis for modern Cost-Benefit Analysis, asserts that an act is potentially Ethical if its Benefits exceed its Costs or Disbenefits. This is in fact the Warrant. The point is that what's Ethical is determined by purely impersonal means, i.e., calculations. Thus, the Evidence consists of a determination of the Benefits and Disbenefits associated with an act, and thus which is greater. The Rebuttal is: "Who determines the Benefits versus Disbenefits? That is, what's Beneficial to whom?"

In sharp contrast, SF/NF Moral arguments consist of deeply personal Moral Beliefs, i.e., what one's close friends, family members, social groups with whom one identifies believe strongly is Righteous and therefore Moral. One of the strongest examples is Pro-Choice versus Pro-Life. The arguments are grounded in deeply personal beliefs in a Woman's Right to Choose versus the Sanctify of Life.

CONCLUDING REMARKS

The Toulmin Argumentation Framework offers a structured way to analyze and present arguments. It breaks an argument into six components: Claim, Data, Warrant, Backing, Qualifier, and Rebuttal. These elements clarify the argument's central point, the Evidence supporting it, the logic connecting the evidence to the claim, additional support for the logic, any conditions or limitations, and counterarguments.

In dealing with messy problems, the framework shines by organizing complex issues into manageable parts. The Claim targets a specific solution or viewpoint, while the Warrant and Data offer reasons and evidence. Qualifiers add nuances, acknowledging that real-world issues rarely have one-size-fits-all solutions. Rebuttals consider opposing views, forcing the argument to confront other perspectives and thereby strengthen its own position.

By dissecting an argument in this manner, the framework exposes underlying assumptions and the quality of existing evidence. It demands rigor in both the logic and the Data supporting an argument, helping identify weak points that may need addressing. This organized approach enables clearer communication and more effective problem-solving, especially in tackling complicated, multi-faceted issues.

COMPREHENSION EXERCISES

1. **Which component of the Toulmin Argumentation Framework states the main point being argued?**
   a) Warrant
   b) Claim
   c) Data
   d) Backing
2. **What does the 'Data' represent in the Toulmin Framework?**
   a) The main argument
   b) Supporting evidence
   c) Counterarguments
   d) Logic connecting the claim to evidence
3. **What is the role of the 'Warrant' in an argument?**
   a) To provide additional support for the claim
   b) To connect the data to the claim
   c) To outline the limitations of the argument
   d) To state the counterargument
4. **What does 'Backing' provide in the Toulmin Framework?**
   a) Counterarguments
   b) Further support for the warrant
   c) The main argument
   d) Limitations of the claim
5. **What are 'Qualifiers' used for in the Toulmin Framework?**
   a) Presenting counterarguments
   b) Specifying conditions or limitations of the claim
   c) Strengthening the warrant
   d) Providing evidence for the claim

6. **What is the purpose of the 'Rebuttal' in an argument?**
   a) To introduce the claim
   b) To provide evidence
   c) To address counterarguments
   d) To support the warrant
7. **Which component is optional in the Toulmin Framework?**
   a) Claim
   b) Data
   c) Qualifier
   d) Warrant
8. **How does the Toulmin Framework help in dealing with 'messy problems'?**
   a) By ignoring them
   b) By simplifying them too much
   c) By breaking them into manageable parts
   d) By focusing only on evidence
9. **What can you identify using the Toulmin Framework?**
   a) Weak points in an argument
   b) The strongest counterargument only
   c) The limitations of the data only
   d) None of the above
10. **Which element of the Toulmin Framework would you examine to understand the underlying assumptions in an argument?**
   a) Data
   b) Warrant
   c) Claim
   d) Rebuttal

REFERENCES

Blair, J. A. (1996). The Possibility and Actuality of Visual Arguments. *Argumentation and Advocacy*, *33*(1), 23–39.

Brockriede, W. (1979). Where Is Argument? *Journal of the American Forensic Association*, *16*, 1–9.

Crosswhite, J. (1996). *The Rhetoric of Reason: Writing and the Attractions of Argument*. University of Wisconsin Press.

Eemeren, F. H. (1992). Argumentation, Communication, and Fallacies: A Pragma-Dialectical Perspective. Lawrence Erlbaum Associates.

Eemeren, F. H. (1996). Fundamentals of Argumentation Theory: A Handbook of Historical Backgrounds and Contemporary Developments. Lawrence Erlbaum Associates.

Ennis, R. H. (1962). A Concept of Critical Thinking. *Harvard Educational Review*, *32*(1), 81–111.

Fischer, M. (1989). Toulmin's Model and the Solving of Ill-Structured Problems. *Argumentation*, *3*(2), 185–204.

Freeman, J. B. (1991). *Dialectics and the Macrostructure of Arguments: A Theory of Argument Structure*. Foris Publications. doi:10.1515/9783110875843

Govier, T. (1987). *Problems in Argument Analysis and Evaluation*. Foris Publications. doi:10.1515/9783110859249

Hitchcock, D. (1998). Toulmin's Warrants. *Argumentation*, *12*(3), 367–380. doi:10.1023/A:1007780507894

Johnson, R. H., & Anthony Blair, J. (2006). *Logical Self-Defense*. IDEA.

Kahane, H. (1971). *Logic and Contemporary Rhetoric: The Use of Reason in Everyday Life*. Wadsworth Publishing.

Kienpointner, M. (1996). How to Classify Arguments. *Argumentation*, *10*(4), 413–430.

O'Keefe, D. J. (1977). Two Concepts of Argument. *Journal of the American Forensic Association*, *13*(3), 121–128.

Perelman, C., & Olbrechts-Tyteca, L. (1969). *The New Rhetoric: A Treatise on Argumentation*. University of Notre Dame Press.

Toulmin, S. (1958). *The Uses of Argument*. Cambridge University Press.

Toulmin, S., Rieke, R., & Janik, A. (1979). *An Introduction to Reasoning*. Macmillan Publishing Co., Inc.

Walton, D. N. (2008). *Informal Logic: A Pragmatic Approach*. Cambridge University Press.

Wenzel, J. W. (1990). Three Perspectives on Argumentation. In R. Trapp & J. Schuetz (Eds.), *Perspectives on Argumentation: Essays in Honor of Wayne Brockriede* (pp. 9–26). Waveland Press.

Willard, C. A. (1989). *A Theory of Argumentation*. University of Alabama Press.

APPENDIX - COMPREHENSION EXERCISES: SOLUTIONS

1. **Which component of the Toulmin Argumentation Framework states the main point being argued?**
   a) Warrant
   b) Claim
   c) Data
   d) Backing

Recommended Answer: B) Claim

2. **What does the 'Data' represent in the Toulmin Framework?**
   a) The main argument
   b) Supporting evidence
   c) Counterarguments
   d) Logic connecting the claim to evidence

Recommended Answer: B) Supporting evidence

3. **What is the role of the 'Warrant' in an argument?**
   a) To provide additional support for the claim
   b) To connect the data to the claim
   c) To outline the limitations of the argument
   d) To state the counterargument

Recommended Answer: B) To connect the data to the claim

4. **What does 'Backing' provide in the Toulmin Framework?**
   a) Counterarguments
   b) Further support for the warrant
   c) The main argument
   d) Limitations of the claim

Recommended Answer: B) Further support for the warrant

5. **What are 'Qualifiers' used for in the Toulmin Framework?**
   a) Presenting counterarguments
   b) Specifying conditions or limitations of the claim
   c) Strengthening the warrant
   d) Providing evidence for the claim

Recommended Answer: B) Specifying conditions or limitations of the claim

6. **What is the purpose of the 'Rebuttal' in an argument?**
   a) To introduce the claim
   b) To provide evidence
   c) To address counterarguments
   d) To support the warrant

Recommended Answer: C) To address counterarguments

7. **Which component is optional in the Toulmin Framework?**
   a) Claim
   b) Data
   c) Qualifier
   d) Warrant

Recommended Answer: C) Qualifier

8. **How does the Toulmin Framework help in dealing with 'messy problems'?**
   a) By ignoring them
   b) By simplifying them too much
   c) By breaking them into manageable parts
   d) By focusing only on evidence

Recommended Answer: C) By breaking them into manageable parts

9. **What can you identify using the Toulmin Framework?**
   a) Weak points in an argument
   b) The strongest counterargument only
   c) The limitations of the data only
   d) None of the above

Recommended Answer: A) Weak points in an argument

10. **Which element of the Toulmin Framework would you examine to understand the underlying assumptions in an argument?**
   a) Data
   b) Warrant
   c) Claim
   d) Rebuttal

Recommended Answer: B) Warrant

Chapter 8
Applying the Concepts:
Case Study of Climate Change and Hurricanes

ABSTRACT

In this chapter the authors apply the concepts presented previously in the book on an example of a complex messy problem: future increase in hurricane frequency and intensity as a result of climate change. They start by outlining the highly interrelated nature of the topic and acknowledge that this is an ill-defined, unstructured, and unbounded problem. Next, they outline some problem treatment approaches as well as mitigation solution timeframes. This evaluation helps break down the larger problem into smaller components as well as assisting us in providing some definition, structure, and boundary. The authors will view the initial complex problem from multiple perspectives (ISTJ, ENFP, and INTJ), where each offers valuable insights, emphasizing the importance of integrating diverse perspectives in understanding and approaching complex problems.

"What I hear I forget, what I see I remember, what I do I know." — Unknown

INTRODUCTION

In this chapter we apply the concepts presented previously in the book on an example of a complex messy problem: future increase in hurricane frequency and intensity as a result of climate change. We start by outlining the highly interrelated nature of

DOI: 10.4018/978-1-6684-6563-9.ch008

the topic and acknowledge that this is an ill-defined, unstructured, and unbounded problem. Next, we outline some problem treatment approaches as well as mitigation solution timeframes. This evaluation helps us break down the larger problem into smaller components as well as assisting us in providing some definition, structure, and boundary. We will view the initial complex problem from multiple perspectives (ISTJ, ENFP, and INTJ)\, where each offers valuable insights, emphasizing the importance of integrating diverse perspectives in understanding and approaching complex problems.

Once a well-specified problem has been delineated, we will apply the five Inquiry Systems in an attempt to identify potential mitigation options. Key/fundamental assumptions will be identified and inventoried. SWOT analyses are used to examine the different facets of the potential mitigations. The Toulmin Argumentation Framework will be leveraged to enhance the mitigation communication to the community. This framework breaks down arguments into their core components, making the logic behind proposals transparent and easily understandable. By presenting the claim, grounds, warrant, backing, rebuttal, and qualifier, the Toulmin method ensures that stakeholders not only understand the what and why of a proposal but also see the evidence and rationale supporting it.

This robust method can be equally applied to various facets of the overarching issue of uncertainty surrounding increased hurricane intensity and frequency. Whether one is examining the socio-economic implications, environmental repercussions, or infrastructural challenges posed by such climatic uncertainties, the structured approach ensures that each dimension is explored with depth, precision, and clarity.

HISTORIC HURRICANE BEHAVIOR AND COMMUNITY RESPONSE

Historically, hurricanes have exhibited seasonal patterns, predominantly forming over warm ocean waters near the equator. These storms gained their energy from the ocean's heat, escalating in strength as they moved over warmer waters. The rotation of the Earth caused them to spin, and they generally moved westward, driven by trade winds. They followed typical paths, with their routes and intensity somewhat predictable based on previous storms and established meteorological models. Over the past century, the frequency of hurricanes has varied, with certain decades experiencing more active hurricane seasons than others.

Communities historically responded to hurricanes with a mix of preparation and reaction. In areas prone to these natural disasters, building codes were established to ensure structures could withstand hurricane-force winds. Mangroves, sea walls, and levees were developed as barriers against storm surges. Evacuation plans were set in place, with designated shelters for residents. Despite these preparations, many communities, especially those without the resources or previous experience with major storms, found themselves vulnerable to the destructive power of these cyclones.

Over time, as meteorological tools advanced, early warning systems became more refined, allowing communities more time to prepare. Satellite imagery, hurricane tracking, and predictive modeling offered a window into the storm's potential path and intensity. This technological progress, combined with increased community awareness and government initiatives, aimed to minimize loss of life and property damage. Yet, despite these advancements, disparate economic socio-status in coastal areas challenged overall community resilience.

CLIMATE CHANGE AND UNCERTAINTY IN FUTURE HURRICANE BEHAVIOR

For our hypothetical case study example, recent global records suggest an upward trend in intense hurricanes. While the total number of storms might not have drastically increased, the frequency of high-category hurricanes, which carry devastating wind speeds and immense water volume, has shown an alarming rise. The once somewhat predictable paths of these storms are now characterized by greater variability. This increased unpredictability, coupled with a trend towards more intense hurricanes, makes preparedness and response efforts challenging for even the most well-equipped communities.

Storm Surge Threat

The rising sea levels, attributed to global climate change, have amplified the threat of storm surges during hurricanes. These surges, which are essentially elevated sea levels driven by the force of the hurricane, wreak havoc on coastal regions. With higher baseline sea levels, even a moderate storm surge can result in devastating flooding, inundating homes, eroding coastlines, and causing billions in property damage. The economic and human toll of such events, especially in densely populated coastal cities, is enormous.

Escalating Wind Speeds

Alongside increased storm surges, hurricanes have been exhibiting higher wind speeds. The destructive power of a hurricane doesn't increase linearly with wind speed; it grows exponentially. This means that a small increase in wind speed can result in significantly higher damage potential. Buildings, infrastructure, and vegetation that might have withstood hurricanes in the past are now at a higher risk. The resultant power outages, structural damages, and transportation disruptions can leave communities crippled for days, weeks, or even longer.

Rainfall Intensity

Beyond storm surges and wind speeds, hurricanes are dropping more rain than they used to. The warmer atmosphere holds more moisture, leading to hurricanes that unleash torrential downpours over areas, causing freshwater flooding. This kind of flooding, separate from the saltwater flooding caused by storm surges, can inundate vast areas, especially if the hurricane moves slowly. Such scenarios were observed in hurricanes like Harvey, which stalled over Houston in 2017, dumping massive amounts of rain and causing catastrophic flooding.

Facing an Uncertain Future

The combined threats of uncertain hurricane paths, greater storm surges, intensified wind speeds, and heavier rainfall present a grim outlook for the future. As the global climate continues to change, understanding and adapting to these shifts is of paramount importance. Communities, governments, and organizations must evolve their strategies and reinforce their infrastructures to brace for these amplified threats and ensure the safety and resilience of vulnerable populations.

UNCERTAINTY OF FUTURE HURRICANE BEHAVIOR AS A COMPLEX MESSY PROBLEM

The uncertainty surrounding the future intensity and frequency of hurricanes epitomizes a complex messy problem. Unlike conventional issues that may have straightforward solutions, predicting the behavior of hurricanes involves myriad interconnected variables, ranging from global temperature changes and sea-level rise to local geographic and sociopolitical factors. These elements don't function in isolation but interact in intricate, often unpredictable ways. This unpredictability is further magnified by feedback loops: for instance, as coastal areas suffer damage and erosion, they may become even more vulnerable to future hurricanes, leading to more extensive damage in subsequent storms. The problem is thus not just about understanding the natural phenomena, but also about grappling with the cascading effects on human systems, economies, and infrastructures.

Confronting Messy Problems

Complex, ill-defined problems, often referred to as "wicked problems", can be daunting due to their intricacies and apparent lack of boundaries. They are ever-evolving, deeply interconnected, and lack a clear, definitive solution. Formulating a clear and concise problem statement on the topic of future hurricane uncertainties is challenging due to the multifaceted nature of the issue.

Hurricanes, as natural phenomena, intersect with a myriad of factors including meteorological patterns, oceanic temperatures, human-induced climate change, and socio-economic elements in coastal regions. Their unpredictability in frequency and intensity further compounds the issue. Additionally, human responses, infrastructural preparedness, and socio-economic disparities among affected communities introduce layers of complexity. It's not merely a scientific or environmental challenge but a socio-economic and political one as well. Distilling such a vast, interconnected web of factors into a singular, concise statement is inherently difficult, as any simplification risks overlooking critical nuances or stakeholder perspectives.

Messy problems are inherently ill-structured and ill-defined, making them particularly elusive to conventional problem-solving approaches. Their ill-structured nature means that they don't fit neatly into established categories or frameworks; they sprawl across disciplines, intertwining with various systems and often producing unexpected interactions and outcomes. Their ill-defined aspect adds to the complexity, as the parameters of the problem are ambiguous, its boundaries are unclear, and there's often no consensus on what the core issue truly is. The inherent vagueness and intricacy in these problems make it challenging to pinpoint a starting point or to determine a direct cause-and-effect relationship. Confronting such problems demands adaptive thinking, multi-disciplinary collaboration, and a tolerance for ambiguity, as traditional linear methods often fall short in providing comprehensive solutions.

Approaching messy problems with potential treatments—absolve, resolve, solve, dissolve—can introduce a semblance of definition and structure to an otherwise ambiguous situation. Each treatment offers a distinct lens, guiding stakeholders in identifying specific intervention strategies. For instance, the 'resolve' approach might spotlight immediate system improvements, whereas 'dissolve' would push for a broader reframing. Further clarity can be achieved by categorizing actions into short-term, medium-term, and long-term timeframes. Short-term actions might focus on immediate relief and rapid response, medium-term actions could center on improving existing infrastructure and systems, and long-term strategies might target foundational changes or transformative innovations. By merging problem treatments with phased actions, we create a systematic roadmap that not only delineates the complex problem but also organizes the path forward, turning abstract challenges into actionable steps.

Problem Treatments

Different problem treatments—absolve, resolve, solve, and dissolve—offer varied approaches to managing the complex messy problem of future hurricane uncertainties. Each treatment offers a unique lens, allowing stakeholders to tailor their strategies according to available resources, community needs, and long-term visions. Let's consider how me might approach each of these treatment strategies of our hypothetical case study.

Absolving

The absolve approach to our complex hurricane problem would entail a passive acceptance of the inevitable forces of nature. Rather than implementing aggressive interventions, this strategy would focus on natural adaptation and recovery. Communities might prioritize post-hurricane rehabilitation and humanitarian aid, embracing the reality of these natural disasters as an inherent part of coastal life. By absolving responsibility for proactive measures, the emphasis shifts to resilience, building mental and emotional preparedness, and ensuring the swiftness of recovery mechanisms after each storm event.

Resolving

Opting to resolve the hurricane challenge means introducing incremental adjustments to our current systems to better cope with these weather phenomena. This could involve refining evacuation procedures, enhancing emergency communication channels, or fortifying existing infrastructure against moderate storms. While not overhauling the entire system, the resolve approach improves and tweaks the present frameworks, ensuring a smoother, more coordinated response when hurricanes strike, ultimately reducing their detrimental impacts on communities.

Solving

The solve treatment delves deeper, seeking to drastically reduce or even eliminate the adverse impacts of hurricanes. This might involve the construction of innovative sea defenses, like advanced sea walls or flood barriers, or the development of state-of-the-art early warning systems using cutting-edge technology. The objective is to not just mitigate but to fundamentally change our relationship with hurricanes, turning high-risk areas into zones where hurricanes pose minimal threats to lives and property.

Dissolving

Dissolving the problem involves a complete reframing of the issue. Instead of zeroing in on hurricanes as isolated events, the focus pivots to broader, systemic concerns—like addressing the global climate change that intensifies these storms. By mitigating root causes, such as greenhouse gas emissions or deforestation, the aim is to alter the very conditions that exacerbate hurricane development and ferocity. It's an acknowledgment that the true solution may lie not in battling individual hurricanes but in reshaping the global environment that spawns them.

Approaches for Mitigation Solutions

Segmenting the problem statement into short-term, medium-term, and long-term efforts provides a structured approach to tackling the vast intricacies of a complex problem. By compartmentalizing the issue into distinct time frames, we can prioritize immediate concerns and methodically build towards more comprehensive, sustainable solutions. The short-term focuses on immediate vulnerabilities and rapid responses, laying the groundwork for the subsequent phases. The medium-term delves deeper, harnessing accumulated data and community engagement to strengthen preparedness. Meanwhile, the long-term vision anchors on systemic transformations, ensuring resilience against future uncertainties. This phased methodology not only makes the challenge more manageable but also ensures that urgent needs aren't overshadowed by future concerns. Instead of feeling overwhelmed by the magnitude of the entire problem, this approach lets stakeholders address the challenge in digestible portions, facilitating continuous progress and adaptation.

In the short term, the immediate goal is to reduce the vulnerability of communities to impending hurricanes. This timeframe may be on the order of months to a few years. This requires a responsive strategy that prioritizes human safety and minimizes property damage. Vulnerability assessments are imperative, pinpointing areas of greatest risk, whether due to geography, infrastructure weaknesses, or population density. Based on this, communities can optimize the allocation of resources, such as reinforcing flood barriers in the most exposed zones or ensuring that evacuation routes are clear and accessible. Concurrently, rapid communication systems must be implemented and tested. These systems would alert residents of imminent threats and provide them with clear instructions for safety, ensuring that even those without personal means of receiving warnings—such as the elderly or disadvantaged—are reached. Potential short-term actions might include:

- **Vulnerability Assessment:** Evaluate current community vulnerabilities to hurricanes by reviewing infrastructure, population distribution, and emergency services. Identify immediate areas for improvement to reduce the impact of impending storms.
- **Emergency Preparedness** Training: Conduct regular community workshops and drills to ensure residents are well-informed about evacuation routes, emergency shelters, and basic survival techniques during intense hurricane conditions.
- **Stockpile Essential Supplies:** Create centralized stockpiles of food, water, medicines, and other essentials that can be swiftly distributed in the immediate aftermath of a hurricane.
- **Enhance Communication Systems:** Upgrade early warning systems to provide timely alerts to residents. This includes the use of apps, SMS, and community radio to relay crucial information.
- **Temporary Infrastructure Reinforcements:** Implement temporary measures like sandbag barriers or portable flood walls to reduce the impact of storm surge in vulnerable coastal areas.
- **Rapid Response Units:** Establish teams equipped with resources like boats, vehicles, and first-aid kits, ready to be deployed for immediate rescue and relief operations during and after a hurricane.
- **Infrastructure Inspection:** Regularly inspect key infrastructure like bridges, roads, and drainage systems to ensure they can withstand increased precipitation and wind speeds, making quick repairs where necessary.
- **Community Relocation:** For extremely vulnerable regions, consider temporary relocations during high-risk periods, moving residents to safer zones to reduce potential casualties.
- **Public Awareness Campaigns:** Launch information campaigns via local media, community meetings, and social media emphasizing the risks of intensified hurricanes and urging residents to take necessary precautions.

The medium term focuses on a deeper understanding and preparedness. This timeframe may be on the order of 5 to 10 years. Analyzing historical hurricane patterns provides insights into possible future scenarios and allows communities to develop contingency plans. With the data at hand, predictive modeling can help in forecasting potential hurricane paths and intensities, thus providing earlier warnings. This period also emphasizes community engagement and education. By conducting workshops, drills, and public awareness campaigns, individuals become better equipped to respond effectively during emergencies. This not only reduces the strain on emergency services but also fosters a culture of self-reliance and community cooperation. Infrastructure updates, though not as extensive as long-term redevelopment, such as improved drainage systems and the establishment of more hurricane shelters, are also key components of medium-term mitigation.

- **Historical Trend Analysis:** Study past hurricane patterns and impacts in the region to discern possible patterns or recurring vulnerabilities, providing a foundation for predictive modeling.
- **Infrastructure Upgrades:** Begin retrofitting existing infrastructure such as bridges, roads, and public buildings to ensure they can withstand stronger hurricanes. Enhance drainage systems to manage increased rainfall effectively and reduce flooding.
- **Urban Planning and Zoning:** Reevaluate and adjust zoning laws in hurricane-prone areas. Prioritize the development of elevated constructions, green buffers, and barriers in vulnerable coastal regions to counteract storm surges.
- **Localized Weather Monitoring Systems:** Invest in more advanced localized weather monitoring and prediction technologies. This can allow for more precise and earlier warnings, granting communities more preparation time.
- **Research and Development:** Allocate funds and resources towards researching new construction materials and techniques that are resilient against strong winds, heavy precipitation, and storm surges. This could also include research into natural barriers like mangrove cultivation, which can act as buffers against storm surges.
- **Educational Initiatives:** Implement school and community college curriculums that educate on climate change, its impacts, and individual roles in mitigation and adaptation. A well-informed populace can make proactive decisions about their safety and property.
- **Insurance and Financial Instruments:** Collaborate with the insurance sector to develop policies that encourage homeowners and businesses to adopt hurricane-resistant measures. Additionally, introduce financial instruments or subsidies that support the adoption of such measures, making it economically viable for a wider section of the population.
- **Elevated Infrastructure and Transportation Networks:** For critical infrastructure within vulnerable zones, consider elevation strategies. Raise key transportation networks, such as roads and railways, above projected flood levels. This would ensure continuity in mobility even during and after severe weather events. When considering new urban transit projects, make elevated or resilient designs standard. Additionally, promote the elevation of vital utilities and services to ensure continuous operation during floods.

- **Green and Blue Infrastructure Integration:** Incorporate green (vegetative) and blue (water) infrastructure within urban planning. This could involve developing green rooftops, permeable pavements, and urban wetlands. These interventions not only absorb excess rainwater, reducing flash flooding risks, but also act as cooling agents, reducing the urban heat island effect. Coupling this with the creation of artificial lakes or expanding existing water bodies can help store excess water and control its release, mitigating flood risks.
- **Clustered Community Design:** Re-envision city planning by promoting clustered communities or nodes, whereby essential services, residential areas, and business zones are concentrated in specific areas, well-protected against extreme weather events. These clusters, strategically positioned, can be interconnected by resilient transport links. This approach reduces sprawl, making it easier to manage and protect urban communities against hurricanes.
- **Retreat and Relocation Strategies:** Recognizing that some areas might become too risky for habitation due to recurrent extreme events, develop a planned retreat strategy. Incentivize residents in highly vulnerable areas to relocate to safer zones through subsidies, tax breaks, or direct financial assistance. Coupled with no-build zoning regulations, this ensures that over time, the most at-risk regions see reduced human habitation, minimizing potential human and economic losses.
- **Elevated Infrastructure and Transportation Networks:** For critical infrastructure within vulnerable zones, consider elevation strategies. Raise key transportation networks, such as roads and railways, above projected flood levels. This would ensure continuity in mobility even during and after severe weather events. When considering new urban transit projects, make elevated or resilient designs standard. Additionally, promote the elevation of vital utilities and services to ensure continuous operation during floods.
- **Green and Blue Infrastructure Integration:** Incorporate green (vegetative) and blue (water) infrastructure within urban planning. This could involve developing green rooftops, permeable pavements, and urban wetlands. These interventions not only absorb excess rainwater, reducing flash flooding risks, but also act as cooling agents, reducing the urban heat island effect. Coupling this with the creation of artificial lakes or expanding existing water bodies can help store excess water and control its release, mitigating flood risks.
- **Clustered Community Design:** Re-envision city planning by promoting clustered communities or nodes, whereby essential services, residential areas, and business zones are concentrated in specific areas, well-protected against extreme weather events. These clusters, strategically positioned, can be interconnected by resilient transport links. This approach reduces sprawl, making it easier to manage and protect urban communities against hurricanes.

- **Retreat and Relocation Strategies:** Recognizing that some areas might become too risky for habitation due to recurrent extreme events, develop a planned retreat strategy. Incentivize residents in highly vulnerable areas to relocate to safer zones through subsidies, tax breaks, or direct financial assistance. Coupled with no-build zoning regulations, this ensures that over time, the most at-risk regions see reduced human habitation, minimizing potential human and economic losses.

The long-term vision involves systemic changes and robust adaptations to the evolving hurricane threat. This timeframe may be on the order of 10 to 50 years. This phase is about resilience and sustainability. Strategic infrastructure redevelopment is central to this approach. Communities might consider relocating critical facilities away from high-risk zones, redesigning urban layouts to minimize flood risks, and enforcing building codes that demand hurricane-resistant designs. Beyond infrastructure, there's a need for continuous research into evolving hurricane behaviors, ensuring that predictive models remain accurate. This might also be the phase where collaborations on larger scales are considered, whether in the form of regional defense strategies, shared research and resources, or international agreements on climate change mitigation, acknowledging the global nature of the challenge.

1. **Coastal Infrastructure Overhaul:** Invest in the redesign and reinforcement of coastal infrastructure, emphasizing the development of sea walls, levees, and breakwaters that can withstand increased storm surges and higher wind speeds.
2. **Urban Planning and Land-Use Revisions:** Rethink urban planning in vulnerable zones, discouraging construction in high-risk areas and promoting the establishment of green belts, buffer zones, and mangrove plantations that naturally dissipate the energy of storm surges and act as flood barriers.
3. **Advanced Warning Systems:** Collaborate globally to develop technologically advanced early warning systems that utilize AI and big data analysis to predict hurricane paths and intensities with greater accuracy. Ensure these systems are universally accessible, especially in regions most vulnerable to hurricanes.
4. **Ecosystem Rehabilitation:** Engage in large-scale mangrove and coral reef restoration projects. These natural barriers play a critical role in reducing the impact of storm surges and in absorbing excess rainwater, helping to mitigate flooding.

5. **Research and Development into Sustainable Architecture:** Encourage and fund research into sustainable and resilient architectural designs that can withstand intense hurricanes. Prioritize the retrofitting of existing structures and the innovation of new building materials and technologies tailored to resist high wind speeds and heavy precipitation.
6. **Climate Change Mitigation Initiatives:** Advocate for international cooperation to address the root causes of climate change. Prioritize the transition to renewable energy sources, encourage reforestation projects, and implement policies that curb carbon emissions, aiming to stabilize global temperatures and, in turn, the factors intensifying hurricanes.

By integrating the problem treatment methodology (absolve, resolve, solve, dissolve) with a temporal action plan (short-term, medium-term, and long-term), one can compartmentalize an overwhelming, complex problem into manageable chunks. This structured approach provides clarity and direction, making the seemingly insurmountable task of tackling vast, interconnected issues more achievable. It's about understanding the problem's dimensions, breaking it down, and addressing it layer by layer, from the immediate to the foundational.

Problem Perspectives

Understanding and appreciating multiple perspectives is pivotal when confronting complex problems. Diverse viewpoints bring a richness of experience, knowledge, and insights that a singular lens might overlook. Each perspective offers a unique vantage point, revealing nuances, challenges, and facets of the issue that might otherwise remain hidden. This multiplicity not only paints a more comprehensive picture of the problem but also helps avoid cognitive traps like confirmation bias, where individuals seek out and value information that confirms their pre-existing beliefs. In embracing various perspectives, we allow ourselves to see the broader context, understand underlying dynamics, and recognize the multifaceted nature of the issue.

Furthermore, incorporating diverse approaches to problem-solving often leads to more innovative, holistic, and resilient solutions. When multiple perspectives converge, they bring with them a range of strategies, methodologies, and tools that can be synthesized and adapted to fit the contours of the specific challenge at hand. This collaborative fusion ensures that the devised solutions are well-rounded, taking into account different facets and stakeholders of the problem. Moreover, it ensures that the strategies implemented are more adaptable to changing circumstances and more resilient to unforeseen challenges. In essence, welcoming a plurality of viewpoints is not just a testament to inclusivity but also a strategic approach to understanding and addressing intricate challenges in our increasingly interconnected world.

The hurricane threat, intensified by climate change, can be viewed and addressed in myriad ways. This case study delves into the topic using various tools and concepts, offering a multi-faceted view from three Myers-Briggs personalities: ISTJ, ENFP, and INTJ. While their strategies differ, each offers valuable insights, emphasizing the importance of diverse perspectives in tackling global challenges.

ISTJ: The Detailed Planner

ISTJs are methodical, practical, and reliable individuals who value traditions and facts. They often enjoy tasks that require attention to detail and show a strong sense of duty. With a grounded perspective, ISTJs trust what is concrete and verifiable through experience or evidence. They typically prefer organized environments and are known for their dependability and commitment to their responsibilities. Integrity and honesty are paramount for ISTJs, and they often take pride in upholding standards and maintaining order.

Complex Systems & Inquiry: ISTJs rely on detail and logic. Viewing climate change as a complex system, the ISTJ would break down the interconnected elements, using analysis and agreement systems. They would consider historical hurricane patterns, matching them against present data.

Messes, Problems & Exercises: ISTJs see messes as challenges to be ordered. They'd classify rising hurricane frequency as a mess, requiring immediate attention.

Problem Formulation: ISTJs would focus on facts. Their formulation: "How have historical hurricane patterns shifted due to recent global temperature changes?"

Problem Treatment: To ISTJs, a solution exists in a concrete action. They'd likely lean towards "solving" – possibly suggesting engineered barriers against rising sea levels.

Conflict Modes: When faced with opposition, ISTJs prefer clear communication and confrontation.

SAST & Toulmin Framework: ISTJs would start with assumptions on hurricane behavior, then methodically work through each, testing their validity. Their arguments would be structured: claim (hurricane patterns have changed), grounds (historical vs. current data), and warrant (rising global temperatures as the causal factor).

ENFP: The Passionate Advocate

ENFPs are enthusiastic, imaginative, and spontaneous souls who thrive on possibilities. They are typically optimistic and genuinely enjoy connecting with others, showing a deep interest in understanding people's motivations and dreams.

ENFPs can easily become the catalysts for change and inspiration in various situations due to their infectious energy and adaptability. However, they may struggle with routine tasks and prefer to follow their inspiration rather than a strict plan. Their free spirit, coupled with their empathetic nature, makes them adept at inspiring and motivating those around them.

Complex Systems & Inquiry: ENFPs, with their intuitive nature, would embrace the systems thinking and multiple perspectives inquiry systems. They might look at socio-economic factors and the broader implications of climate change.

Messes, Problems & Exercises: ENFPs are motivated by values. To them, the threat of hurricanes is not just an environmental mess but a humanitarian one.

Problem Formulation: Their question: "How can society rally to mitigate the dangers posed by increasing hurricanes due to climate change?"

Problem Treatment: ENFPs might lean towards "dissolving" the problem, advocating for societal shifts towards sustainable practices.

Conflict Modes: ENFPs, empathetic and persuasive, would navigate disagreements through collaboration and understanding.

SAST & Toulmin Framework: ENFPs would present their assumptions (like how society's actions impact climate change). Their arguments: claim (society can mitigate hurricane threats), grounds (evidence of successful green initiatives), and warrant (the connection between societal practices and climate effects).

INTJ: The Strategic Visionary

INTJs are strategic, analytical, and deep thinkers who approach the world with a thirst for knowledge and a penchant for planning. They value logic, clarity, and efficiency, often able to see patterns and solutions that others might miss. While they tend to be reserved, it's not due to a lack of confidence but rather a preference for introspection. INTJs are independent and decisive, setting high standards for themselves and others. They are often visionary in their thoughts, focused on future possibilities, and can chart a path forward with meticulous precision.

Complex Systems & Inquiry: INTJs, with their analytical minds, would gravitate towards the dialectic and analysis systems, diving deep into climate models and future predictions.

Messes, Problems & Exercises: For INTJs, messes are opportunities. They'd view the hurricane threat as a chance for innovation.

Problem Formulation: Their formulation would be: "Given the current trajectory, what strategies can future-proof our cities against enhanced hurricanes?"

Problem Treatment: INTJs might opt for "resolving", devising future-oriented solutions.

Conflict Modes: INTJs would confront conflict analytically, dissecting opposing views for inconsistencies.

SAST & Toulmin Framework: Their arguments would be well-structured and forward-thinking. They'd start with assumptions about future hurricane patterns, working systematically. Their arguments: claim (strategies exist to future-proof cities), grounds (data on effective urban planning), and warrant (projections indicating escalating hurricane threats).

Leveraging Different Perspectives

For the pragmatic ISTJ, the hard facts and historical data reveal a clear pattern that cannot be ignored. Detailed records and meticulous analyses consistently point towards the escalation of these natural disasters, demanding action based on empirical evidence. The visionary ENFP, driven by passion and concern for communities, recognizes the emotional and societal implications of these climatic shifts. By acknowledging the stories of those affected and imagining a world where such catastrophes are commonplace, they're motivated to inspire change. Meanwhile, the strategic INTJ perceives the broader systemic implications and long-term trajectories.

Using a structured and analytical approach, they can project potential scenarios and strategize on the best ways to mitigate or adapt. By integrating the detail-oriented diligence of the ISTJ, the empathetic motivation of the ENFP, and the foresighted analysis of the INTJ, we find a comprehensive understanding of the issue—one that's rooted in fact, fueled by emotion, and forward-thinking in its approach. Together, these perspectives form a compelling call to action, urging us to address the looming challenges that intensified hurricanes present.

FORMULATION OF A WELL-DEFINED PROBLEM

Having performed some initial structuring and bounding of our future hurricane intensity/frequency challenge, we can generate strategy plan to address one of the problem aspects. There is always the ability to scale the problem-solving team, but it is most important to recognize that one can only effectively tackle one thing at a time. We can start by looking at which of the identified long-term visions we would like to most address. From there, we can identify several related medium-term goals, and from that list, we can articulate one initial short-term accomplishments that start us off on our journey.

Long-Term Vision - Urban Planning and Land-Use Revisions: Rethink urban planning in vulnerable zones, discouraging construction in high-risk areas and promoting the establishment of green belts, buffer zones, and mangrove plantations that naturally dissipate the energy of storm surges and act as flood barriers.

Medium Term Aims - Urban Planning and Zoning: Reevaluate and adjust zoning laws in hurricane-prone areas. Prioritize the development of elevated constructions, green buffers, and barriers in vulnerable coastal regions to counteract storm surges.

Short-Term Initiative - Vulnerability Assessment: Evaluate current community vulnerabilities to hurricanes by reviewing infrastructure, population distribution, and emergency services. Identify immediate areas for improvement to reduce the impact of impending storms.

By nesting these efforts, we have the ability to frame a larger issue (long-term and medium-term), but initiating a feasible and implementable first step (short-term) to get the process started. Perhaps we even narrow the initial focus to be:

Vulnerability Assessment: Evaluate current community vulnerabilities to hurricanes in Sweethaven County by reviewing critical facilities (hospitals, prisons, limited mobility populations) and evacuation ability/preparedness to identify facilities that may need to be relocated in order to limit the need for evacuation due to storm surge, excessive wind, intense precipitation, and extended power outages (more than 48 hours).

EVALUATING THE PROBLEM WITH INQUIRY SYSTEMS

Agreement

The "agreement" inquiry system seeks consensus among involved stakeholders, focusing on shared values and perspectives to collaboratively address a given challenge. In the context of Sweethaven County's vulnerability assessment related to hurricanes, this inquiry system would involve the following steps:

1. **Stakeholder Identification and Engagement:** Begin by identifying and gathering all key stakeholders, including representatives from critical facilities like hospitals and prisons, local government officials, emergency response teams, community leaders, and representatives from limited mobility populations.

2. **Shared Vision Development:** Facilitate sessions to establish a collective understanding of the importance of assessing vulnerabilities. Frame the assessment around the common goal: ensuring the safety and well-being of Sweethaven County's residents, especially during hurricane events.
3. **Data Collection and Sharing:** Compile data on current infrastructure, population density, historical hurricane impacts, and existing evacuation routes and capabilities. This data should be transparently shared among stakeholders, ensuring everyone operates from a shared knowledge base.
4. **Collaborative Risk Evaluation:** Engage stakeholders in mapping out critical facilities' vulnerabilities, emphasizing those areas most at risk from storm surge, excessive wind, and intense precipitation. Special attention should be given to facilities housing limited mobility populations, as their relocation during emergencies may be challenging.
5. **Evacuation Preparedness Review:** Collaboratively review the current evacuation capabilities, specifically focusing on the potential challenges during extended power outages. Share best practices and learn from previous evacuation experiences.
6. **Recommendation Development:** With input from all stakeholders, develop a set of recommendations. These could range from enhancing current facilities to be more resilient, adjusting evacuation procedures, or potentially relocating certain critical facilities to safer zones.
7. **Feedback Loop:** Throughout the process, maintain an open feedback loop. Ensure that the voices of those directly impacted by hurricanes are at the forefront of the decision-making process.
8. **Final Consensus and Implementation Plan:** Once all data is reviewed and recommendations are put forth, seek agreement on the best way forward. This may involve trade-offs, but the shared vision and collaborative spirit fostered through the agreement inquiry system will facilitate a consensus-driven approach to Sweethaven County's hurricane preparedness.

Analysis

The "analysis" inquiry system focuses on breaking down complex problems into manageable parts and understanding the relationships between those parts. It emphasizes data-driven, objective evaluation and systematic approaches to derive conclusions. For Sweethaven County's hurricane vulnerability assessment, this inquiry system would involve:

1. **Data Collection:** Start by gathering detailed data on the location, structure, and capacity of critical facilities like hospitals, prisons, and places housing limited mobility populations. Compile information on past hurricane impacts, infrastructure resilience, and existing evacuation procedures.
2. **Facility Risk Analysis:** Systematically assess each facility's risk using data on its proximity to high-risk zones, structural strength, and surrounding infrastructure. Use predictive models to estimate potential damages from storm surge, wind, and intense precipitation.
3. **Evacuation Capability Analysis:** Evaluate existing evacuation routes, transport means, and capacity. Consider factors like road resilience to flooding, accessibility, and potential bottlenecks. Analyze the logistical challenges and timeframes involved in evacuating limited mobility populations.
4. **Extended Power Outage Impact:** Analyze the backup power capabilities of critical facilities. Identify those that may not sustain more than 48 hours of power outage and understand the cascading effects of such outages on emergency services and the community.
5. **Cost-Benefit Analysis:** For facilities identified as high-risk, conduct a cost-benefit analysis comparing the cost of relocating the facility versus upgrading it to withstand potential hurricane impacts. This should factor in both tangible costs and the intangible impact on human lives.
6. **Scenario Modelling:** Using predictive analytics, model various hurricane scenarios to anticipate potential challenges. For example, what would happen if two critical facilities were impacted simultaneously? Or if a major evacuation route was blocked?
7. **Recommendation Development:** Based on rigorous analysis, develop actionable recommendations. This could involve suggesting facility relocations, infrastructural upgrades, or revised evacuation plans.
8. **Validation and Review:** To ensure robustness, validate findings using alternative data sources or modeling techniques. Engage external experts for a peer review of the assessment's methodologies and conclusions.

By deploying the analysis inquiry system, Sweethaven County would gain a comprehensive, data-driven understanding of its vulnerabilities to hurricanes. This approach ensures that decisions are based on objective criteria, providing a strong foundation for future preparedness initiatives.

Multiple Realities

The "multiple realities" inquiry system recognizes that different stakeholders often have distinct perspectives on a situation, influenced by their experiences, values, and priorities. This approach seeks to understand and reconcile these varying viewpoints to gain a more holistic understanding of the issue at hand. In configuring a vulnerability assessment for Sweethaven County using this inquiry system:

1. **Stakeholder Identification:** Begin by identifying all potential stakeholders involved or affected by hurricane vulnerabilities. This would include representatives from critical facilities, local government, emergency services, resident groups, and particularly the limited mobility populations.
2. **Facilitated Workshops:** Organize workshops with these stakeholders to understand their unique concerns, experiences, and viewpoints regarding hurricane vulnerabilities. For instance, hospital administrators might focus on medical equipment and patient safety, while a prison warden might be concerned about security during evacuations.
3. **Diverse Data Collection:** Beyond just empirical data, gather qualitative data like personal anecdotes, historical narratives, and community stories related to past hurricane experiences. This adds depth to the understanding of vulnerabilities.
4. **Scenario Exploration:** Present multiple potential hurricane scenarios and gather feedback on how each stakeholder perceives the risks and challenges. This can reveal blind spots or concerns that may not be immediately apparent from a purely analytical perspective.
5. **Collaborative Mapping:** Using insights from the workshops, collaboratively map out areas of consensus and disagreement. For instance, while there might be agreement on the vulnerability of a particular facility, there might be differing opinions on whether to relocate or reinforce it.
6. **Integrated Vulnerability Profiles:** Develop vulnerability profiles that integrate the diverse inputs from stakeholders. These profiles offer a more rounded view of risks, incorporating both quantitative data and qualitative insights.
7. **Iterative Feedback Loops:** As potential strategies are formulated, loop back with stakeholders to gather feedback and refine the plans. This iterative process ensures that multiple perspectives continue to shape the assessment's outcomes.
8. **Final Recommendations:** While it might be challenging to find solutions that cater to every perspective, the goal is to find strategies that are most inclusive and considerate of the multiple realities represented by the community.

By embracing the "multiple realities" inquiry system, Sweethaven County can ensure that its hurricane vulnerability assessment is not only robust but also deeply attuned to the diverse needs, concerns, and insights of its community. This inclusive approach can foster greater community buy-in and enhance the effectiveness of the strategies implemented.

Dialectic

The "dialectic" inquiry system is based on the principle of thesis, antithesis, and synthesis. It seeks to uncover deeper truths by pitting opposing viewpoints against each other, facilitating a debate, and ultimately synthesizing a new, more comprehensive understanding. Here's how it would be applied in Sweethaven County's context:

1. **Thesis Formulation:** The initial position or argument regarding hurricane vulnerabilities is stated. For instance, a thesis could be that critical facilities in Sweethaven are currently well-protected against hurricane threats and that only minor adjustments are needed.
2. **Antithesis Identification:** The opposing viewpoint is presented. Contrary to the thesis, the antithesis might argue that many critical facilities are severely underprepared for hurricanes, and major interventions, including relocations, are necessary.
3. **Structured Debates:** Organize structured debates between proponents of the thesis and antithesis. Representatives from critical facilities, local government, emergency services, and particularly affected communities can present their arguments and counterarguments.
4. **Data-Driven Examination:** In parallel with debates, gather empirical data on the current state of critical facilities, evacuation capabilities, and potential hurricane impacts. This data serves as an unbiased anchor in the discussions, ensuring debates remain rooted in reality.
5. **Synthesis Creation:** After thorough debate and data examination, a synthesis is formed—a new viewpoint or plan that integrates the strengths of both the thesis and antithesis while discarding their weaknesses. For instance, the synthesis might acknowledge the preparedness of certain facilities but recognize the vulnerability of others, leading to a targeted relocation and fortification strategy.
6. **Stakeholder Collaboration:** Engage with a broad range of stakeholders to refine the synthesized strategies. By including voices from all affected parties, from hospital administrators to limited mobility populations, a richer, more inclusive solution can be shaped.
7. **Implementation Plan:** Once the synthesized strategies are agreed upon, develop a clear implementation plan. This plan should detail the roles of various stakeholders, timelines, resources required, and potential challenges.
8. **Continuous Evaluation:** The dialectic inquiry system acknowledges the evolving nature of problems and solutions. As the environment changes or new data emerges, it's crucial to revisit the thesis, antithesis, and synthesis, adjusting strategies as needed.

By using the dialectic inquiry system, Sweethaven County can ensure a deep, well-considered understanding of its hurricane vulnerabilities. By embracing opposition and debate, it can unearth innovative solutions that balance a wide range of needs and perspectives. This process, though rigorous, promises strategies that are resilient, comprehensive, and adaptive to the dynamic challenges posed by hurricanes.

Systems Thinking

Unbounded Systems Thinking (UST) operates on the idea that problems aren't confined within predefined boundaries but interact with other systems and evolve over time. This holistic approach acknowledges that factors affecting one system might originate outside its apparent borders. Here's how UST would be employed for Sweethaven County's hurricane vulnerability assessment:

1. **Holistic Contextualization:** Begin by understanding the broader context of Sweethaven County. This means not just looking at its facilities and populations, but also at its geography, history, socio-economic factors, political landscape, and more. This ensures that the assessment captures all relevant factors, not just the most apparent ones.
2. **Interconnection Mapping:** Identify how the various systems in the county interact. For example, how do evacuation strategies impact limited mobility populations? Or how might the economic implications of moving a hospital affect the wider community? By drawing these connections, Sweethaven can anticipate ripple effects and secondary challenges.
3. **External Influences:** Recognize that influences on hurricane vulnerabilities might come from outside the immediate system. For instance, state or federal policies, global climate change trends, or even shifts in global economics might play a role. By including these external factors in the assessment, Sweethaven ensures it's not blindsided by unforeseen challenges.
4. **Adaptive Strategy Formulation:** Given the evolving nature of unbounded systems, the strategies derived need to be adaptive. This means not only preparing for current threats but also building in flexibility to adjust as new challenges or information arise.
5. **Stakeholder Engagement:** Recognizing that everyone is part of an interconnected system, engage a wide array of stakeholders. This can range from residents and facility managers to experts in adjacent fields, like environmental scientists or urban planners. This diversity of input ensures that the assessment isn't myopic but benefits from a range of insights.

6. **Scenario Planning:** Given the unpredictability inherent in unbounded systems, engage in scenario planning. Develop multiple future scenarios based on different assumptions (e.g., frequency of hurricanes, changes in population demographics) and strategize how Sweethaven might respond in each case.
7. **Continuous Feedback Loops:** Set up mechanisms to gather continuous feedback. This could be in the form of regular community forums, data collection efforts, or partnerships with research institutions. This ongoing feedback ensures that as the system evolves, Sweethaven's strategies evolve alongside it.

By employing Unbounded Systems Thinking, Sweethaven County can ensure its hurricane vulnerability assessment is comprehensive, forward-looking, and adaptable. It recognizes that the challenge isn't static but is influenced by a myriad of factors, many outside its immediate control. This kind of thinking ensures that the county isn't just reacting to the latest hurricane but is proactively planning for an uncertain future.

Leveraging all Inquiry System Tools

Sweethaven County decides to leverage all five Inquiry Systems for their evaluation. They begin with the Unbounded Systems Thinking (UST) method to provide an holistic understanding; then using "multiple realities" inquiry where diverse stakeholder perspectives are considered. "Agreement" is then used to seek consensus on primary vulnerabilities, while the "analysis" phase delves into quantitative assessments, turning these realities into actionable data. Post-analysis, the findings are rigorously examined using the "dialectic" inquiry system, presenting counterarguments and probing initial conclusions for potential weaknesses. The result is a comprehensive and adaptive strategy well-suited to address the multifaceted challenges of hurricanes.

Let's examine these steps in closer detail:

- **Unbounded Systems Thinking (UST):** The starting point for Sweethaven County's hurricane vulnerability assessment is UST, where problems aren't isolated but interconnected and continually evolving. In this holistic context, Sweethaven begins by understanding its broader environmental, socio-economic, and political landscape. Through this lens, the county identifies interconnections, acknowledges external influences from global or state policies, and anticipates possible future scenarios.

In the initial application of the UST inquiry system, the ISTJ personality, known for their methodical and detail-oriented approach, would likely emphasize the historical patterns and well-documented facts about hurricanes and their impact on Sweethaven County. The ENFP, with their broad-mindedness and focus on human experiences, would integrate anecdotal evidence and qualitative narratives, bringing a broader, more holistic perspective to the assessment. The INTJ, possessing a natural ability to forecast and strategize, would highlight the potential long-term implications of current trends and the necessity of continuous reassessment in an ever-changing environment.

- **Multiple Realities:** With the expansive perspective provided by UST, Sweethaven then adopts the "multiple realities" inquiry system, recognizing that different stakeholders might perceive the problem in varied ways. This system aims to uncover these multiple perspectives to generate a more comprehensive understanding.

As the assessment segues into the "multiple realities" phase, the ISTJ's pragmatic nature would ensure that different perspectives are not only identified but also organized systematically. The ENFP would play a pivotal role in gathering these diverse perspectives, reaching out with genuine curiosity and understanding, ensuring that every stakeholder feels heard. Meanwhile, the INTJ, with their innate ability to discern patterns, would begin to identify common threads across these realities, hinting at more universal truths or concerns.

- **Agreement:** Here, Sweethaven seeks a consensus on the baseline realities of the hurricane vulnerabilities. This involves facilitating dialogues between various stakeholders, such as residents, facility managers, urban planners, and environmental scientists, to agree upon the most pressing vulnerabilities. This agreement is vital as it serves as a foundation upon which further analyses are built.

In the "agreement" inquiry phase, the ISTJ would drive consensus through their reliance on proven facts and tried-and-true methods. ENFPs would utilize their empathetic and diplomatic skills, ensuring that disagreements are addressed with compassion, bridging gaps and finding common ground. The INTJ, being naturally strategic, would focus on aligning these agreements with the county's overarching goals, ensuring that the collective vision remains forward-thinking and robust.

- **Analysis:** Once there's agreement on baseline vulnerabilities, Sweethaven delves into an analytical assessment. This involves quantitative methods like risk assessments, cost-benefit analyses of potential interventions, and modeling potential hurricane impacts. The analysis system transforms the agreed-upon realities into actionable data.

The "analysis" phase would witness the ISTJ meticulously organizing data, ensuring that it's accurate and ready for thorough evaluation. The ENFP would champion the qualitative aspects, reminding the team of the human stories behind the numbers and advocating for solutions that prioritize well-being. The INTJ would contribute by delineating logical pathways, making connections between data points, and proposing efficient strategies based on the analysis.

- **Dialectic Inquiry System:** After consolidating insights from the aforementioned systems, Sweethaven employs the "dialectic" inquiry system to challenge the derived results. This is crucial for ensuring robustness in the findings. Counterarguments or alternative interpretations of the data are presented, probing the initial conclusions for weaknesses. For example, if the analysis suggests relocating certain facilities based on future hurricane predictions, the dialectic approach might challenge the reliability of these predictions or present alternate, more cost-effective mitigation measures.

In the "dialectic" inquiry, the ISTJ's steadfastness in their beliefs and values, grounded in reality, would serve as a strong foundation against counterarguments. The ENFP, always considering the bigger picture, would present challenges based on societal and emotional implications. The INTJ would critically evaluate the entire methodology, exposing any inconsistencies or flaws and ensuring that the conclusions drawn are both sound and sustainable.

This rigorous challenge serves two main purposes: Firstly, it ensures that the county's plans are not only based on consensus and data but have also been tested against counterarguments. Secondly, it prepares Sweethaven for potential criticisms from external entities or changes in the future, ensuring that their strategies are resilient and adaptable.

By weaving through these inquiry systems, Sweethaven County ensures that its hurricane vulnerability assessment is not only comprehensive but also robustly challenged, making it well-equipped to address the multi-dimensional challenges posed by future hurricanes.

Incorporating ISTJ, ENFP, and INTJ perspectives within each inquiry phase ensures a balanced, thorough, and strategic approach to Sweethaven County's vulnerability assessment, aptly addressing the multifaceted challenges hurricanes present.

VULNERABILITY ASSESSMENT FINDINGS

Our initial holistic examination identified that Sweethaven County's coastal positioning and low-lying areas make it particularly susceptible to the storm surges and flooding associated with hurricanes. Over time, this vulnerability has been exacerbated by rising sea levels and changing weather patterns, presenting an even greater threat to critical facilities located near the coast.

Through consultation with various stakeholders, including emergency services, residents, and local officials, diverse perspectives were collated. While emergency services stressed the logistical challenges of evacuating certain facilities during hurricanes, residents of low-lying areas expressed feelings of anxiety and insecurity about the adequacy of existing storm infrastructure. Local officials, while aware of these concerns, raised budgetary and land availability issues as constraints to immediate action.

There was a unanimous consensus among stakeholders that critical facilities, especially hospitals and prisons, are of paramount concern. A particular hospital located in a vulnerable zone was consistently flagged by all groups. Its current location not only places patients and staff at risk during severe weather events, but its potential inoperability during such times could pose a broader health crisis for the county.

Detailed analysis of the hospital's location revealed its proximity to a flood-prone zone. Data from the past decade showed that during major storms, access routes to the hospital were often inundated, leading to delayed emergency responses. Moreover, the hospital's backup power infrastructure was found to be outdated, with a significant risk of failure during extended power outages.

Challenging these findings, some parties argued that relocating or heavily fortifying the hospital would be too costly and that funds could be better utilized in widespread community education and evacuation readiness programs. Others counter-argued that the hospital's centrality to the county's health and emergency response made its fortification or relocation a non-negotiable priority.

Based on the comprehensive evaluation using the five inquiry systems, it's evident that Sweethaven County's hospital in the identified vulnerable zone presents a significant risk in the face of future hurricanes. Immediate actions, either through fortification, the establishment of alternative emergency medical centers, or potential relocation, are imperative to safeguard community health and ensure uninterrupted emergency medical services during severe weather events.

TRACKING FUNDAMENTAL ASSUMPTIONS

During the course of the vulnerability evaluations, Sweethaven County's evaluation team identified and inventoried key assumptions. These assumptions included the following:

- Sea-Level Rise: It is assumed that the rate of sea-level rise will continue at the current pace, or possibly even accelerate, leading to more frequent and severe flooding in low-lying areas of Sweethaven County.
- Weather Patterns: The findings are based on the assumption that weather patterns, influenced by climate change, will lead to hurricanes becoming more intense and frequent over time.
- Infrastructure Durability: It's assumed that the current infrastructure, especially around critical facilities, is built to past standards and may not be robust enough to withstand the increasing severity of hurricanes.
- Evacuation Efficiency: The current evacuation plans and routes are assumed to be efficient for past hurricane scenarios and may not be adequate for future, more severe events.
- Power Infrastructure: The assumption is that the backup power systems at critical facilities, especially the hospital, are outdated and not up to the standards required to handle prolonged power outages.
- Budget Constraints: The findings take into account the assumption that local authorities face budget constraints, which may limit the immediacy and scale of response actions.
- Community Preparedness: It's assumed that the broader Sweethaven County community might not be adequately educated or prepared for major hurricane events, influencing the priority of certain mitigation measures.
- Land Availability: The findings operate on the assumption that land availability for relocating critical facilities, like the hospital, might be limited or might involve complex logistical challenges.
- Stakeholder Perspectives: The vulnerability findings are based on the assumption that the perspectives collected from different stakeholders are comprehensive and represent the broader views of the Sweethaven County community.
- Economic Factors: The findings assume that relocating or fortifying critical facilities would have economic implications, both in terms of immediate costs and long-term community economic resilience.

Acknowledging and inventorying core fundamental assumptions is pivotal for the integrity and relevance of any evaluation or study. At the heart of every decision-making process, assumptions serve as the foundation upon which conclusions and recommendations are built. When these assumptions go unexamined, there is a risk that the entire structure of conclusions becomes shaky or flawed. By clearly laying out the presumptions at the onset, researchers and stakeholders can have a clear roadmap, outlining the base beliefs and theories that guide their inquiries. This transparency helps in ensuring that all involved parties have a shared understanding and can contribute more effectively to the discourse.

Furthermore, the dynamic nature of many subjects, especially in areas like climate science, urban planning, and community resilience, means that situations can change rapidly. Assumptions that may have been valid at one point in time may no longer hold true as new data emerges or as the external environment shifts. By having a well-documented inventory of core assumptions, future evaluations can systematically revisit and challenge these foundational beliefs. This iterative process not only ensures that conclusions remain relevant but also fosters adaptability and agility in response strategies.

Lastly, acknowledging assumptions promotes intellectual honesty and rigour. It provides a mechanism for stakeholders, peers, and critics to challenge and validate the underpinnings of a study. By opening up these fundamental beliefs to scrutiny, the evaluation becomes more robust, and potential blind spots are minimized. The practice of regularly scrutinizing assumptions helps in keeping the evaluation process grounded, ensuring that conclusions and recommendations are both valid and actionable in the real world.

PROPOSED MITIGATION

In light of Sweethaven County's primary vulnerability to hurricanes, immediate actions centered around the protection and continuity of critical medical services are essential. The county has prioritized the fortification of existing medical facilities, ensuring they can withstand the brunt of hurricanes, from powerful winds to the potential flooding brought on by storm surges. As a proactive measure, plans are in motion to establish alternative emergency medical centers strategically located in areas less prone to these threats. These auxiliary centers will serve as backup facilities, ensuring that emergency medical care remains accessible even when primary hospitals face operational challenges.

Moreover, there's an active exploration into the feasibility of relocating some of the most at-risk medical facilities to safer regions within the county. The goal is to diminish their exposure to severe weather threats altogether. Relocation, although resource-intensive, could provide a long-term solution, significantly reducing the risk of disruption in medical services during catastrophic events. Sweethaven County is unwavering in its commitment to guaranteeing that residents have reliable access to emergency medical care, regardless of the weather challenges they face.

A SWOT analysis for a proposed mitigation plan offers a comprehensive framework for understanding the internal and external factors that can impact the plan's success. By identifying the strengths, the analysis illuminates what the project can leverage to its advantage. The weaknesses spotlight areas of improvement, allowing for pre-emptive strategies to address potential pitfalls. Furthermore, opportunities shed light on external factors or trends that can be harnessed to enhance the mitigation effort, while threats provide insights into possible challenges and external risks that could jeopardize the plan. In essence, a SWOT analysis allows stakeholders to proactively anticipate and respond to challenges, ensuring a more robust, resilient, and well-informed mitigation strategy.

Given the previously discussed vulnerability for Sweethaven County, which involves the proximity of critical facilities (like hospitals and prisons) to zones at risk for hurricane impacts, here's a SWOT analysis for a proposed mitigation plan:

Strengths (S):

1. **Improved Safety:** Relocating or reinforcing critical facilities reduces the risk to human life and ensures continuous operation during emergencies.
2. **Cost Savings in the Long Run:** Although there's an upfront cost, the long-term benefits in avoiding damages and disruption can lead to significant savings.
3. **Enhanced Community Confidence:** Demonstrating proactiveness in addressing known vulnerabilities can boost public trust in local governance.

Weaknesses (W):

1. **High Initial Investment:** The costs associated with relocating or retrofitting facilities can be substantial.
2. **Disruption during Transition:** The process of moving or fortifying structures can disrupt services temporarily.
3. **Land Availability:** Finding suitable and safe zones to relocate can be a challenge, especially in densely populated areas.

Opportunities (O):

1. **Leverage Federal and State Funding:** Many government programs offer funding for disaster preparedness and mitigation projects.
2. **Public-Private Partnerships:** Engaging with private entities can provide additional resources, expertise, and funding avenues.

3. **Incorporate Modern Design and Technology:** The move or upgrade can incorporate state-of-the-art designs that are not only resilient but also more efficient and user-friendly.

Threats (T):

1. **Public Resistance:** Residents might resist changes due to attachment to existing structures or concerns about changes in accessibility.
2. **Environmental Concerns:** Relocation or construction projects may face challenges related to environmental regulations or unintended ecological impacts.
3. **Unpredictable Future Threats:** Climate change and other variables might bring about unforeseen challenges, rendering today's mitigation strategies less effective in the future.

Given this SWOT analysis, it's essential for Sweethaven County to carefully consider its strengths and opportunities while actively addressing its weaknesses and potential threats to develop a holistic and forward-looking vulnerability mitigation strategy.

COMMUNICATION THE MITIGATION

The Toulmin Argumentation Framework offers a structured approach to presenting arguments, making it invaluable for understanding and conveying potential mitigation solutions for Sweethaven County. By dissecting an argument into its foundational elements—Claim, Grounds, Warrant, Backing, Rebuttal, and Qualifier—the framework provides clarity to stakeholders, allowing them to see the basis for proposed solutions, the logic connecting data to the recommendations, and any potential counterarguments. This method ensures that solutions are not merely presented as assertions but are grounded in evidence and rationale. Additionally, by anticipating and addressing potential objections within the framework, Sweethaven County's planners can better foster trust and consensus among the community and stakeholders. In essence, the Toulmin Argumentation Framework streamlines communication, ensuring that proposed mitigations are both transparent and compelling.

TAF for Fortifying Hospitals

Claim: Fortifying existing medical facilities in Sweethaven County is a crucial and immediate step towards ensuring continuous medical services during hurricanes.

Grounds (Data): Hurricane assessments for Sweethaven County indicate an increased threat to critical infrastructure, including hospitals and medical centers. These facilities are essential for providing emergency medical care, especially during and after severe weather events. Current building structures are susceptible to damages from powerful winds, flooding from storm surges, and other associated hurricane risks.

Warrant (Connection between Grounds and Claim): Medical facilities play a pivotal role in saving lives, especially during emergencies. Ensuring their operational continuity during hurricanes is not just about preserving buildings but, more critically, about safeguarding human lives. Thus, if these structures can't withstand hurricane threats, the consequences can be dire for the community.

Backing (Support for Warrant): Studies have shown that fortified structures have a significantly higher chance of withstanding the impacts of hurricanes compared to their non-fortified counterparts. Regions that have previously fortified their medical facilities witnessed fewer disruptions in medical services during severe weather events.

Rebuttal (Address Counterarguments): While some might argue that the financial cost of fortification is high, the cost of inaction can be far greater. The loss of a medical facility during a hurricane could result in lost lives, not to mention the economic toll of rebuilding post-disaster.

Qualifier (Statement of the Claim's Limitations): While fortification can significantly enhance the resilience of medical facilities against hurricanes, it is important to note that no mitigation measure can offer a 100% guarantee against all possible hurricane damages. However, fortification dramatically reduces the risk.

Considering the imperative nature of medical services during emergencies, fortifying existing medical facilities emerges as an essential and immediate action to safeguard Sweethaven County residents during hurricanes.

TAF for Relocating Hospitals

Claim: Relocating critical medical facilities in Sweethaven County to safer zones is an urgent and necessary measure to ensure uninterrupted emergency medical care during hurricane events.

Grounds (Data): The vulnerability assessment for Sweethaven County highlights that several medical facilities are located in zones of high hurricane risk, prone to storm surges, powerful winds, and heavy rainfall. The geographical location of these facilities places them at an increased threat level during hurricanes.

Warrant (Connection between Grounds and Claim): Ensuring the safety and operational continuity of medical facilities during extreme weather conditions is vital for the well-being of Sweethaven's residents. If the existing locations of these facilities pose a constant threat to their operation, relocating them becomes not just a strategic choice, but a moral imperative.

Backing (Support for Warrant): Other regions with similar vulnerabilities have adopted relocation strategies, demonstrating a significant decrease in disruptions to medical services during adverse weather events. Relocated facilities, being out of immediate danger zones, have proven more resilient and capable of serving their communities when needed most.

Rebuttal (Address Counterarguments): There are arguments regarding the high costs and logistical challenges of relocating medical facilities. While these are valid concerns, the potential loss of lives and the long-term economic repercussions of having non-operational medical centers during a crisis can far outweigh the one-time costs and challenges of relocation.

Qualifier (Statement of the Claim's Limitations): While relocating medical facilities to safer areas can drastically reduce their vulnerability to hurricanes, it's essential to understand that no location is entirely immune. The aim is to minimize risk and optimize response capabilities during severe weather events.

For the long-term health and safety of Sweethaven County's residents, relocating critical medical facilities to zones of lower hurricane risk becomes not just a logistical consideration but a necessary action to guarantee continued medical assistance during dire times.

TAF for Establishing Alternative Locations

Claim: Setting up alternative emergency centers in strategic, safer locations within Sweethaven County is a crucial step to provide uninterrupted emergency medical care during hurricanes.

Grounds (Data): The vulnerability assessment shows that, while Sweethaven County has critical medical facilities, they lie in high-risk hurricane zones. Past hurricane events have led to disruptions in emergency medical care, with significant delays in patients receiving the necessary attention.

Warrant (Connection between Grounds and Claim): Given the unpredictability and increasing severity of hurricanes, it's essential to have redundancy in the emergency medical system. By having alternative emergency centers, the county can ensure that when one center is compromised, others can take over without losing precious time.

Backing (Support for Warrant): Studies from other hurricane-prone regions have shown that having multiple emergency response centers distributed geographically reduces the strain on any single facility and ensures wider coverage during emergencies, ultimately saving more lives.

Rebuttal (Address Counterarguments): Some may argue that the costs involved in setting up new centers can be prohibitive, and resources could be better spent on improving the existing infrastructure. However, considering the potential loss of life when a primary facility is incapacitated, the investment in alternative centers proves to be cost-effective in the long run.

Qualifier (Statement of the Claim's Limitations): While alternative emergency centers can play a crucial role during severe weather events, their efficiency depends on factors like staffing, equipment, and accessibility. It's vital to ensure that these centers are not just structures but are adequately equipped and staffed.

The establishment of alternative emergency centers in Sweethaven County, strategically placed in safer areas, would significantly enhance the county's ability to respond to emergencies during hurricanes, ensuring that residents always have access to vital medical services.

CONCLUSION

In addressing the multifaceted challenges presented by complex issues, a systematic approach is vital to ensure clarity, accuracy, and thoroughness. One initial step is to delineate potential problem treatments by considering whether the issue can be absolved, resolved, solved, or dissolved. Each treatment presents a unique path to approach the problem, ranging from natural self-correction to proactive change. Segregating actionable steps into short-term, medium-term, and long-term horizons further adds granularity, allowing for a phased approach that acknowledges varying time, resources, and strategic priorities. This structured approach ensures that efforts are not diluted by attempting to tackle every facet of a problem simultaneously, and instead, they're channeled towards the most pressing needs first.

Upon this foundation, crafting a well-specified problem statement becomes crucial. This statement should be concise yet comprehensive, capturing the essence of the challenge and serving as a focal point for all subsequent efforts. With a clear problem statement in hand, the five inquiry systems—unbounded systems thinking, multiple realities, agreement, analysis, and dialectic—can be applied sequentially. These systems allow for a multi-dimensional exploration of the problem, facilitating a holistic understanding by capturing a variety of perspectives, assumptions, and potential solutions.

An integral part of this process is the inventory of all fundamental assumptions. Assumptions, often implicit, can influence the trajectory of problem-solving. By making these assumptions explicit, we can ensure that they are critically examined, validated, or refuted. This exercise illuminates potential biases or gaps in the analysis, ensuring a more rigorous and objective evaluation.

Subsequently, a SWOT analysis—assessing strengths, weaknesses, opportunities, and threats—is employed for each identified mitigation option. This analysis presents a comprehensive picture of each option's viability, potential benefits, challenges, and external factors that might influence its success. By contrasting the positive attributes with potential pitfalls, decision-makers can make informed choices that align with the community's best interests and available resources.

Finally, to communicate the proposed mitigation solutions effectively to stakeholders, the Toulmin Argumentation Framework is harnessed. This framework breaks down arguments into their core components, making the logic behind proposals transparent and easily understandable. By presenting the claim, grounds, warrant, backing, rebuttal, and qualifier, the Toulmin method ensures that stakeholders not only understand the what and why of a proposal but also see the evidence and rationale supporting it. This transparency fosters trust, enabling more informed discussions and decisions. In essence, this multi-step process—from problem treatment identification to argumentative presentation—ensures a holistic, thorough, and transparent approach to complex problem-solving.

The systematic process, rooted in delineating problem treatments, segregating actions across time horizons, employing inquiry systems, identifying assumptions, and using strategic tools like SWOT analysis and the Toulmin Argumentation Framework, is not restricted solely to Sweethaven County's vulnerability assessment. This robust method can be equally applied to various facets of the overarching issue of uncertainty surrounding increased hurricane intensity and frequency. Whether one is examining the socio-economic implications, environmental repercussions, or infrastructural challenges posed by such climatic uncertainties, the structured approach ensures that each dimension is explored with depth, precision, and clarity. By adapting this comprehensive methodology, stakeholders can holistically understand the multi-dimensional challenges, formulate strategies grounded in rigorous analysis, and communicate proposals effectively, ensuring that the complex nature of these uncertainties is addressed in a well-rounded and informed manner.

Conclusion

This book aimed to arm readers with Tools to navigate and overcome the challenges of complexity rather than be immobilized by it.

We presented an initial take on problems with which we are presented in everyday life and guidance on how to frame complex problems, an overview of problem treatments, as well as introduction to the four phases of problem solving (Chapter 1). Chapter 2 introduced the concept of Systems, which recognizes and acknowledges the multi-faceted composition of the larger world we live in.

We explored (Chapter 3) different attitudes and mental states, through the Jungian Personality Framework (JPF), which is fundamental in understanding why different Personality Types relate differently to problems affect our ability to confront different kinds of problems.

Chapter 4 outlined the use of Inquiry Systems (ISs) to collect relevant knowledge to the complex challenge at hand. Namely, what kinds of Knowledge Producing Systems are most appropriate and thereby are needed for which kinds of problems.

An overview of the Strategic Assumptional Analysis Technique (SAST) for uncovering and analyzing key assumptions was presented in Chapter 5. Assumptions are pivotal in structuring productive discussions when faced with differing opinions and thoughts on decisions needing to be made.

We presented an overview of various conflict modes and provide available modes of addressing and confronting conflict (Chapter 6), which can overcome the immobilizing sense of 'Freezing," the fear-induced "Flight" response, or conflict escalating "Fight" response.

Chapter 7 presented the Toulmin Argumentation Framework (TAF), which is crucial in examining the different types of arguments that people give in responding to different types of problems and issues in general. The TAF provides a powerful framework for analyzing the structure of arguments and can be used to outsmart Complexity by appropriately structuring arguments that integrate the multiple Tools presented in this book and honing in on solutions to problems that are not oversimplified and speak to the many different associated perspectives and beliefs.

Finally, we presented a synthetic case study that applied the concepts presented in the book to one hypothetical complex messy problem: future increase in hurricane frequency and intensity because of climate change. The highly interrelated nature of the topic is outlined and acknowledge that it's an ill-defined, unstructured, and unbounded problem. Problem treatment approaches and mitigation solution timeframes were outlined, which aided in breaking down the larger problem into smaller components as well as assisting us in providing some definition, structure, and boundary. The initial complex problem is considered from multiple perspectives (ISTJ, ENFP, and INTJ), where each offers valuable insights, emphasizing the importance of integrating diverse perspectives in understanding and approaching complex problems.

Compilation of References

Ackermann, F., & Eden, C. (2011). Strategic Management of Stakeholders: Theory and Practice. *Long Range Planning*, *44*(3), 179–196. doi:10.1016/j.lrp.2010.08.001

Ackoff, R. L. (1974). *Redesigning the Future: A Systems Approach to Societal Problems*. John Wiley & Sons.

Ackoff, R. L. (1978). *The Art of Problem Solving: Accompanied by Ackoff's Fables*. John Wiley & Sons.

Ackoff, R. L. (1981). *Creating the Corporate Future: Plan or be Planned For*. John Wiley & Sons.

Ackoff, R. L. (1981). *Creating the Corporate Future: Plan or Be Planned For*. John Wiley & Sons.

Ackoff, R. L. (1981). The Art and Science of Mess Management. *Interfaces*, *11*(1), 20–26. doi:10.1287/inte.11.1.20

Ackoff, R. L. (1999). *Ackoff's Beset His Classic Writings on Management*. John Wiley & Sons.

Ackoff, R. L. (1999). *Ackoff's Best: His Classic Writings on Management*. John Wiley & Sons.

Ackoff, R. L. (1999). *Re-creating the corporation: a design of organizations for the 21st century*. Oxford University Press.

Ackoff, R. L., & Emery, F. E. (1972). *On Purposeful Systems*. AldineTransaction.

Ackoff, R. L., & Gharajedaghi, J. (1971). Towards a System of Systems Concepts. *Management Science*, *17*(11), 661–671. doi:10.1287/mnsc.17.11.661

Ackoff, R. L., & Rovin, S. (2003). *Redesigning Society*. Stanford University Press.

Ackoff, R. L., & Rovin, S. (2003). *Redesigning Society. Stanford*. Business Books.

Ackoff, R., & Greenberg, D. (2008). *Turning learning right side up putting education back on track*. Wharton School Pub.

Ansell, C. (2011). *Pragmatist Democracy: Evolutionary Learning as Public Philosophy*. Oxford University Press. doi:10.1093/acprof:oso/9780199772438.001.0001

Argyris, C. (1964). *Integrating the Individual and the Organization*. Transaction Publishers.

Argyris, C. (1982). *Reasoning, Learning, and Action: Individual and Organizational*. Jossey-Bass.

Argyris, C. (1990). *Overcoming Organizational Defenses: Facilitating Organizational Learning*. Allyn & Bacon.

Argyris, C. (1993). *Knowledge for Action: A Guide to Overcoming Barriers to Organizational Change*. Jossey-Bass.

Argyris, C. (1999). *On Organizational Learning*. Blackwell.

Argyris, C., & Schön, D. A. (1978). *Organizational Learning: A Theory of Action Perspective*. Addison-Wesley.

Argyris, C., & Schön, D. A. (1996). *Organizational Learning II: Theory, Method, and Practice*. Addison-Wesley.

Ashby, W. R. (1958). Requisite variety and its implications for the control of complex systems. *Cybernetica*, *1*, 83–99.

Axelrod, R., & Cohen, M. D. (2000). *Harnessing Complexity: Organizational Implications of a Scientific Frontier*. Free Press.

Banathy, B. H. (1991). Systems Design of Education: A Journey to Create the Future. *Educational Technology*.

Barabba, V. P., & Ian, I. Mitroff. (2014). Business Strategies for a Messy World - Tools for Systemic Problem Solving. New York: Palgrave Macmillan.

Bar-Yam, Y. (1997). *Dynamics of Complex Systems*. Addison-Wesley.

Beyer, H., & Holtzblatt, K. (1998). *Contextual Design: Defining Customer-Centered Systems*. Morgan Kaufmann Publishers.

Blair, J. A. (1996). The Possibility and Actuality of Visual Arguments. *Argumentation and Advocacy*, *33*(1), 23–39.

Blake, R. R., & Mouton, J. S. (1964). *The Managerial Grid: The Key to Leadership Excellence*. Gulf Publishing Co.

Bostrom, R. P., & Stephen Heinen, J. (1977). MIS Problems and Failures: A Socio-Technical Perspective, Part I: The Causes. *Management Information Systems Quarterly*, *1*(3), 17–32. doi:10.2307/248710

Brillinger, D. (2002). John Tukey: His Life and Professional Contributions. *Annals of Statistics*, *30*(6), 1535–1575. doi:10.1214/aos/1043351246

Brockriede, W. (1979). Where Is Argument? *Journal of the American Forensic Association*, *16*, 1–9.

Checkland, P. (1981). *Systems Thinking, Systems Practice*. John Wiley & Sons.

Checkland, P. (1999). *Soft systems methodology: a 30-year retrospective*. John Wiley & Sons.

Cherns, A. (1976). The Principles of Socio-Technical Design. *Human Relations*, *29*(8), 783–792. doi:10.1177/001872677602900806

Churchman, C. W. (1968). *The Systems Approach.* Dell.

Churchman, C. W. (1971). *The Design of Inquiring Systems: Basic Concepts of Systems and Organization.* Basic Books.

Churchman, C. W. (1979). *The Systems Approach and Its Enemies.* Basic Books.

Clegg, C. W. (1988). Psychology of Employee Lateness, Absence, and Turnover: A Methodological Critique and an Empirical Study. *The Journal of Applied Psychology, 73*(1), 88–101. doi:10.1037/0021-9010.68.1.88

Coakes, E. (2011). *Sociotechnical and Soft Approaches to Information Requirements Elicitation in the Post-Millennium Era.* Researching the Future in Information Systems.

Courtney, J. F. (2001). Decision making and knowledge management in inquiring organizations: Toward a new decision-making paradigm for DSS. *Decision Support Systems, 31*(1), 17–38. doi:10.1016/S0167-9236(00)00117-2

Crosswhite, J. (1996). *The Rhetoric of Reason: Writing and the Attractions of Argument.* University of Wisconsin Press.

Dewey, J. (1963). *Experience and education.* Collier Books.

Dreu, D. (1997). Using conflict in organizations. Sage.

Dumas, J. S., & Redish, J. C. (1993). *A Practical Guide to Usability Testing.* Intellect Books.

Eden, C., & Huxham, C. (1996). Action research for management research. *British Journal of Management, 7*(1), 75–86. doi:10.1111/j.1467-8551.1996.tb00107.x

Edwards, A. W. F. (2004). *Cogwheels of the mind: The story of Venn diagrams.* Johns Hopkins University Press. doi:10.56021/9780801874345

Eemeren, F. H. (1992). Argumentation, Communication, and Fallacies: A Pragma-Dialectical Perspective. Lawrence Erlbaum Associates.

Eemeren, F. H. (1996). Fundamentals of Argumentation Theory: A Handbook of Historical Backgrounds and Contemporary Developments. Lawrence Erlbaum Associates.

Emery, F. E. (1959). *Characteristics of socio-technical systems.* Tavistock Institute.

Emery, F. E., & Trist, E. L. (1965). The Causal Texture of Organizational Environments. *Human Relations, 18*(1), 21–32. doi:10.1177/001872676501800103

Ennis, R. H. (1962). A Concept of Critical Thinking. *Harvard Educational Review, 32*(1), 81–111.

Euler, L. (1768). *Lettres à une Princesse d'Allemagne sur divers sujets de physique et de philosophie.*

Fischer, M. (1989). Toulmin's Model and the Solving of Ill-Structured Problems. *Argumentation, 3*(2), 185–204.

Fisher, R., Ury, W., & Patton, B. (1981). *Getting to Yes: Negotiating Agreement Without Giving In*. Penguin.

Flood, R. L., & Carson, E. R. (1993). *Dealing with Complexity: An Introduction to the Theory and Application of Systems Science*. Plenum Press. doi:10.1007/978-1-4757-2235-2

Flood, R. L., & Jackson, M. C. (1991). *Creative Problem Solving: Total Systems Intervention*. John Wiley & Sons.

Flood, R. L., & Jackson, M. C. (1993). Total systems intervention: A practical face to critical systems thinking. *Systems Practice*, *6*(4), 341–355.

Folger, J. P., Poole, M. S., & Stutman, R. K. (1997). *Working through conflict: Strategies for relationships, groups, and organizations*. HarperCollins College Publishers.

Forrester, J. W. (1961). *Industrial Dynamics*. MIT Press.

Forrester, J. W. (1968). *Principles of Systems*. Productivity Press.

Freeman, J. B. (1991). *Dialectics and the Macrostructure of Arguments: A Theory of Argument Structure*. Foris Publications. doi:10.1515/9783110875843

Gharajedaghi, J. (2005). *Systems Thinking: Managing Chaos and Complexity - A Platform for Designing Business Architecture*. Butterworth-Heinemann.

Gharajedaghi, J. (2005). *Systems Thinking: Managing Chaos and Complexity: A Platform for Designing Business Architecture*. Butterworth-Heinemann.

Gharajedaghi, J. (2006). *Systems thinking: managing chaos and complexity: a platform for designing business architecture*. Elsevier.

Gould, J. D., & Lewis, C. (1995). Designing for usability: Key principles and what designers think. *Communications of the ACM*, *28*(3), 300–311. doi:10.1145/3166.3170

Govier, T. (1987). *Problems in Argument Analysis and Evaluation*. Foris Publications. doi:10.1515/9783110859249

Grimaldi, R. P. (2004). *Discrete and Combinatorial Mathematics: An Applied Introduction*. Addison-Wesley.

Henrion, M. G. (1990). *Uncertainty: A Guide to Dealing with Uncertainty in Quantitative Risk and Policy Analysis*. University of Cambridge.

Hitchcock, D. (1998). Toulmin's Warrants. *Argumentation*, *12*(3), 367–380. doi:10.1023/A:1007780507894

Holland, J. H. (1998). *Emergence: From Chaos to Order*. Oxford University Press.

Holland, J. H. (2014). *Complexity: A Very Short Introduction*. Oxford University Press. doi:10.1093/actrade/9780199662548.001.0001

Holt, J. (1902). A Set of Postulates for the Logic of Classes. *Transactions of the American Mathematical Society*, *3*(3), 343–370.

Introna, L. D. (2005). Disclosive Ethics and Information Technology: Disclosing facial recognition systems. *Ethics and Information Technology*, *7*(2), 75–86. doi:10.100710676-005-4583-2

Introna, L. D. (2011). Phenomenological Approaches to Ethics and Information Technology. In E. N. Zalta (Ed.), *The Stanford Encyclopedia of Philosophy*. Stanford University.

Introna, L. D. (2014). Towards a post-human intra-actional account of sociomaterial agency (and ethics). In J. McIntyre-Mills (Ed.), *Systemic Ethics and Non-Anthropocentric Stewardship* (pp. 31–53). Springer.

Jehn, K. A. (1995). A Multimethod Examination of the Benefits and Detriments of Intragroup Conflict. *Administrative Science Quarterly*, *40*(2), 256–282. doi:10.2307/2393638

Johnson, R. H., & Anthony Blair, J. (2006). *Logical Self-Defense*. IDEA.

Kahane, H. (1971). *Logic and Contemporary Rhetoric: The Use of Reason in Everyday Life*. Wadsworth Publishing.

Kauffman, S. A. (1995). *At Home in the Universe: The Search for the Laws of Self-Organization and Complexity*. Oxford University Press.

Keeney, R. L., & Raiffa, H. (1976). *Decisions with Multiple Objectives: Preferences and Value Tradeoffs*. Wiley.

Kesten, H. (1968). *An Introduction to Probability Theory and Its Applications* (Vol. 1). John Wiley & Sons.

Kienpointner, M. (1996). How to Classify Arguments. *Argumentation*, *10*(4), 413–430.

Kilman, R. H. (2021). *Creating a Quantum Organization, The Whys and Hows of Implementing Eight Tracks for Long-Term Success*. Newport Coast: Kilman Diagnostics LLC.

Kilmann, R. H. (1975). Quantifying a Theoretical Model of Managerial Conflict. *Decision Sciences*, *6*(1), 57–67.

Kilmann, R. H. (1982). Conflict and Negotiations. In *Handbook of Industrial and Organizational Psychology* (pp. 771–826). Consulting Psychologists Press.

Kilmann, R. H., & Thomas, K. W. (1977). Developing a Forced-Choice Measure of Conflict-Handling Behavior: The 'MODE' Instrument. *Educational and Psychological Measurement*, *37*(2), 309–325. doi:10.1177/001316447703700204

Klein, J. K., & Delbridge, M. A. (1996). Sociotechnical Criteria for Designing Integrated IT Systems. *Management Information Systems Quarterly*, *20*(1), 31–44.

Kolb, D. M., & Williams, J. (2000). Breakthrough Bargaining. *Harvard Business Review*, *78*(1), 130–137. PMID:11213701

Leavitt, H. J. (1965). Applied Organizational Change in Industry: Structural, Technological and Humanistic Approaches. In J. G. March (Ed.), *Handbook of Organizations* (pp. 1144–1170). Rand McNally.

Leavitt, H. J., & Pondy, L. R. (1964). Leadership: A Special Type of Role. In H. J. Leavitt, (Eds.), *Readings in Managerial Psychology* (pp. 58–71). University of Chicago Press.

Linstone, H. A. (1999). *Decision Making for Technology Executives: Using Multiple Perspectives to Improved Performance*. Artech House.

Mason, R. O., & Mitroff, I. I. (1973). A Program for Research on Management Information Systems. *Management Science, 19*(5), 475–487. doi:10.1287/mnsc.19.5.475

Mason, R. O., & Mitroff, I. I. (1981). *Challenging Strategic Planning Assumptions: Theory, Cases, and Techniques*. John Wiley & Sons.

Meadows, D. H. (2008). *Thinking in Systems: A Primer*. Chelsea Green Publishing.

Midgley, G. (2000). *Systemic Intervention: Philosophy, Methodology, and Practice*. Kluwer Academic/Plenum Publishers. doi:10.1007/978-1-4615-4201-8

Minsky, M. L. (1967). *Computation: Finite and Infinite Machines*. Prentice-Hall.

Mitroff, I. I. (1983). *Stakeholders of the Organizational Mind*. Jossey-Bass.

Mitroff, I. I. (2018). *The Essential Guide to Managing Corporate Crises: A Step-by-Step Handbook for Surviving Major Catastrophes*. Oxford University Press.

Mitroff, I. I., & Denton, E. A. (1999). A study of spirituality in the workplace. *MIT Sloan Management Review, 40*(4), 83–92.

Mitroff, I. I., & Kilmann, R. H. (1978). *Methodological approaches to social science: Integrating divergent concepts and theories*. Brooks/Cole Publishing Company.

Mitroff, I. I., & Linstone, H. A. (1993). *The Unbounded Mind, Breaking the Chains of Traditional Business Thinking*. Oxford University Press.

Mitroff, I. I., & Linstone, H. A. (1993). *The Unbounded Mind: Breaking the Chains of Traditional Business Thinking*. Oxford University Press.

Mitroff, I. I., & Mason, R. O. (1976). Business Policy and Metaphysics. *Academy of Management Review, 1*(2), 67–74.

Mitroff, I. I., & Pauchant, T. C. (1990). Strategic Assumption Surfacing and Testing. In *We're So Big and Powerful Nothing Bad Can Happen to Us: An Investigation of America's Crisis Prone Corporations*. Birch Lane Press.

Mitroff, I. I., & Pauchant, T. C. (1992). *Transforming the Crisis-Prone Organization: Preventing Individual, Organizational, and Environmental Tragedies*. Jossey-Bass.

Morin, E. (2008). *On Complexity*. Hampton Press.

Mumford, E. (1983). Designing Human Systems. In *The ETHICS method.* Manchester Business School.

Nielsen, J. (1993). *Usability Engineering.* Morgan Kaufmann Publishers. doi:10.1016/B978-0-08-052029-2.50007-3

Norman, D. A. (1990). *The Design of Everyday Things.* Basic Books.

O'Keefe, D. J. (1977). Two Concepts of Argument. *Journal of the American Forensic Association, 13*(3), 121–128.

Pasmore, W. A. (1988). *Designing Effective Organizations: The Sociotechnical Systems Perspective.* John Wiley & Sons.

Perelman, C., & Olbrechts-Tyteca, L. (1969). *The New Rhetoric: A Treatise on Argumentation.* University of Notre Dame Press.

Preece, J., Rogers, Y., & Sharp, H. (1994). *Human-Computer Interaction.* Addison-Wesley.

Prigogine, I., & Stengers, I. (1984). *Order out of Chaos: Man's New Dialogue with Nature.* Bantam Books.

Pruitt, D. G., & Carnevale, P. J. (1993). *Negotiation in Social Conflict.* Brooks/Cole.

Putnam, L. L., & Wilson, J. M. (1988). Communicative Strategies in Organizational Conflicts: Reliability and Validity of a Measurement Scale. *Communication Yearbook 11. Sage.*

Puyt, R. W., Lie, F. B., & Wilderom, C. P. M. (2023). The origins of SWOT analysis. *Long Range Planning, 56*(3), 102304–. doi:10.1016/j.lrp.2023.102304

Rahim, M. A. (1983). A Measure of Styles of Handling Interpersonal Conflict. *Academy of Management Journal, 26*(2), 368–376. doi:10.2307/255985 PMID:10263067

Raiffa, H. (1968). *Decision Analysis: Introductory Lectures on Choices Under Uncertainty.* Addison Wesley.

Raiffa, H., Richardson, J., & Metcalfe, D. (2002). *Negotiation Analysis: The Science and Art of Collaborative Decision Making.* Harvard University Press.

Ramage, M., & Shipp, K. (2009). *Systems Thinkers.* Springer. doi:10.1007/978-1-84882-525-3

Richardson, G. P., & Pugh, A. L. III. (1981). *Introduction to System Dynamics Modeling with DYNAMO.* MIT Press.

Rittel, H. W. J., & Webber, M. M. (1973). Dilemmas in a general theory of planning. *Policy Sciences, 4*(2), 155–169. doi:10.1007/BF01405730

Rubin, J. Z., Pruitt, D. G., & Kim, S. H. (1994). *Social Conflict: Escalation, Stalemate, and Settlement.* McGraw-Hill.

Schwaninger, M. (2002). Methodologies in conflict: Achieving synergies between system dynamics and organizational cybernetics. *Systems Research and Behavioral Science*, *19*(4), 341–358.

Senge, P. M. (1990). The Fifth Discipline: The Art & Practice of The Learning Organization. Doubleday/Currency.

Senge, P. M. (1990). *The Fifth Discipline: The Art & Practice of The Learning Organization*. Currency Doubleday.

Shneiderman, B. (1998) Designing the User Interface: Strategies for Effective Human-Computer Interaction. (3rd ed.). Addison Wesley Longman.

Simon, H. A. (1969). *The Sciences of the Artificial*. MIT Press.

Simon, H. A. (1973). The structure of ill-structured problems. *Artificial Intelligence*, *4*(3-4), 181–201. doi:10.1016/0004-3702(73)90011-8

Stacey, R. D. (1996). *Complexity and Creativity in Organizations*. Berrett-Koehler.

Sterman, J. D. (2000). *Business dynamics: Systems thinking and modeling for a complex world*. Irwin/McGraw-Hill.

Sveiby, K.-E. (1987). *Managing Knowhow: Increase Profits by Harnessing the Creativity in Your Company*. Bloomsbury.

Thomas, K. W. (1996). The Social Construction of Conflict. *The Social Construction of Difference and Inequality*. Mayfield Publishing.

Thomas, K. W. (1976). Conflict and Conflict Management. In *Handbook of Industrial and Organizational Psychology*. Rand McNally.

Thomas, K. W. (1992). Conflict and Conflict Management: Reflections and Update. *Journal of Organizational Behavior*, *13*(3), 265–274. doi:10.1002/job.4030130307

Thomas, K. W. (2000). *Intrinsic Motivation at Work: Building Energy & Commitment*. Berrett-Koehler Publishers.

Thomas, K. W., & Kilmann, R. H. (1974). *Thomas-Kilmann Conflict Mode Instrument*. Xicom.

Tjosvold, D. (1986). Effects of Approach to Controversy on Superiors' Incorporation of Subordinates' Information in Decision Making. *Academy of Management Journal*, *29*(2), 233–246.

Toulmin, S. (1958). *The Uses of Argument*. Cambridge University Press.

Toulmin, S., Rieke, R., & Janik, A. (1979). *An Introduction to Reasoning*. Macmillan Publishing Co., Inc.

Trist, E. L. (1981). *A Socio-Technical Critique of Scientific Management*. Knowledge and Action.

Trist, E. L., & Murray, H. (1990). *The Social Engagement of Social Science: A Tavistock Anthology*. University of Pennsylvania Press.

Tufte, E. R. (1983). *The Visual Display of Quantitative Information.* Graphics Press.

Tukey, J. W. (1962). The future of data analysis. *Annals of Mathematical Statistics, 33*(1), 1–67. doi:10.1214/aoms/1177704711

Tukey, J. W. (1977). *Exploratory Data Analysis.* Addison-Wesley.

Turner, B. (1976). The organizational and interorganizational development of disasters. *Administrative Science Quarterly, 21*(3), 378–397. doi:10.2307/2391850

Ulrich, W. (1983). *Critical heuristics of social planning: A new approach to practical philosophy.* Haupt.

Ulrich, W. (1983). *Critical Heuristics of Social Planning: A New Approach to Practical Philosophy.* Haupt.

Venn, J. (1880). On the Diagrammatic and Mechanical Representation of Propositions and Reasonings. *The London, Edinburgh and Dublin Philosophical Magazine and Journal of Science, 9*(59), 1–18. doi:10.1080/14786448008626877

Vickers, G. (1965). *The Art of Judgment: A Study of Policy Making.* Chapman & Hall.

Vickers, G. (1968). *Value Systems and Social Process.* Basic Books.

Vickers, G. (1970). *Making Institutions Work.* John Wiley & Sons.

Vickers, G. (1972). *Freedom in a Rocking Boat: Changing values in an unstable society.* Penguin.

Vickers, G. (1980). *Responsibility – Its Sources and Limits.* Intersystems Publications.

Vickers, G. (1983). *Human Systems are Different.* Harper & Row.

Waldrop, M. M. (1992). *Complexity: The Emerging Science at the Edge of Order and Chaos.* Simon & Schuster.

Wall, J. A. Jr, & Callister, R. J. (1995). Conflict and its management. *Journal of Management, 21*(3), 515–558. doi:10.1177/014920639502100306

Walton, D. N. (2008). *Informal Logic: A Pragmatic Approach.* Cambridge University Press.

Weick, K. E. (1995). *Sensemaking in Organizations.* Sage.

Wenzel, J. W. (1990). Three Perspectives on Argumentation. In R. Trapp & J. Schuetz (Eds.), *Perspectives on Argumentation: Essays in Honor of Wayne Brockriede* (pp. 9–26). Waveland Press.

Whitworth, B., & Whitworth, A. P. (2010). The social environment model: Small heroes and the evolution of human society. *First Monday, 15*(11), NP–NP. doi:10.5210/fm.v15i11.3173

Willard, C. A. (1989). *A Theory of Argumentation.* University of Alabama Press.

Winograd, T. (Ed.). (1996). *Bringing Design to Software.* Addison-Wesley. doi:10.1145/229868

About the Authors

Rune Storesund has a BA in Anthropology from UC Santa Cruz and a BS in Civil Engineering, part of a joint 'dual degree' program between the two schools which intended to 'diversity' engineering students. He has a Master of Civil Engineering and Doctorate of Civil Engineering from UC Berkeley. He is a Professional Geotechnical and Civil Engineer, Board Certified Diplomat of the National Academy of Forensic Engineering, and Fellow of the American Society of Civil Engineers. Dr. Storesund is the CEO and President of his boutique engineering and risk consulting firm Storesund Consulting, the CEO and President of his civil works construction company Storesund Construction, Inc. the CEO and President NextGen Mapping,Inc., an innovative software development company, and the CEO/President of his non-profit "SafeR3" that focuses on the Safety, Reliability, Resilience, and Risk-Reduction of critical infrastructures. He is the Executive Director of the Center for Catastrophic Risk Management at UC Berkeley specializing in state-of-the-art research and application of safety and reliability of critical infrastructure systems.

Ian I. Mitroff is credited as being one of the principal founders of the modern field of Crisis Management. He has a BS, MS, and a PhD in Engineering and the Philosophy of Social Systems Science from UC Berkeley. He Is Professor Emeritus from the Marshall School of Business and the Annenberg School of Communication at USC. Currently, he is a Senior Research Affiliate in the Center for Catastrophic Risk Management, UC Berkeley. He is a Fellow of the American Psychological Association, the American Association for the Advancement of Science, and the American Academy of Management. He has published 41 books. His most recent are: Techlash: The Future of the Socially Responsible Tech Organization, Springer, New York, 2020. The Psychodynamics of Enlightened Leadership; Coping with Chaos, Co-authored with Ralph H. Kilmann, Springer, New York, 2021. His latest is: The Socially Responsible Organization: Lessons from Covid 19, Springer, New York, 2022.

Index

F

G

H

I

J

K

L

M

O

P

R

S

T

U

V

W

www.ingramcontent.com/pod-product-compliance
Ingram Content Group UK Ltd.
Pitfield, Milton Keynes, MK11 3LW, UK
UKHW050945290926
15470UKWH00005B/1647